PSYCHOLOGY

Abraham P. Sperling, PhD

Advisory editor
Kenneth Martin, MSc

MADE SIMPLE
B O O K S

Made Simple Books
An imprint of Butterworth-Heinemann Ltd
Linacre House, Jordan Hill, Oxford OX2 8DP

 PART OF REED INTERNATIONAL BOOKS

OXFORD   LONDON   BOSTON
MUNICH   NEW DELHI   SINGAPORE   SYDNEY
TOKYO   TORONTO   WELLINGTON

First published 1967
Reprinted 1970, 1971, 1972, 1974, 1975
Revised and reprinted 1977
Reprinted 1979, 1980
Revised and enlarged edition 1982
Reprinted 1984, 1985, 1986, 1987, 1989, 1990, 1992

© Butterworth-Heinemann Ltd 1982

All rights reserved. No part of this publication
may be reproduced in any material form (including
photocopying or storing in any medium by electronic
means and whether or not transiently or incidentally
to some other use of this publication) without the
written permission of the copyright holder except in
accordance with the provisions of the Copyright,
Designs and Patents Act 1988 or under the terms of a
licence issued by the Copyright Licensing Agency Ltd,
90 Tottenham Court Road, London, England W1P 9HE.
Applications for the copyright holder's written
permission to reproduce any part of this publication
should be addressed to the publishers

British Library Cataloguing in Publication Data
Sperling, Abraham, P.
   Psychology made simple. – rev. and enl. ed.
   repr. – (Made simple books, ISSN 0265–0541)
   1. Psychology
   I. Title   II. Martin, Kenneth   III. Series
   150 BF151

ISBN 0 7506 0720 3

Printed in England by Clays Ltd, St Ives plc

Foreword

This book is designed to show the reader how psychology has developed over its relatively brief period as a science in its own right and to introduce some of the areas which are the concern of the contemporary psychologist. It will also be found useful to students taking courses both in social sciences and education. No one introductory text can hope, however, to cover all current areas and it is appreciated that some readers will wish to develop their understanding to a greater degree than is possible in a book of this nature. A list of texts for 'Suggested Further Reading' is therefore given at the end of each chapter.

The subject matter of psychology is behaviour and the task of the psychologist is to study, understand and explain behaviour. Clearly this can present difficulties and the contemporary psychologist can in no way claim to have answered all the questions and solved all the problems which have been posed. It is worth remembering, however, that as a separate science psychology is a comparative newcomer. The roots of psychology are to be found, in particular, within philosophy and physiology and it was only some one hundred years ago that the scientific approach of controlled laboratory experiment began to be utilised by psychology. There have been many advances during the last century and a variety of techniques for investigation have been introduced and developed. Psychology has also not been afraid to draw on the findings from such apparently diverse sources as biochemistry to engineering in the quest for greater understanding of our behaviour. Today the scope and applications of psychology continue to be wide. Psychologists will be found not only in academic institutions but, in particular, applying their knowledge in industry, education and hospitals where they provide a valuable service.

From time to time we hear in conversation phrases such as 'psychologically speaking' and it is not unusual for the layman to be heard to claim to being 'something of a psychologist'. Clearly this is a field which proves fascinating to many and it is hoped that the reader who begins a more systematic study of the subject through this book will gain a more critical understanding of himself and the social environment in which he lives.

KENNETH MARTIN

Contents

Contents

1

A SCIENTIFIC APPROACH TO THE STUDY OF HUMAN NATURE

Of all the many wonders that man has probed on earth, in the sea and in the sky, the most interesting of all seems to be man himself. One need only examine current books, films, television programmes to see that most people are really much more interested in human nature than they are in Mother Nature.

By and large, people are not impressed by arguments that 'prove' how insignificant the individual is compared to the immense universe. Even though astronomy long ago showed that the earth is nowhere near the centre of the solar system, mankind continues to hold a central place in the imagination. Actually, man does occupy at least *one* kind of physical centre. A human being is just about as many times *larger* than the *smallest* object in the universe (an electron) as he is *smaller* than the universe itself.

However, man does not need any such justification of his intense self-curiosity. There are other, sufficient reasons why he continuously probes the mysteries of human nature.

WHY MEN STUDY HUMAN NATURE

The interest of some people in human nature is motivated only by curiosity. They want to know just for the sake of knowing. In exactly the same way that some people want to understand rocks or stars, others want to understand human beings. They agree with the poet Alexander Pope that 'the proper study of mankind is man'. In effect, they want to know what it means to be a human being.

Some have a more practical interest in acquiring knowledge about human nature. They believe it would be possible to solve social problems if enough were known about their causes. Such people feel that man-made difficulties can be overcome, that man-made institutions can be changed, given sufficient knowledge of man. They want to abolish, or at least diminish, industrial unrest, racial conflict, crime, international tensions and war.

Still another kind of practical interest motivates studies of man: the desire to 'get along with other people'. They realize that in order to work and live as harmoniously as possible with others, they must know why people think and feel and act the way they do. There is

1

also a business as well as a social interest of this sort. Thus employers want to know what kind of personalities are most likely to succeed in particular jobs. Parents want to know what kind of children gain the most out of life.

Perhaps the strongest practical interest in human nature comes from our intense curiosity about ourselves.

How do I become aware of things? How do I perceive things? How do I learn, remember, and forget? Am I wasting my intelligence and talent? How did my personality develop? Can I learn to control my emotions? Do my motives conflict? How can I make the best possible adjustment between the complex world and my equally complex but unique self?

In asking these questions, people are following the 2,500-year-old dictum of Socrates, 'Know thyself'.

SOURCES OF KNOWLEDGE ABOUT HUMAN NATURE

People have almost as many sources of information about human nature as they can have reasons for wanting it. Broadly speaking, there are four sources of such information: **proverbs, myths, and generalizations; literature and other arts; personal experience; science.**

Proverbs, Myths, and Generalizations. Over the centuries, humanity has accumulated a vast body of statements about human nature, called proverbs. These statements vary in form from one nation to another, but are essentially the same the world over. This constancy is not surprising, since by definition *human* nature is a trait of the species, not of a mere cultural group.

Unfortunately, proverbs are neither detailed nor reliable enough to satisfy our human need for self-understanding. They do not give sufficient information about many important areas of human nature. In other areas they contradict one another. Everyone can think of many contradictory pairs of proverbs, such as:

'Absence makes the heart grow fonder'

versus

'Out of sight, out of mind'

and 'Two heads are better than one'

versus

'Too many cooks spoil the broth'

Other proverbs are unreliable because they are simply not true. In the third edition of JOHN FREDERICK DASHIELL'S *Fundamentals of General*

Psychology, the author lists twenty common proverbs whose truth or falsity he invites the reader to judge. The twenty are:

1 A rose by any other name would smell as sweet.
2 As the twig is bent, so the tree's inclined.
3 Forbidden fruit is sweetest.
4 Misfortunes make us wise.
5 Necessity is the mother of invention.
6 Once a knave, always a knave.
7 Once bitten, twice shy.
8 Practice makes perfect.
9 Scalded cats don't fear cold water.
10 Still waters run deep.
11 The fairer the paper, the fouler the blot.
12 The fairest apple hangs on the highest bough.
13 The master's eye makes the horse fat.
14 The watched pot is slow to boil.
15 Unto the pure, all things are pure.
16 What soberness conceals, drunkenness reveals.
17 What the heart thinks, the pulse betrays.
18 When children stand quiet, they have done no harm.
19 When the fox preaches, beware of your geese.
20 Zeal is fit only for wise men, but found mostly in fools.

These proverbs are not meant to be taken literally, of course, but are to be understood as metaphorical statements about human nature. Before reading the next paragraph, which gives the professional opinion of Professor Dashiell on the truth and falsity of these proverbs, determine which seem *true* to you and which seem *false*.

According to Dashiell, the 1st, 6th, 8th, 9th, 10th, 15th, 18th, and 20th, are *false*, and the others are true. He admits having no proofs for his judgements—but he is trying to show the necessity for proofs of statements claiming to give the entire truth of *all* human nature.

Ignorant myths (in the popular sense of the term) about various ethnic or national groups are often equally unreliable. It is regrettable that in civilized countries boasting universal literacy, unreliable statements like the following are still made and believed:

> 'The English have no sense of humour.'
> 'The French are obsessed with sexuality.'
> 'Americans have no culture.'

Other unjustified generalizations that circulate among uncritical people underlie such common epithets as 'tight Scotsman', 'dumb Irish', 'cheap Jew', 'mad Russian', and 'greasy Italian'. The reasons why these generalizations are made and believed are themselves worthy of investigation. Leaving the problem for later consideration, we might merely cite the sometimes reliable proverb about 'the pot calling the kettle black'.

Literature and Other Arts. Another route to understanding human nature is the indirect path through literature, history, biography, and autobiography. The reliability of the knowledge thus gained varies with the experience, insight, and honesty of the writer, all of which qualities are hard to verify. Another drawback is the fact that what is true of one person, fictional or real, may not necessarily be true of another. The detailed and overwhelmingly convincing analyses of characters made in the novels of Dostoevsky, for example, differ markedly from the equally convincing analyses made by Henry James. In turn, they both differ from the self-revelations of Proust, which again are not identical with the 'confessions' of Poe, or Rousseau, or St. Augustine.

Since a literary artist is after all only one man, we cannot expect him to have Godlike omniscience. Even Shakespeare didn't know *everything* there is to know about the nature of man. Thus we can say that the poet Pope was exaggerating when he claimed that 'Nature and Homer were the same'.

Personal Experience. The same arguments that apply to individual writers apply to individuals who feel that their personal experiences give them complete comprehension of human nature. Experience indeed may give them *sufficient* comprehension, but it certainly does not give them *complete* comprehension.

Our own personal experience may show us that those people who claim to understand others so well, actually understand neither other people nor themselves. There is often an ironic relationship between their opinions and their own make-up. Too often, what they believe to be true about others is usually true of themselves. This tendency to confuse one's own traits with those of others, the psychologist calls 'projection'.

We see in personal experience several major drawbacks to its efficiency as a basis for understanding people. First there is the inescapable *limit* to the amount of experience, insight, and intelligence that any *one* person can have. Then there is the all-too-human failure of our ability to be sufficiently aware of our *own* prejudices, preferences and other blind spots, which interfere with true interpretation of reality.

Scientific Method. The human race has developed a remarkable method for overcoming the intellectual limitations of its individual members. This is, of course, the scientific method of study, or science. Essentially, science is the pooling of individual attempts to understand experience. That is, scientific knowledge results from the accumulation of innumerable 'personal experiences'.

These experiences are always accumulated in a particular way. The process actually resembles subtraction more than it does addition, for science *retains* only as much of one investigator's personal experience as completely agrees with the personal experience of other investigators. Obviously, complete agreement can best be detected by measurements. The first step in the scientific method, then, is careful measurement of all the factors in a situation.

Cause and correlation. The fact that two aspects go together—that is, are **correlated**—does not prove that one **causes** the other.

The search for causes. Science does not always stop at the level of correlation. It is also interested in discovering causes. There is a particular way to find out which of all the factors in a situation is the cause. If all the factors but *one* can be kept from changing, then any changes in the situation must be caused by the change in that one factor. By varying *one* factor at a time, we can discover the exact contribution that *each* factor makes to the total situation.

To sum up, the **scientific method** includes several steps; **finding and measuring all the factors contributing to a situation; correlating the factors; varying the factors one at a time to see the particular result of each.**

SCIENCES OF HUMAN NATURE

When the scientific method is used to study human behaviour and experience, several different bodies of knowledge are accumulated, according to the prime interest of the investigator.

Suppose, for instance, that you are interested in the so-called races of mankind, their origin, distribution, and peculiarities. You would be studying the science of **ethnology.** If the emphasis of your racial studies was on their cultures, arts, customs and practices, you would be called an **anthropologist.** Some social scientists ignore racial considerations entirely, and concentrate on the origins and evolutions of the form, institutions, and functions of human social groups. Such men are called **sociologists.**

In contrast to these **social scientists,** there are scientists who study individual men, in part or as a whole. If your studies were concentrated on gaining an understanding of the parts of the body, you would be an **anatomist.** If it were the functions of the body that you studied, you would be a **physiologist.** Suppose, however, that you were interested in the interrelationship of anatomy and physiology. You would then become a **physician.** If you specialized in mental and emotional illnesses, you would be called a **psychiatrist.** If you treated victims of these ailments in the particular way originated by SIGMUND FREUD, you would be a **psychoanalyst.**

We have left to the last another science that attempts to understand and explain the behaviour of man—**psychology.**

Not just any opinion or information about human nature is psychology, nor is everyone a psychologist who knows his fellows adequately.

To call an effective salesman a good psychologist, is as inaccurate as to call an adding machine operator a mathematician. Only the knowledge of human nature that is arrived at **scientifically** is truly **psychological** knowledge.

SCIENTIFIC METHODS IN PSYCHOLOGY

One form of psychological knowledge comes from **objective laboratory experiments.** The laboratory scientist is trained to be able to distinguish between what he wants to believe and what he actually finds to be the case, if experiments show that the two differ.

The laboratory is also the ideal place for controlling an experimental situation so that all of its aspects and factors can be scientifically determined and measured.

For example, suppose we want to test a person's ability to locate the directions of sources of sound. In a laboratory, unlike the outside world, we can eliminate every possible helping cue but the sounds themselves. We can sound-proof the room. We can conceal the sources of sound. We can adjust the signals to the same musical pitch. We can set them off in random order, so that the person with whom we are experimenting cannot anticipate the direction of the next sound. In this way, we can exclude every factor but the one whose effect we want to test.

Some experiments need not be made in a laboratory, if the situations permit the essential scientific conditions to prevail—namely, keeping all factors constant but one. For example, imagine that we want to discover how much faster children will learn spelling if we praise them than they will if we make no comment on their work. Our first step would be to divide a class into two groups. One group would be praised whenever possible; the other group, called a control group, accepted but neither praised nor blamed. To make sure both groups are as similar as possible, we would not only make them the same size, but would also give each group as fair a share as possible of children with equal probable abilities. The two groups ought to *match* in age, grade, school marks, intelligence scores, and home background. In other words, they should be equated in all respects. Then we can be more certain that any differences in performance that may result are due to the absence or presence of the factor being tested, namely the element of 'praise'.

Statistical Descriptions. Postponing to appropriate chapters discussion of the tests by which such factors as intelligence would be measured, let us turn to the scores that are made on such tests. For *any* trait of personality, whether of physique, temperament, ability, or sociability, *most* human beings tend to fall around the middle value between the two possible extremes of 0 and 100 per cent of that trait. Taking *height* as an example, the class of children referred to in the preceding experiment would almost surely include a few 'shorties', with one real shorty, a great many children of medium height, and a few 'longfellows', with one real 'stretch'. Let's assume that there are thirty children in a group. If it were a typical class in a typical school, you can be fairly certain that the children would form the following kind of profile if lined up in size place:

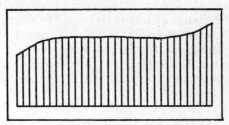

Fig. 1. Thirty children in size place

How can we describe this profile? We might point out the *most common* height. In statistical language, this is called the **mode.** We might pick the height of the child in the *middle* of the line. The statistical term for this is the **median.** We might add the height in inches of all the children and divide by the number of children, to get what statisticians call the **mean,** or in popular language, the **average** height.

In the example given, the 'mode', the 'median', and the 'mean' coincide. They do not always do so. Just one more very tall child would raise the mean. A difference of a fraction of an inch in one of the middle children might make *two* heights equally common. And in any case, the median tells us nothing of the *range* of heights, or the *number* of children in the group.

The Normal Distribution Curve. Psychologists have found that the most graphic device for describing the pattern of a given group's possession of a particular trait is the **distribution curve.** This is a simple graph.

Let us see how we would plot such a graph for a class of thirteen-year-old children. First, we would see just how tall the tallest child is and just how short the shortest child is. Let us say, to use an exaggerated example, 6 feet and 4 feet, respectively. This would give a **range** of 2 feet between the shortest and tallest child. We would next break up this range into smaller **spreads** or **steps** of 2 inches each. Then we would note on our graph *how many* children fall into *each* spread of 2 inches. This might be indicated by a rectangular box on the graph drawn above the part of the range line that represented that spread.

In this way a pictorial representation or 'graph' would be formed to show the distribution of the varying heights of thirty children in randomly selected thirteen-year-olds.

It is a very important fact about human nature that almost always, if this were a typical class group selected at random, the resulting graph would look something like this:

Fig. 2. Height distribution of a class of thirty thirteen-year-old children

As larger and larger classes were to be measured, the psychologists would use smaller spreads, until the profile would assume the following smooth form:

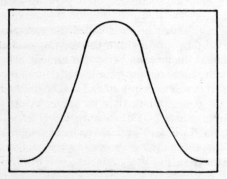

Fig. 3. The normal distribution curve

This line is called the **normal distribution curve,** precisely because most traits, when measured in sufficiently large groups of people, are found to be distributed in just this way.

The importance of the normal distribution fact emerges when psychological theories of **personality types** are raised which attempt to divide humanity into two groups, such as introverts *versus* extraverts, or tall *versus* short, or any of the other 'sheep *versus* goats' system of typing mankind. None of these theories is justified. When put to the objective test of measurement, the crucial trait is always found to be **distributed normally** among the population at large. *Most* people are *neither* tall *nor* short, *neither* totally extraverted *nor* totally introverted, *neither* aggressive *nor* submissive, but somewhere in the middle.

Objective Observation. Unfortunately, it is not always possible to arrange easily controlled **experiments** for determining psychological effects and their causes.

Psychologists must often rely on **observations** for knowledge of certain aspects of human nature. For example, consider the problem of tracing the mental and behavioural development of the individual from conception to maturity. The process raises many intricate questions about the influences of heredity and environment, the conditions favourable to normal growth, and the factors that produce such abnormalities as delinquency and insanity. Some of the questions *can* be clarified experimentally. Tests and laboratory methods can be used to measure the stage of development reached at particular ages, and for determining the upward curve of growth. But to make a really decisive experiment on child development, you would have to be in total control of the conditions in which a large group of children were reared. You would also have to subject half of the children deliberately to conditions presumed to be unfavourable.

As a substitute for experiment, psychologists use the **observational method.** It is neither possible nor necessary to record *everything*. You need to record only the events required to prove or disprove a **hypothesis** you want to test.

Another form of observation is called the **case-history** method. In this, the psychologist gathers data about the *past* experiences of a person in order to understand better his *present* behaviour. By comparing many case histories of people with similar complaints, it is often possible to detect patterns of cause and effect.

Sometimes the people studied are no longer living, or are otherwise unavailable for interviewing. They may nevertheless be studied profitably by the **biographical** method. As an example of what can be learned in this way, consider C. M. COX's comparative study of the life stories of several hundred geniuses. By comparing such evidences of intellectual achievement as the ages at which they learned to read, tell time, and write poems during childhood, Cox demonstrated that in most cases an adult whom the world calls a genius will have shown his superiority in childhood.

Perhaps the simplest observational technique of all is the **field-study method.** This consists simply of making observations with no attempt to control conditions or to get the co-operation of your subjects. In fact, field studies are usually most successful when the subjects are unaware of being observed. Great use of this method was made in England during the Second World War. To determine how well morale was holding up, trained observers successfully 'spied' on the people. The field-study method differs from personal experience in two ways. Actual counts are made, and more people are encountered than most individuals can meet.

Objectivity and Subjectivity. Experimenting and observing are both **objective** methods of study. The emphasis is on **external** events, speech or other acts of **behaviour** which may be accurately recorded. However, there are many **internal** events that cannot be studied objectively. Feelings, thoughts, and visions can be known only **subjectively,** in our own experience alone.

Of course, you can try to be as objective as possible about your inner experiences. But you can never be sure that what you are experiencing is the same as it would be if you were not paying attention to yourself.

This process of examining closely your own mind is called **introspection.** It used to be the primary method of the early psychologists for studying human nature. However, from the point of view of more recent scientific psychology, it was found to have the following drawbacks:

1 The possibility, already mentioned, that introspection may alter the quality of inner experience.

2 The fact that its results cannot be verified by another person.

3 Its uselessness with animals, small children, or inarticulate adults.

4 The fact that many mental activities are partially or entirely unconscious.

As we shall see in later chapters, this last fact is of more importance than as a mere argument against introspection. However, at this point it can be quite helpful to the reader to focus our discussion upon experiments that prove the existence of the '**unconscious**'. Perhaps the most familiar of these are concerned with the phenomenon of **hypnosis.**

Hypnosis and the Unconscious Mind. Hypnosis, as understood by the psychologist, might be described as a state of excessive **suggestibility** in which a person temporarily relinquishes conscious control of his behaviour and accepts the suggestions at the 'unconscious level' of one who has hypnotized him.

While we understand a good deal more about hypnotism today than we did in the days of MESMER (when it was called 'mesmerism'), there is still much about the hypnotic state which remains a mystery.

We know, for example, that in the hypnotic state an individual can bring up memories from the 'unconscious mind' which have long been forgotten and cannot be recalled in the conscious or waking state. This is termed 'age-regression' by hypnotic practitioners. There is good experimental evidence that under hypnosis average adults, aged twenty to forty, can be 'induced' to recall events, names, and places from their childhood as far back as age six which they cannot recall when not in the hypnotized state. The question of just how far back this age-regression memory can be carried under hypnosis is a moot point.

While a person under hypnosis is in a deep state of exaggerated suggestibility, it is confined to the individual who induced the trance state. It requires no special power to induce this hypnotic state. Anyone can learn to induce a hypnotic trance state in a willing subject. Generally speaking, an individual cannot be hypnotized against his will. There are, however, exceptional instances. There are cases on record which indicate that despite all efforts to resist, certain persons will drift into a trance state through hypnotic suggestion.

It is a characteristic of the hypnotic state that the hypnotized person will accept suggestions from the hypnotist to be carried out *later*, in his *waking* or *conscious* state. Such suggestion is termed **post-hypnotic suggestion.** Its nature is excellently described in a passage from Albert Moll's classic work, *Hypnotism*.

> We have here a hypnotized subject to whom I say when he wakes he is to take a flower-pot from the window-sill, wrap it in a cloth, put it on the sofa, and bow to it three times. All of which he does. When asked for his reasons he answers, 'You know, when I woke and saw the flower-pot there I thought that as it was rather cold the flower-pot had better be warmed a little, or else the plant would die. So I wrapped it in the cloth, and then I thought that as the sofa was near the fire I would put the flower-pot on it, and I bowed because I was pleased with myself for having such a bright idea.'

It is interesting to note that the hypnotized person tends to invent a reason why he ought to perform the suggested act. This tendency to **rationalization** is an important fact of human nature. It will be discussed more fully in the chapter on 'Personality Adjustment and Maladjustment'.

At the moment we are primarily interested in this demonstration of the fact that unconscious attitudes can influence conscious thought or behaviour. Leaving the implications for later study, we may merely conclude at this time that conscious introspection can be of no more real value than any other form of personal experience as a guide to psychological understanding. Indeed, the study of human nature became the science of psychology *only* when objective methods replaced introspection and theorizing.

The Era before Scientific Psychology. Attempts to understand human experience and behaviour are as old as recorded history. The first theory put forth to explain human nature attributed man's consciousness to an inner spirit, a 'little man' located somewhere in the body. Later thinkers—e.g. the Greeks Plato and Aristotle—spoke of the *psyche*, or soul, as the centre of experience. 'Psychology' took its name from this word.

Later, philosophers continued to theorize about the nature of human experience and behaviour. In 1690, the Englishman JOHN

LOCKE, in his *Essay Concerning Human Understanding*, put forth the idea that human knowledge is acquired during life, is not inherited or based on 'innate' ideas. It so happens that Locke was right. But he might just as easily have been wrong. There was then no way of telling. Another Lockean theory—that habits are merely associations of particular acts—has been found to be only partially true. Without objective testing, theories are only guesses, however good.

SOME SCHOOLS OF PSYCHOLOGY

The Structuralists. In 1879, WILHELM WUNDT, a German physiologist, founded psychology as a separate science by setting up the first experimental laboratory in psychology. In his earliest studies he investigated sensations and imagery. Soon after this, there arose many psychological laboratories in Europe and America.

Wundt and his followers were called **structuralists,** because they claimed that complex mental experiences were really 'structures' built up from simple mental states, much as chemical compounds are built up from chemical elements. They worked on the premise that it was the prime business of the psychologist to explore the 'structure' of consciousness and evolve the laws of its formation. Their primary approach was by introspective analysis but under more controlled conditions than previously.

The Functionalists. About twenty years later, a school of psychology was formed by psychologists who were dissatisfied with the structuralist emphasis on mental states. Instead of asking, 'What is consciousness?' as the structuralists did, they asked, 'What is consciousness for? What is its purpose or function?' Because they wanted to study the way that individuals *used* mental experience in adjusting to the environment, they were called **functionalists.** The leaders in this group among the psychologists were WILLIAM JAMES and JAMES R. ANGELL. Naturally, they tended to concentrate their attention on the **learning process.** JOHN DEWEY, the famous American philosopher and educator, was another major exponent of the functionalist school.

The Psychoanalysts. The beginning of the 1900s, when the functionalists split off, was also the time of the founding of the **psychoanalytic school.** The advances in the field of medical psychology, and the practices of the early school of hypnosis, prompted the development of this psychoanalytic movement. Under the leadership of SIGMUND FREUD, the psychoanalysts emphasized the **unconscious mental processes.** Freud was a medical man, a psychiatrist and neurologist who was essentially concerned with the understanding and cure of mental disorders. He had very little interest in the traditional problems of academic psychology such as the nature of sensation, perception, thinking and intelligence. Thus, Freud ignored the problems of 'consciousness' and directed his efforts to an understanding and description of what he termed 'the unconscious'. In his judgment, this was a facet of mental make-up which could not be probed by the current methods of 'introspection' or 'laboratory experimentation'. It was in the 'unconscious' that the primary source of conflicts and mental disorders was to be found, in terms of the Freudian theories. Therefore, in order to study these phenomena, he developed the new and specialized technique of psychoanalysis which is based largely on an interpretation of the patient's 'freely associated stream of thoughts' and dream analysis. This viewpoint at the time represented a radical departure in both content and method. Over the years, the psychoanalytic approach has had a stormy career with much modification, and has gathered as many supporters as detractors.

The Behaviourists. During the First World War, a group of American psychologists called **behaviourists** attracted considerable attention with an attitude that was as sceptical as the psychoanalytic about the importance of 'consciousness'. However, the behaviourists did not discard consciousness from their work because they believed it concealed an unconscious mind. Indeed, Freud's ideas were repugnant to them. The behaviourists were led by JOHN B. WATSON, whose initial interest had been animal experimentation in which the traditional approaches of the early psychologists through 'consciousness', 'introspection' and the 'unconscious' were of no practical value. What the animal experimenters could observe was primarily **behaviour.** To the behaviourists, this was its greatest virtue because it was **objective** and eliminated the subjectivity of the studies of 'consciousness', 'introspective report' and the 'free association from the unconscious'. The behaviourist transferred his techniques of studying animal behaviour to the study of human behaviour. The behaviourists leaned heavily on physiology and their great contribution to psychology has been their work on **conditioned responses.** While much of Watson's behaviourism was later challenged, his systematic objective approach has been carried forward in later objective psychology in the work of CLARK HULL, EDWARD TOLMAN, and others.

The Gestaltists. While in enforced exile during the First World War, a German psychologist named WOLFGANG KÖHLER made certain experiments on the learning processes of apes that convinced him of the great importance of **insight** in learning. Köhler's work seemed to confirm the theories of MAX WERTHEIMER that the whole pattern of an experience is more important than its individual parts in determining its meaning, and even its appearance. The school of psychology which these men founded has therefore been called the **Gestalt** school, after the German word for 'pattern'.

Table I, based on a chart in the third edition of Floyd L. Ruch's *Psychology and Life* (Scott, Foresman and Co., Chicago, 1948), shows important facts about the main schools of psychology.

Contemporary Psychology. Many practising psychologists feel that no one school has a monopoly of psychological truth. A glance at the 'main topics' listed in Table I will indeed show that the five chief schools more closely resemble the five fingers of one hand than they do five separate hands. In the remainder of this book, we shall not hesitate to present the valid findings of *all* schools. The next chapter, for instance, is largely based on discoveries begun by the **psychophysical structuralists,** while the chapter after that draws heavily upon the discoveries of the **Gestaltists.** We shall not always bother to label particular points with the name of the schools that made them, since their acceptance into the mainstream of modern psychology signifies their general scientific **validity.**

Table I. Historically important schools of psychology

Name	Main Topics	Methods	Leaders	Approximate Date of Origin
Structuralist (Psychophysical)	Sensations	Introspection Experiment	WUNDT TITCHENER	1879
Functionalist	Behaviour (particularly Learning)	Introspection Observation	ANGELL DEWEY	1900
Psychoanalytic	Mental disorders Unconscious processes	Clinical Observation	FREUD ADLER JUNG	1900
Gestalt	Perception Memory	Introspection Observation Experiment	WERTHEIMER KÖHLER KOFFKA LEWIN	1912
Behaviourist	Stimulus—Response Animal behaviour	Observation Experiment	PAVLOV WATSON DASHIELL	1913

Another reason for avoiding labels has to do with the technical jargon in which the members of particular schools often express their findings. Too often, enthusiastic followers of one system of thought forget that naming is not explaining. To call a habitual thief of useless objects a 'kleptomaniac' does not tell us anything about his reasons for stealing, nor does it help us better to understand his behaviour. To call *every* act of learning an instance of 'conditioning' is a waste of time, unless the process can be shown to have occurred in each case.

THE PLAN OF THIS BOOK

To save the reader an arduous job of translating the private language of each school, the important findings of each school have been put into simple English. Only terms used throughout psychology have been retained. All such technical terms are clearly explained.

When the reliable findings of the various schools are pooled in this way, a logical order of subject matter can be imposed upon them. To be sure, the various topics of psychology are so closely interrelated that a good case can be made for several *different* orders of presentation. We might have begun with learning and memory, since our thoughts and actions at any time depend upon what we have previously learned. Or the book could begin with the 'psychology of infancy', since we all begin our lives as infants. Then again, a good place to enter psychological studies is in the field of adjustment and maladjustment. Indeed, it is common that interest in general psychology begins with a particular psychiatric problem.

We shall begin this survey of modern psychological knowledge with **sensation,** the topic whose study began the science of psychology. The reason, however, is not merely to conform to the historical order, but to ground the reader in a firm understanding of the most *objective* part of psychological knowledge. Only when the physiological aspects of psychology are mastered will the reader be able fully to judge for himself the ultimate worth of the more speculative theories.

To the body functions that underlie the mental functions, therefore, we now turn our attention.

SUGGESTED FURTHER READING

Many readers will want to expand the basic psychological knowledge they have gained from this book. To guide their reading, a list of books for further study has been added after each chapter. It is hoped that the lists will be useful to readers who want to study more of modern psychology than it has been possible to give in a book of this nature.

Brown, G., Cherrington, D. H., and Cohen, L., *Experiments in the Social Sciences*. Harper and Row: London, 1975.

Brown, J. A. C., *Freud and the Post Freudians*. Penguin: London, 1961.

Dobson, C. B., Hardy, M., Heyes, S., Humphreys, A., and Humphreys, P., *Understanding Psychology*. Weidenfeld and Nicolson: London, 1981.

Gardiner, J. M., and Kaminska, Z., *First Experiments in Psychology*. Methuen: London, 1975.

Hall, C. S., *A Primer of Freudian Psychology*. Mentor: New York, 1954.

Hardy, M., and Heyes, S., *Beginning Psychology*. Weidenfeld and Nicolson: London, 1979.

Legge, D., *An Introduction to Psychological Science*. Methuen: London, 1975.

Medcof, J., and Roth, J. (Eds.), *Approaches to Psychology*. Open University Press: Milton Keynes, 1979.

Miller, G. A., *Psychology. The Science of Mental Life*. Penguin: London, 1967.

Miller, S., *Experimental Design and Statistics*. Methuen: London, 1975.

Robson, C., *Experiment, Design and Statistics in Psychology*. Penguin: London, 1973.

Rycroft, C. (Ed.), *Psychoanalysis Observed*. Penguin: London, 1968.

Thomson, R., *The Pelican History of Psychology*. Penguin: London, 1968.

2

SENSATION AND PERCEPTION

Everything we experience comes to us by means of our sense organs. These may be thought of as receiving stations for stimuli which come from outside and from within our body.

Human beings and other higher animals are distinguished by the fact that the sense organs are highly specialized for receiving specific kinds of stimuli. We have eyes for seeing, ears for hearing, the tongue for taste. In the most simple forms of animal life such as the one-celled amoeba, there is no differentiation as regards sense organs. The whole body is equally sensitive to heat, to cold, to pressure, and light.

It may be well for us to define the terms most commonly employed by the psychologist in describing sensory behaviour.

A **sense organ,** sometimes referred to as a **receptor,** is a **specialized part of the body which is selectively sensitive to some types of changes in its environment and not to others.** For example, the eye is a receptor for sensations of light waves but is impervious to sound stimuli. To a deaf individual whose sense of hearing is totally impaired, it would make no difference whether you held a gently ringing alarm clock next to his ear or a wailing siren.

A **stimulus** is any kind of mechanical, physical, or chemical change that acts upon a sense organ. The important feature is the element of 'change'. In 'applied' psychology, we make maximum use of this idea when we want to hold an individual's attention. The advertiser, the teacher, the actor, and the engineer—for example—employ this principle continuously.

Ordinarily, a red light over a door serves as a warning. Left there long enough, we get used to it and its effectiveness as a stimulus is diminished. If we then change its nature by making it a blinking red light, it again serves as an effective stimulus. For the same reason, the advertiser puts motion into his otherwise stationary window displays. The actor changes his position from one spot on the stage to another when he delivers a long oration. The effective schoolteacher changes the pitch of her voice as an aid in sustaining interest.

The behavioural reaction brought forth by a stimulus is termed a **response.** In effect, **every human response is preceded by a stimulus.** (Later, we will have more to say about the nature of this **stimulus–response** activity.)

17

It has been traditional to speak of man's *five* senses—seeing, hearing, smelling, touching, and tasting. Psychological experimentation, however, has expanded our knowledge about sensory functions. We can now identify possibly *eleven* sensory mechanisms. A knowledge of the way in which these organs function provides an understanding of some very common, although interesting, variations of everyday human reactions.

THE SENSE OF SIGHT

Vision is probably the most complicated of our sensory functions. The eyes are the sense organs of sight. They are generally likened to a camera in the way they operate.

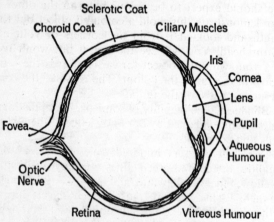

Fig. 4. Horizontal sketch of the eyeball

How We See. Light waves from an object enter the eye through the **pupil** and pass through the **lens.** They focus on the **retina** which is the photographic back plate of the eye or the true **receptor** of visual stimuli. The **optic nerve** attaches to the retina and serves as a medium for carrying the visual impulses to the brain.

The retina has two kinds of receiving cells—**rods** and **cones,** so named because of their shape. The cones are concentrated in the centre of the retina and the rod cells on the outer margin. The proportion of cone cells to rod cells decreases as we proceed from the centre to the outer edge of the retina. In the very centre of the retina is a small depression which is called the **fovea.** It is the point of greatest concentration of the cone cells and hence the area of sharpest vision in daylight.

The **rods** are used for twilight vision or light of low intensity and enable us to make only colourless discriminations.

The **cones** are responsible for daytime levels of light intensity and also enable us to see colours.

To confirm the fact that the **rod cells** (used for twilight vision) are located on the periphery of the retina, conduct this test: in the evening, try to pick out some distant stars of low magnitude. If you gaze directly at them, you will find it difficult to spot any. Then, turn your head to one side and look out of the corners of your eyes. You will suddenly find that several faint stars have come into view. The reason—the concentration of rod cells on the periphery of the retina.

How We See Colours. To examine a function of the **cone cells** (which make possible colour vision), you can try an experiment frequently demonstrated in the psychology laboratory. Since the cones are responsible for colour vision and are concentrated in the centre of the retina, we should expect to be colour blind in the outer edge of the retina. To demonstrate this, hold a coloured object out to the side at arm's length and look at it from the corners of your eyes without turning your head. You will see the object but won't recognize the colour. As you swing the object forward towards the centre of your vision, you will recognize the colour. The reason—the cones are concentrated in the centre of the retina.

Colour Blindness. The inability of some people to distinguish certain colours is partially explained by our knowledge of the relative function of rod cells and cone cells.

About three out of every hundred males are colour blind for the colour qualities of red and green. They see only five distinct colours, namely, yellow, blue, black, white, and grey. All red and green objects appear to them as shades of grey, just as such objects appear to any of us when they are held out to the side and viewed from the corners of the eyes as in the experiment described above.

Many individuals report variations of colour blindness other than the red–green pattern. In all such cases, it is believed that the colour blindness is due to some defect in the **fovea** of the retina where the cones are maximally concentrated. However, it must be emphasized that physiologists and psychologists are agreed that we do not yet have a full understanding of the phenomenon of colour vision.

Light and Dark Adaptation. We are continuously adapting our vision to increasing darkness or increasing brightness in our surroundings. To accomplish this, the retina becomes more or less responsive to light, as the case may be. It is aided by the pupil of the eye which narrows or widens to let in more or less light. Whether the change is towards brightness or darkness, vision is affected and a period of time is needed for the eyes to become accustomed to the surroundings. This is known as **light and dark adaptation.**

Being temporarily blinded by the glare of oncoming headlights is a defect of eye-adaptation. (Since so many of us are prone to this condition, motor-car manufacturers have developed a headlight in which the beam is automatically focused down by the light of an oncoming car.)

The importance of **dark adaptation** has been recognized in warfare. Men who are assigned as lookouts at night or as night patrol stay in the dark for half an hour before going on duty so that they will be fully 'dark adapted'.

Night Vision and the Purkinje Phenomenon. As noted previously, for daylight vision we rely on cone cells and for night vision on rod cells. However, as the daylight blends into night, we distinguish what is called twilight. At this point it is believed that **cone vision** and **rod vision,** as they are called, overlap and that both function together.

The safety engineer is vitally interested in this for the reason that in any 24-hour period the greatest percentage of car accidents occur during the twilight hour when daylight blends into night.

Evidence of how the eye adapts to varying situations is seen in the individual's ability to discriminate colours as the day fades into night. At the first part of twilight one can still distinguish red, yellow, green, and blue, although they appear somewhat blacker and greyer. Then at a particular point of diminished light, the reds begin to darken appreciably and the greens and blues to lighten. This change is called by psychologists the **Purkinje phenomenon,** after the physiologist who first described it in 1825. Finally, in complete night vision (a moonless night with the clouds obscuring the stars) all colours are seen as shades of black, grey, and white. The cone cells responsible for day vision and colour vision are ineffectual in illumination of such low intensity.

Night Blindness. It is generally known that some people have the condition called **night blindness.** When they came to the attention of medical men, they complained of an inability to see properly at night. At first they were thought to be hypochondriacs and were described by some psychologists as neurotic or over-fearful of the dark.

However, it was ultimately learned that these persons suffered from a visual inability to adapt to conditions of low illumination. These night-blind persons were found to have defective rod cells. Their difficulty stemmed from a deficiency in the pigment layer of the retina which supplies an essential substance known as 'visual purple'. This is a chemical compound which decomposes in the presence of light and recombines in darkness. Chemical analysis of visual purple has shown that it depends upon Vitamin A for nutrition. Experimentation has indicated that taking large quantities of Vitamin A, when a deficiency exists, has improved the capacity for twilight and night vision.

The Blind Spot. At one point in the retina there are neither cones nor rods. It is, in fact, not sensitive to any light stimulation and is referred to as the **blind spot.** This is the point where the optic nerve is attached to the retina. You can check your blind spot in each eye by following the simple directions in Fig. 5. Close the left eye. Hold the page 10 inches in front of the right eye. Stare directly at the plus sign with the right eye. Move the book a little nearer or farther away. When the right distance is found the white spot will disappear.

Fig. 5. Blind spot

After-images. If you have been staring at a bright object intently and it is removed suddenly, you will continue to see images of the object. You are apt to feel you are 'seeing things' which aren't there. This *is* the case. It is a common visual experience termed the **after-image,** a phenomenon readily demonstrated and explained in the psychology laboratory.

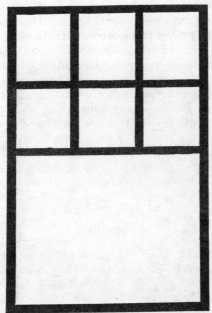

Fig. 6. Development of an after-image

By definition, **after-image is the visual sensory experience which persists after the external stimulus has been removed.** The longer the original stimulus, the stronger will be the after-image.

After-images are explained by the fact that the nerve impulses set up in the retina by a stimulus outlast the stimulus. This is considered to be due to the time-lag between the period when the stimulus is removed and the time it takes to travel along the paths of the nervous system or conscious mental processes.

We experience what are termed 'positive' after-images and 'negative' after-images.

In the **positive after-image,** the same kind of detail, brightness and colour of the *original impression* is experienced after the object is removed. Positive after-images are not very common in everyday experiences. A good example is the yellowish 'spots before your eyes' after you look into the sun. By staring for a few moments at Fig. 6 and then looking away you can create an after-image experience.

In the **negative after-image,** you see a colour or pattern which is **complementary** to that of the original image. For example, if you look at a jet-black surface for a minute, the after image will be white or greyish. You can test this vividly by gazing steadily at a square of bright-red paper for about one minute. Then turn your gaze to a neutral grey background. You will get an after-image having a greenish appearance (because green is the complement of red). Try this with the image of the well-known historical character in Fig. 7.

Fig. 7. Negative of a well-known person

Fix your gaze for about a minute on this impression. Shift quickly to a blank sheet of white paper. You will then see a complementary image of the figure portrayed.

Eye Movements and Reading Efficiency. Clear vision occurs when the eyes and the object being viewed are motionless in relation to each other. The act of seeing is like taking pictures with a camera. To register an image on the retina there must be a period of exposure.

Types of Eye Movements. Laboratory observations reveal that in the act of reading, the eye does not move smoothly along a line, but rather progresses in jerks, taking in two or three words at a time.

The eye movements employed in reading are technically referred to as **saccadic.** These are distinguished from what is termed **pursuit** movements as when you watch a moving train and **compensatory** movements as when you fixate on a stationary object and turn your head from side to side to view it from all angles. A fourth type of eye movement is described as **convergence and divergence,** which occurs when the eyes adjust to an object that is moving directly towards or away from you.

Eye Movements in Reading. For practical application, the general psychologist and educational psychologist, in particular, have been most interested in **saccadic** eye movements.

Detailed studies of eye movements in reading have shown that individuals differ in their habits. In a typical line of story reading matter, containing 10 to 15 words, the average adult uses 5 to 7 eye movements per line. Some individuals use only 4 movements and others as many as 8, 10 or 15, stopping at each word.

Efficiency in reading is directly related to the number of stops and starts or **fixations** the eye makes in moving across a line of type. Other factors related to reading efficiency are the tendencies of some individuals to fixate on the wrong words and to make wasteful **regressive** movements, as they are called.

Characteristic eye movements normally vary with (*a*) the nature of the reading material, (*b*) our familiarity with the information and (*c*) the individual's intelligence.

Easy story reading reveals a minimum number of stops or fixations per line, whereas reading mathematical or chemical formulae entails a maximum number of fixations.

The results of studies tell us that the poorest readers fixate too *long*, look back too *often*, and move forward with too *many* jerky and halting eye movements.

Reading Improvement. While it is admittedly not an easy task, it is generally agreed that most of us can improve our reading efficiency because so few of us practise optimal habits.

In adult courses for improving reading efficiency, emphasis is placed on four features: (1) teaching the reader to move the eyes forward in more even and regular progressions; (2) practice in reducing the number of fixations per line; (3) consciously inhibiting any attempts at regressions (returning to a word already passed); (4) concentration on habits of vocabulary study.

THE SENSE OF HEARING

In several ways our auditory sense has much in common with our visual sense. Together, sight and hearing are the primary mechanisms for bringing to us experiences from the outside. They are sometimes classed as the distance senses because they make possible a judgement of the relative distance from which a stimulus emanates. They are both activated by **wave** movements in the atmosphere. Thus, we speak of 'light waves' and 'sound waves'.

Vision and hearing are obviously of the greatest importance in bringing us into contact with the pleasures of aesthetic experience. Lacking either, we would be deprived of a vast store of sensory experiences in the world about us. It has been pointed out that man's capacity for speaking and hearing words is probably the greatest single factor which separates man from primates.

No profound evidence is needed to convince the reader of the radical changes in behaviour brought by any serious impairment of the hearing sense. For this reason, an understanding of the workings and phenomena of the hearing mechanism has an important place in the traditional curriculum of general psychological study.

How We Hear. Hearing occurs when sound acts as a stimulus to the auditory sense. **Sound** consists of alternate waves of condensation and rarefaction in the form of vibrations in the air. This is what the physicist calls **sound waves.** (For a comprehensive description of the physical nature of sound, read Chapter XI, *Physics Made Simple*, by Ira M. Freeman.) When the sound waves strike the tympanic membrane of the human ear, we experience sound in the psychological sense.

In structure and function the ear is a highly complex organ. We recognize three major parts of the ear—the outer, middle, and inner ear. The **outer ear** serves as a horn to catch sound waves. The **middle ear** acts as a sort of sound transformer while the **inner ear** contains the sensitive receptors.

Sound waves strike the **tympanic membrane** or eardrum. Behind the eardrum is the middle ear containing three small bones (ossicles) which interlock and serve to conduct the sound impulses from the eardrum to the inner ear. They are popularly termed the 'hammer', 'anvil', and 'stirrup' because of their characteristic shapes.

These bones are frequently involved when younger persons are hard of hearing. Their difficulty may be due to a reduction in the flexibility of the joints between the bones. In some cases the joints become 'fixed' as a result of *otosclerosis*, with resulting deafness.

Such a hearing loss is referred to as **conduction deafness.** These persons can benefit by a hearing-aid which employs a bone conduction receiver placed on the mastoid bone just behind the ear.

The **middle ear** is filled with air and is connected with the throat by the **eustachian** tube, named after EUSTACHUS, the sixteenth-century Italian anatomist who first described it. The eustachian tube is closed where it connects with the throat, but it opens when we swallow. In this way it serves to equalize the air pressure in the middle ear with

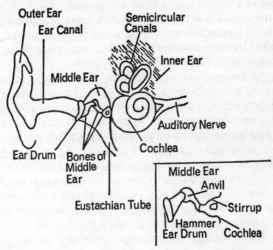

Fig. 8. Diagram of the ear

the outside atmospheric pressure. Thus, when you first get up to a high altitude you feel an uncomfortable bulging of the eardrums because of the lower outside atmospheric pressure. To relieve the discomfort it is advisable to open the mouth and swallow air.

The **inner ear** connects with the middle ear by an oval-shaped window into which is fitted the 'stirrup'. The inner ear is filled with lymph fluids and contains a highly important small, snail-like structure, the **cochlea.** Just above the cochlea is found the **semicircular canal,** which plays no part in hearing but is related to our sense of balance.

Within the cochlea is a section called the **Organ of Corti** containing minutely sensitive **hair cells.** These hair cells are considered to be the fundamental units of the auditory receptors, corresponding to the rods and cones in vision. Much has been written by the physiological psychologists about the Organ of Corti in their attempt to find an answer to this crucial question: how do human beings take in vibratory movements of the atmosphere and convert them into an electro-chemical message to be psychologically interpreted by the brain?

THEORIES OF HEARING

We are not certain about the exact mechanics of hearing. Several theories have been advanced. The longest held is known as the **piano**

theory, developed by the renowned physiologist, HELMHOLTZ. It was his premise that each element or hair cell of the Organ of Corti responded to a specific vibration to which it is tuned much like the strings of a piano. Because of this fixed tuning, we presumably distinguish different vibrations as different sounds.

Another hypothesis is termed the **wave-pattern theory.** This holds that variable sound qualities of pitch result from the combined action of many nerve fibres rather than any single element. Thus, the transmission of *low*-frequency sounds would require combined action of a *few* nerve fibres, and sounds of *higher* frequency would entail co-operative action of a proportionately *greater number* of nerve fibres. It is thought that both pitch and intensity could possibly be explained on a like basis.

A rather remarkable experiment performed by Drs. Wever and Bray seems to support the wave-pattern theory, although it does not prove it. By means of a surgical operation they attached electrodes to the auditory area of a cat's brain. It had previously been established that nerve activity releases electrical energy. Therefore, Drs. Wever and Bray attached a powerful audio-amplifier by means of wires to the electrodes which were in contact with the cat's brain. The audio-amplifier magnified weak electrical currents to a point where they operated a loudspeaker. Next, the cat was placed in a sound-proof room with the wires leading out to the audio-amplifying set. Phonograph music was started in the sound-proof room. To the surprise of the experimenters, the loudspeaker outside the sound-proof room played back the identical music.

While this remarkable Wever–Bray experiment did not prove the 'wave-pattern' theory of hearing, it demonstrated that **the auditory nerve transmits an electrical energy pattern corresponding exactly to the soundwave pattern that hits the ear.** This in itself has been received by experimental psychologists as having great significance. It showed that hearing **is not a symbolic response** in which the nervous mechanism of the ear would have the job of recombining a pattern of air waves into another configuration.

What We Hear. To the question 'what do we hear, wave lengths or sounds?' we know now that the answer is: sounds. We have learned that the ear has the unique function of organizing air vibrations into integrated sound patterns. At this point in most books on general psychology it is a common practice to describe the physical characteristics of sound and the implications of pitch, tonal qualities, intensity, and loudness. But this information belongs more appropriately in a text on general physics. (See *Physics Made Simple*, Chapter XII, by Ira M. Freeman.) For our purposes, we are primarily concerned with hearing and its effect **on behaviour.**

Our Range of Hearing. Not all sound waves are heard by the human ear. In general, the ear responds to sound waves having a vibration frequency from 25 per second to 20,000 vibrations per second. We specify 'human' for the reason that many animals respond to **high-frequency** sounds beyond the 20,000 range which are not usually audible to the human ear.

A dog can respond to a tone too high for human beings to hear. A favourite practice with showmen dog trainers is to teach dogs to respond to these inaudible high-frequency sounds. At the same time they talk to the dog in a conversational manner and give the audience the impression that the dog is carrying out complicated verbal instructions.

Age and Hearing Loss. Within the generally audible ranges, it has been shown that *age* is the dominant factor in causing differences among people in their hearing acuity. Experimenting with several hundred persons varying in age from twenty to seventy years, Dr. S. J. Crowe has made some interesting discoveries about hearing. He found that the lower tones—those having a frequency of less than 1,000—were heard equally well by all the age groups. However, he found that, in general, hearing acuity decreases for the higher frequency ranges (above 8,000) as age increases. The upper limit for individuals between twenty and forty years of age was near the 16,000 frequency; between age forty and sixty, to the 10,000 frequency; and above sixty, to the frequency of 8,000.

Having demonstrated this progressive loss in acuity of hearing for high tones, Dr. Crowe sought to learn the reason. His explorations are of interest to the psychologist because we tend to ascribe such things to 'old age' without finding out the fundamental reasons. Dr. Crowe's experiments in this connection were rather ingenious.

Employing the surgical technique used by Wever and Bray with a cat, Dr. Crowe attached some weights to the tympanic muscle which controls the articulation of the three bones (ossicles) of the middle ear. When large weights were attached to the muscle, greatly increasing the muscle tension, he found that the capacity to transmit low-frequency sounds was impaired, whereas the transmission of high-frequency sounds was not affected. In one case, tones below a frequency of 1,000 were inaudible but tones above the 4,000 range were not affected.

To investigate the reverse situation, he severed the tendon of the tympanic muscle, thereby releasing all tension on the ossicles of the middle ear. This time he found the ability to transmit high-frequency sounds was reduced or destroyed entirely although the transmission of low-frequency sounds was not affected.

From Dr. Crowe's research it was concluded that **the usual decrease in hearing ability with increasing age is due to the loss of muscle tone of the tympanic muscle.**

Acuity of Hearing in Infants and Children. At the *lower* age extreme, researchers have found that infants and monkeys are closest to the lower animals in their capacity to hear sounds in the higher frequency ranges.

In several investigations with chimpanzees, Dr. J. H. Elder found their hearing acuity to be well above the range of human adults. He also found that infants and young children had a range of hearing close to that of the chimpanzee.

Schoolteachers who have had occasion to conduct hearing tests in routine examinations at various times confirm these observations about the hearing of children. In all such group testing, the youngest children have always been found to have the most acute hearing. Being aware of these facts, the experienced elementary schoolteacher or parent will quickly recognize the presence of a hearing defect when any child of school age shows difficulty in hearing in the normal speech range.

The 'Sixth Sense' or 'Facial Vision' of the Blind. If a chair is placed in the path of an alert blind person, you will observe that he is able to avoid it. Very likely, he will also know when another person is before or beside him. Many people consider this ability to be a 'sixth sense', a mysterious kind of 'facial vision' akin to the supposed ability of normal people to tell when someone is staring at their backs.

Experiments show that these ideas are absolutely without foundation. You cannot dependably tell when you are being watched from behind. Try it experimentally and keep tally of your score. Make sure to stuff your ears with cotton-wool, however, to ensure that no slight sounds help your decisions.

As for the 'facial vision' of the blind, three Cornell University psychologists have shown that it is not mysterious at all. Before showing just what this so-called 'sixth sense' really is, let us say that it is *not* the effect of atmospheric pressure on the skin, electromagnetic vibrations, or slight changes in temperature. By alternately covering the face of their subjects, covering the exposed parts of the skin, eliminating the ability to smell, and plugging the ears, Karl Dallenbach, Michael Supa, and Milton Cotzin found that **the blind 'perceive' objects by their sense of hearing.**

Experiments on hundreds of blind people have shown that their sense of hearing is no more powerful than normal. However, it has been trained by adversity and experience. The blind person's inability to see had made it necessary for him to pay more attention to what he hears, often without his knowing it.

Indeed, some *normal*-sighted people have developed their hearing to the point where they too could 'see' in the dark.

OUR SENSE OF TASTE AND SMELL

Descriptions of taste and smell as sensory mechanisms are traditionally linked in books on general psychology. There is a good reason for this. Investigations by psychologists have shown that many of the things we believe we are tasting, are only susceptible to discrimination by our sense of taste plus smell.

You may not readily believe it, but with your eyes closed and your nose clogged, you could not accurately taste the difference between a slice of an apple and a potato.

Taste Receptors. The taste receptors are microscopic hair cells within the 'taste buds'. These are located in the **papillae** of the tongue, epiglottis and soft palate. The hair cells in each taste bud are connected to a nerve and react to chemicals in the liquids of foods when they penetrate the pits in the tongue.

Taste is considered a **chemical sense** and requires a liquid solution for stimulation. Solids will not arouse a sensation of taste until the fluids of the mouth have dissolved them. You can demonstrate this with a little experiment.

Get some cube sugar and rock salt. Find a co-operative friend and dry his or her tongue with a towel. Place a dry piece of cube sugar or rock salt on his tongue. He will be unable to discriminate between he sugar or salt unless you leave them there long enough for the saliva to begin to dissolve them.

The Basic Taste Sensations. There are five basic taste sensations that can be distinguished by taste alone. These are *sweet*, *sour*, *bitter*, and *salty*, plus the taste of *metallic* substances.

Some specialization of these tastes exists in different parts of the tongue. Receptor cells for *sweetness* are concentrated near the tip of the tongue while those sensitive to *bitter* are towards the back. Sensitivity to *sour* occurs mostly along the sides of the tongue and *salt* seems to be uniform over the entire tongue. A bitter pill will not taste as bitter at the tip of the tongue as it will towards the back. Try it.

Mingling of Sense Responses. In the usual situation, what we describe as the taste of a particular food is actually a combination of the basic tastes plus **smell, temperature** or our sense of **touch** in the cheeks. It would be difficult to describe an egg, milk or a grilled steak in terms of the categories of the four basic tastes. Unconsciously, we tend to associate with the 'taste' of milk its coolness, and with steak its sizzling warmth.

In most cases the sense of **smell** supplements our **taste** associations. A popular experiment to demonstrate this is one in which a subject is blindfolded and his nostrils are plugged with cotton wool. Then he is asked to distinguish between the taste of an onion and an apple. In general, the responses are no more accurate than a 50–50 guess.

Further evidence of the intermingling of smell and taste is seen when the person suffering with the common cold complains that everything he eats is 'tasteless'. The stuffed nose has blocked the smell of the foods and shows the limitations of our sense of taste alone. The youngster who holds his nose when taking an unpleasant medicine has benefited by bitter experience. By so doing, he minimizes the unpleasantness.

Very often our preference for a food or beverage in a particular form is due to the fact that it combines several sensory responses rather than just taste. An interesting example is the widespread popularity of carbonated beverages. When you order tonic water in preference to water, one reason is that you like the *feel* of the bubbles of carbon dioxide as they burst and tickle your palate. If you let any sweet carbonated drink stand until the carbonation is removed, what's the usual complaint? 'Flat!' The *taste* is the same as when it is fully carbonated: the only thing missing is the tickling sensation of the bubbles inside of the mouth. Your displeasure is due to absence of the *touch* sensation in the inside of the mouth and is not a complaint against the 'taste'.

Changing Tastes. It is generally recognized that children show differences in taste preferences from those of adults. Most infants show a favourable response to sweet-tasting foods and an initial negative response to bitter, sour, and salty foods. In the early school years, individual differences in children's taste preferences begin to develop. Many display a strong liking for salty and bitter foods. Others dote on sweets. All of us are more sensitive in our taste responses in childhood. For this reason we tend to use more seasoning and exotic flavours as we mature.

Although physiological in its basis, learning plays a large part in shaping taste preferences and habits. We learn to 'cultivate a taste' for many foods. Very few persons like beer or olives the first time they are tasted but rather have to cultivate a taste for them with repeated experiences.

Eating foods under conditions of pleasant or new associations aids in developing a liking for certain foods. Every mother has expressed amazement at the foods Johnny eats at someone else's house which he wouldn't touch at home.

Professional tea tasters and coffee tasters report that they 'develop' their sense of taste by training in much the same way that the blind person cultivates his sense of hearing which, as we have said, is not basically more acute than that of the average sighted individual. In utilizing the sense of taste, as in most physical and physiological aspects of behaviour, it is apparent that 'practice improves'.

Smell. Smell or **olfaction,** as it is called, is also a chemical sense. Our sense of smell is activated when gaseous particles of a substance reach the nasal fluids. The receptors for smell are spindle-shaped cells embedded in the olfactory tissues, which are connected to the olfactory nerve.

The olfactory nerve endings are in the roof of the nasal passages and not in the direct path of inspired and expired air. This arrangement protects the olfactory receptors against over-stimulation. Being so located, it makes it necessary for us to sniff vigorously when we want to 'get a good whiff' of faint odours, as the saying goes. The most volatile substances which break down into the minutest particles smell the strongest because more of them reach the smell sense receptors.

Classifying Smells. As in the sense of taste, experimentation has enabled us to identify a group of **basic smell classifications** as follows:

Spicy: cloves.
Flowery: violet, rose.
Fruity: orange rind.
Resinous: pine, pitch, turpentine.
Scorched: burned tar.
Putrid: decaying fish or meat.

It has been questioned whether any such classification can be complete. It is pointed out that most substances represent a blend of at least two or more of these odour categories. Taken alone, it would be difficult to classify many familiar foods and everyday substances. It would be difficult to obtain agreement on which of these primary odours is found in such familiar items as ammonia, petroleum, alcohol, garlic, and lemon juice.

Much of this type of psychological laboratory experimentation has been introspective and subjective. It is by no means exhaustive and should not be considered as such by the reader.

Smell Capacities of Children. What we have learned from such experimentation is that individuals vary greatly in their smell sensitivities. Children respond more readily to smell stimuli than adults. For whatever implications we can draw from it, children are closer to animals. Their sense of smell is vastly more responsive than that of human adults. There is a physiological basis for this in that the **olfactory lobes,** the 'smell brain' of man, are much smaller, proportionately, than those of animals.

Smell Adaptability. An important characteristic of our sense of smell is its ready adaptability. If you come into the presence of a strong and unpleasant smell, although seemingly unbearable at first, the unpleasantness will not disturb you as much after several minutes.

Sanitation personnel and others are able to work in refuse dumps, fish glue factories, perfumeries and other 'impossible smelling places' all day long without real discomfort. It has been demonstrated that after a relatively brief period of intense stimulation most of our sensory organs show a greatly diminished response. This 'adaptability' may be thought of as a natural protective mechanism.

THE FEELING SENSES

In the skin, where formerly only the sense of touch was thought to prevail, we now distinguish four individual senses—**touch or pressure, pain, warmth** and **cold.** Receptors for these sensations are not limited to the skin. Internal organs, to a much lesser degree, also respond to sensations of touch, pain and temperature.

For each type of **cutaneous** or skin sensation, there are believed to be specialized nerve endings which react to the specific type of stimuli. For example, the application of heat to the skin activates different nerve endings than those which respond to tactile pressure. The sensory tracts for impulses of pain, pressure, and temperature follow separate paths through the spinal cord to the brain.

Evidence for this dissociation of closely related skin sensitivities is seen in a relatively rare disease called *syringomyelia*. In this circumstance, the victim loses sensitivity to heat and cold but retains the sense of touch. Such persons may lean against hot stoves and sustain bad burns without any feeling of discomfort.

Sensations of Hot and Cold. Reactions to heat and cold are separate sensations rather than extremes of the same sensation. Different nerve endings in the surface of the skin carry the messages of heat and cold stimuli. This has been demonstrated by mapping actual hot and cold receptor areas on the skin with heated and chilled needle points.

There is an odd exception to the separate action of hot and cold receptors on the surface of the skin. Cold spots will respond to the application of intense heat and warm spots will react to an application of intense cold. These reverse sensations are referred to by the psychologist as **paradoxical cold** and **paradoxical warmth.** They explain the effects of the familiar trick of blindfolding a victim and telling him that he is to be branded with a hot iron while pressing a piece of ice against his back. Often a victim will scream because momentarily he really feels he is being scorched. Another example is that of the youngster who has been playing with snowballs for a half hour and comes into the house crying that his 'hands are burning' when they are really freezing. However, his confusion is understandable. The intense cold has activated the hot spots as well as the cold spots on the surface of his hands.

The Sensitive Areas of the Skin. By means of interesting and painstaking explorations with two-pointed styluses, bristle brushes and heated needles, experimental psychologists have literally mapped out the surface of the body with reference to the feeling senses.

You can accept the psychologists' findings or explore them for yourself. By way of generalization they tell us that different parts of the body have different degrees of sensitivity for the various stimuli. Some parts are more responsive to touch, others to pain, some to heat and some to cold.

The lips and fingertips are most responsive to **touch** or pressure. This may be the basis of kissing and handshaking as forms of greeting. The fingertips are almost equally responsive to **pain.** One square centimetre on the tip of the finger is reported to have sixty pain spots. The cornea of the eye is said to have many *pain* spots but no *touch* spots.

The calf area of the leg is relatively insensitive to cold. That is why sheer nylon stockings can keep women warm.

Occasionally we find reports in the newspapers about persons who are insensitive to any feelings of pain or pressure, or hot and cold. These have been explained by a possible damage to the specific region of the brain (at the top of the head) that receives messages from the nerves carrying the 'feeling sensations'.

Pain Sensation. Specialized receptor nerve-endings for **pain** are located deeper in the skin tissue. To cause pain by such means as pinching, cutting or pricking the skin, the stimulation needs to go below the general protective layer of skin. Extreme temperatures of heat and cold which penetrate the skin also register sensations of pain.

Although not entirely insensitive, the internal organs contain few pain receptors. For this reason, once the surgeon gets into the viscera, his knife-cut produces little pain. This fact also explains how diseases of internal organs, such as cancer and tuberculosis, can make great headway before they make themselves felt.

Intense or continued stimulation of other sense organs gives rise to pain. We speak of 'eye strain' after a full day's use of the eyes in poor light. The constant din of noise can cause an 'earache' or a 'headache'. Pain sensations of this nature are **protective.** They can sometimes serve as a signal of excessive stresses and strains, and if persistent may indicate some internal disease or incubating infection.

SENSE OF BALANCE

When you begin to fall and catch yourself in time, you are apt to say, 'I almost lost my balance.' The normal ability to maintain an upright position and a 'sense of balance' is controlled by a delicate sensory mechanism called the **semicircular canals.**

Within the labyrinth of the inner ear, in addition to the cochlea, we find the semicircular canals which are receptors for sensations of position and balance. There are three semicircular canals about the diameter of a pinhead in size, which are bent like pretzels and arranged in three perpendicular planes corresponding to the back, side, and top of the head. The canals are filled with a lymph-like fluid and contain hair cells attached to nerve endings as were found in the cochlea. It is believed that movements of the head which set the fluids in motion, stimulate the hair cells and thus register a sensation of change in position.

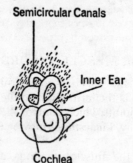

Fig. 9. The semicircular canals

The position and movements of the head control the body position in space. Anyone learning to drive or do acrobatics soon learns to take advantage of this fact. What happens is that with repeated experiences they are learning to interpret the sensations of equilibrium in the semicircular canals. This ability is referred to as a capacity for orienting one's self in space. Some individuals come by this ability naturally. However, it can be improved with training.

Overstimulation of the semicircular canals causes dizziness and a loss of balance. Every youngster soon learns that if he spins himself around in circles, when he stops, he will feel that his surroundings are still spinning. This is explained by the fact that the fluids in the canals are continuing to swish around, owing to momentum.

Symptoms of dizziness or **vertigo,** as it is technically termed, can frequently be traced to some disturbance of the semicircular canals. Individuals rising suddenly out of bed will occasionally complain of feelings of dizziness. This is thought to be due to the sensation created by the sudden movement of the head in overcoming the inertia of the fluids in the semicircular canals. Others with an ear inflammation or respiratory infection that affects the inner ear, will report spells of dizziness.

Visual effects are known to be closely connected through the nervous system with the sense of equilibrium. Figure skaters and twirling ballet dancers prevent themselves from getting dizzy by momentary fixations of the eyes on a spot each time they twirl around. They are also aided by a conditioning of their sense of equilibrium through constant practice. Looking at the ground from a great height while watching a stream of traffic can cause dizziness. Children in a motor-car trying to follow the scenery with their eyes may become dizzy and affected by nausea.

Feelings of nausea and vertigo are closely associated through a similar proximity of the nerve patterns. A classic example of the close relationship between these two sensations is seen in the intermittent spells of nausea and dizziness which so often plague the pregnant woman.

SENSE OF MUSCLE CO-ORDINATION

Very closely linked to the sense of equilibrium is what we call the **kinaesthetic** sense. This is the term given to the sensory impulses from muscles, tendons, and joints which control the co-ordination of body movements. More simply, **kinaesthesis may be defined as the awareness of body movements.**

Nerve endings from the muscles, tendons, and joints connect with the nerve pathways to various parts of the brain for registering kinaesthetic sensations. We use the sensations from our muscles and tendons as cues for performing a multitude of muscular activities from the simple act of reaching out for an object to the highly complex act of performing a fancy high-dive off a springboard.

In everyday situations, we do not usually give conscious attention to the responses of our muscle and tendon senses. However, in certain physical abnormalities where they are impaired, we gain a conscious appreciation of the implications of the kinaesthetic sense. This is most tragically brought to our awareness when we observe victims of the crippling disease known as **muscular dystrophy.** Their impaired kinaesthetic sensory mechanism makes it a hardship for their muscles and joints to carry out the dictates of an unimpaired intellect.

The kinaesthetic sense mechanisms and the semicircular canals co-operate in maintaining muscle control. Animals whose semicircular canals have been removed will stagger around aimlessly in a limp way. However, after a period of time they recover much of the lost motor control and improve the accuracy of their movements when the muscle senses apparently have had a chance to take over. In prize fighting, a knockout blow to jaw or head will make the victim go limp. This is thought to be caused by the shock to the semicircular canals, producing a temporary loss of muscle tone in the entire body.

VISCERAL SENSES

As suggested by the term itself, the visceral senses pertain to the sensory responses thought to originate from the internal organs such as the stomach, intestine, liver, heart, bladder, and genitalia.

Surgical experience over the years yielded the information that without the benefit of anaesthetics, intestinal organs could be cut and cauterized without arousing pain. For this reason it was once thought that the internal organs did not produce sensory responses. However, laboratory experimentation has indicated that the internal organs do respond to stimuli of warmth, cold, and stretching of the walls. It has been further noted that sensations from the visceral organs are not as accurately localized as those other senses like hearing, taste, or equilibrium. Because of the vagueness of the exact origin of the various visceral sensations, many psychologists question whether the viscera can be classified as true sensory organs.

Regardless of whether we label the viscera as true sense organs, they do respond to specific stimuli and register characteristic body sensations which influence behaviour. We refer to sensations of hunger, thirst, fatigue, and sexual excitement, which indisputably have their origin in the internal organs. Dryness of the throat contributes to the sensation of thirst. Contractions of the walls of the stomach are interpreted as hunger sensations. Pressure of faecal matter against the walls of the large intestine becomes the signal for a call to excrete. Reverse waves of peristalsis in walls of the stomach cause feelings of nausea.

While some receptor mechanisms for visceral sensations are found in the digestive, circulatory, and excretory organs, we do not as yet know the exact mechanisms by which they are created. For example, we know that generalized feelings of sexual pleasure and emotional depression originate to some extent to the internal organs. However, a more accurate answer as to just what mechanism gives rise to those sensations must await further experimentation and analysis.

To the reader, this inquisitiveness of the psychologist as to the origin of certain sensory experiences may at first seem like a quest for a scientific answer only for its own sake. This is not necessarily the case, for it is hoped that such disclosures may help in furthering our comprehension of some little-understood aspects of human behaviour. For example, it is possible that a more exact knowledge of the origin of internal sensory experiences may contribute to our understanding of the mechanism of some forms of emotional or mental illness. The development of the alkaloid drugs, by which we have been able to produce in volunteer subjects various agitated states of emotional unbalance, would seem to confirm the theories that some forms of emotional deviations can have a specific internal organic basis. A knowledge of just which internal sense organ or organs are affected by the drugs must await further investigation.

SUGGESTED FURTHER READING

Blundell, J., *Physiological Psychology*. Methuen: London, 1975.

Gregory, R. L., *Eye and Brain*. 2nd Edn, Weidenfeld and Nicolson: London, 1972.

Moray, N., *Listening and Attention*. Penguin: London, 1969.

Padgham, C. A., and Saunders, J. E., *The Perception of Light and Colour*. G. Bell and Sons: London, 1975.

Thompson, R., *Introduction to Physiological Psychology*. Harper and Row: London, 1975.

Zusne, L., *Visual Perception of Form*. Academic Press: London, 1970.

3

PERCEPTION

Perception *versus* **Sensation.** Psychologically, a fine discrimination is made between the processes of sensation and perception.

Sensation, we have said, is the act of receiving a stimulus by a sense organ.

Perception is the act of interpreting a stimulus registered in the brain by one or more sense mechanism.

While the mechanics or physiology for receiving stimuli are similar from one individual to the next, our interpretation of these stimuli may easily differ.

To illustrate the difference between sensation and perception, a common analogy compares a *photograph* of a scene with an artist's *painting* of the scene. The photograph would record the scene as the sense organ **receives** it whereas the painting depicts the scene as the artist **perceives** it. Succinctly stated, we might say, the eye 'receives' while the mind 'perceives'.

Sensation Without Perception. Instances of pure sensation in human experiences are rare. If you hear a strange noise, no matter how unusual, you immediately associate it with something familiar. If you see a completely strange and foreign object, you unconsciously attempt to relate it to some form or shape you have seen before. The nearest circumstance to a pure sensation might be the instant in which a colour is presented for the first time to a person who has been blind from birth and suddenly gained the power to see.

No one of us can look at an object, hear a voice or taste food and receive these sensations without projecting into them some facet of past experience. At whatever age, the accumulations of a lifetime of all sensory experiences go into our perceptions. An orange might be perceived by an infant as just another coloured ball with which to play. To an adult in the United States, at this time, it represents a commonplace breakfast fruit served usually in the form of juice. To some youngster in Great Britain during the Second World War when oranges were very scarce, it would have represented a curiosity and a luxury to be enjoyed in its entirety as a rare treat. Thus, in describing the phenomenon of perception, we come to the psychological truism aptly stated by the philosopher Immanuel Kant: 'We see things not as they are but as we are.' In other words, perception represents our apprehension of a present situation in terms of our past experiences.

What we perceive at any given time, therefore, will depend not only on the nature of the actual stimulus, but also on the background or setting in which it exists—our own previous sensory experiences, our feelings of the moment, our general prejudices, desires, needs, attitudes and goals.

Although these various elements are present in a general way in our perceptions, one feature will be more influential than another in

Fig. 10. Closure, or wholeness, in perception

affecting our perceptual reactions to specific aspects of the environment. For convenience in analysing and understanding the role of each of these essential elements of perception, we might list them as follows:

The sensory nature of the stimulus.
The background or setting.
Previous related sensory experience.
Personal feelings, attitudes, drives, goals.

How We Perceive. Ordinarily we are not aware of the processes that determine our perceptions. Whether they are perceptions of sight, hearing or touch, we rarely stop to analyse the incoming sensations and the basis of our interpretations. We know only that we see, hear and respond to situations in meaningful contexts. This is a characteristic human approach to everything that is familiar in the environment. Thus, we are accustomed to organizing things in our mind into a form, a shape, a melody, or a scene that makes up a meaningful whole. Whatever the perception, it is a unified experience. If we look at a clock, for example, we don't 'see' its parts, we perceive the 'whole' instrument which we recognize as a timepiece. If we pick up an apple and bite into it, we are not aware of a group of 'taste sensations' such as bitter, sweet, etc.—we taste an apple.

To prove to yourself this tendency to perceive things as an organized total, look at Fig. 10. You don't just see a few sketched-in black lines. You see a man, wearing a hat and glasses and smoking a pipe. This particular concept of 'how we perceive' is the important hypothesis of the **Gestalt school of psychology.**

The Gestalt Concept of Perception. The Gestalt adherents point out that in our perceptions we are prone to organize stimuli along the lines of certain natural tendencies which might be related to an organizing and grouping function in the brain.

Some contemporary psychologists maintain that these so-called 'natural tendencies' are the results of learned experiences. Whatever their origin, all agree that the tendencies do exist and follow almost universal patterns.

For ease of study, these patterning tendencies have been classified descriptively as factors of (1) **similarity,** (2) **proximity,** (3) **continuity,** (4) **closure.** As you review the examples of perception illustrating each of these factors it will be noted that—primarily—they fall into the **first** of the four categories in that they are most influenced by the sensory nature of the stimulus.

PERCEPTION AND THE NATURE OF THE STIMULUS

Similarity. Items of the same size, shape, or quality are more likely to be viewed as a group or pattern than dissimilar elements. In Fig. 11 there is a strong tendency to see four alternating groups of double rows because of our inclination to unite the similar x's and o's even though the rows are evenly spaced.

XXXXOOOOXXXXOOOOXXXXOOOOXXXXOOOO
XXXXOOOOXXXXOOOOXXXXOOOOXXXXOOOO

Fig. 11. The effect on perception of similarity

By reason of this same organizing tendency, when we view a landscape from a vantage point high on a hill, we set off in our mind's eye images of planted fields of corn, potatoes, rows of fruit trees in an orchard and other areas of patchwork. Anyone travelling over a large city in an aeroplane cannot help but pick out the clusters of similar houses here and there which represent recent building developments.

Proximity. Items that are close together tend to be 'grouped' in our perceptions. In viewing Fig. 12,

dis   abl   est   ish

Fig. 12. The effect of proximity on perception

we see four groups of three letters each. Even though they are meaningless in this form, we see them as dis/abl/est/ish/. However, were we to bring them close together you would no longer see four groups but rather the one equally meaningless word *disablestish*.

Continuity. In viewing a pattern such as Fig. 13 two factors are prevalent. We see the dots as straight lines and not as separate dots.

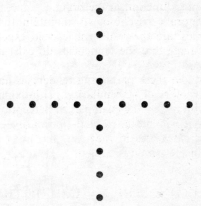

Fig. 13. The effect of continuity on perception

Further, the dots group themselves as two continuing lines rather than as four short lines meeting at a central focus. This is called the factor of **continuity** and illustrates our natural opposition to break the continuous flow of a line, pattern or design in our perceptual awareness.

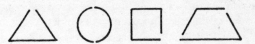

Fig. 14. The effect of closure on perception

Closure. If we look at the geometrical shapes in Fig. 14, we see them as a triangle, square, and circle. Although they are not complete, there exists a strong inclination to perceive them as unified wholes. Thus we tend to fill in mentally or 'close' the triangle, the circle, the square, and the trapezium.

This is referred to as the phenomenon of **closure** in perception. It might best be described as **an organizing tendency to complete an incomplete pattern.**

PERCEPTION AND THE BACKGROUND OR SETTING OF THE STIMULUS

Everyone has probably had the experience of remarking how different an object or event appeared in a different setting. This is related to the fact that we do *not* perceive objects as isolated elements. Because of our inherent tendency to see things in an organized totality, we always

Fig. 15. The effect of context on the perception of size

visualize them in a context or setting. And the total context or background in which certain stimuli occur will influence our perception of those stimuli.

The popular picture of the fisherman, Fig. 15, is used in many books on psychology to illustrate the effects of context on perception of size. You will note that the fish appears to be relatively larger in relation to the man and smaller in relation to the hand.

As you stand in the railway station and the train moves out, there's no question in your mind that you are standing still while the train is moving. However, as you sit looking out of the window of your train at the one on the next track, you tend to think your own train is

Fig. 16. Seeing is believing

moving when the other one starts out of the station. Your misapprehension is due to the unfamiliar frame of reference when you are sitting in a train as compared with standing on a station platform.

Making comparative judgements about the size of objects in relation to their background leads us to commit many unsuspected errors. For

Fig. 17. Fluctuations of perception

example, look at the drawing of the table in Fig. 16. What is your judgement about whether you can place a small coin inside the area of the table-top without touching an edge? Try it and see to what extent the total setting had influenced the accuracy of your perception.

Fluctuations of Perception. It has been observed that in some situations the setting or background of a stimulus is not definitive. In such cases we experience the phenomenon of shifting perceptions. This is best illustrated in what is termed psychologically as the **figure-ground relationship.**

Look at Fig. 17. At first you are apt to see a black goblet on a white background. Look again and note your observations.

In Fig. 18, we have what is known as the **Köhler cross.** At first glance you see the black cross and white background. After gazing at

Fig. 18. The Köhler cross

it for a while you will see a white cross against a black background. If you continue to stare at the figure, you may time yourself to see how frequently a shift occurs as to which is the figure and which is the background.

An equally popular illustration of this figure-ground relationship is pictured in Fig. 19, which is referred to as the 'shifting staircase'.

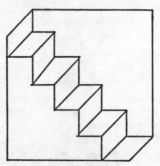

Fig. 19. The shifting staircase

Do you see the staircase from above or below?

Perception of Relationships. While investigating the 'context' or 'setting' aspect of perceptions, many psychological studies have shown that animals learn to respond to relationships between stimuli as well as to specific stimuli. One of the earliest and best known of such experiments was performed by WOLFGANG KÖHLER, a leader in the Gestalt school of psychology. He first demonstrated that a chicken can be taught to avoid a dark grey square and to approach a medium grey square. If after learning this, the chicken is presented with a medium-grey square and another square of lighter grey it will go to the lighter grey square. Thus it is shown that the chicken has learned to respond to the relationship of one stimulus being *lighter than* another.

PERCEPTION IN TERMS OF PREVIOUS RELATED EXPERIENCE

The way in which we perceive any present situation is inevitably related to some previous sensory experience. If the previous experience occurs frequently, our reaction becomes one of habit. The popular expression that 'man is the victim of habit' is scientifically true where his perceptual responses are concerned. It is probable that 90 per cent of our daily sensory experiences are perceived in an habitual manner based on repeated previous experiences.

Reaction to Cues and Symbols. Because so much of our daily activity is dependent upon previous experience, we have learned to react to **cues** and **symbols** rather than to the total original stimuli. Thus, in most situations, **perception is largely a process of inference based on past experiences.** We see a moving outline in the sky and 'infer' that it is an aeroplane although we cannot actually see what it is. We hear a rhythmic sputter and without turning, we assume the sound to be coming from the exhaust of a car. In practice, many of our daily activities consist of responses to familiar cues or symbols. We smell coffee percolating and visualize breakfast being prepared. The young child hears the garage door open and concludes that bedtime is near and father has just come home.

In reacting to cues, we have in reality trained ourselves to jump to conclusions from partial and familiar stimuli where common sensory perceptions are concerned. Depending as we do upon habit and past experiences rather than critical observation, we frequently commit many errors in perception. Some of our perceptual errors in gauging external situations are so common that they are referred to in psychology as 'normal illusions'.

Illusions. When there is a definite discrepancy between what we perceive and the actual facts, the experience is termed an **illusion.** For example, if you put a pencil into a cup of water, the pencil will appear bent. But you know, of course, that it is not. Your perception of the pencil as bent is a false one—an illusion.

Our senses can be deceived in many ways and these deceptions extend to any of the senses. However, in psychological experimentation, **visual illusions** have received the greatest amount of attention.

Illusion of Length. The best known of the visual illusions is the **Mueller–Lyer illusion** pictured in Fig. 20. (This phenomenon is named

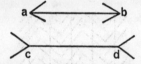

Fig. 20. The Mueller–Lyer illusion

after the two experimenters who first demonstrated it in original papers.) Look at horizontal lines *ab* and *cd* and decide which is shorter. Then measure them.

Illusion of Area. In Fig. 21 the inner circle of *a* appears larger than that of *b*. Measure the diameters of both inner circles.

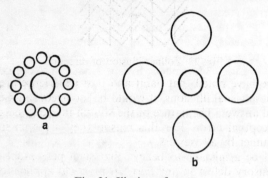

Fig. 21. Illusion of area

Illusions of Distortion. In Fig. 22 lines *a* and *b* appear to bulge and the circle *c* appears distorted. Hold the book on a line with your vision

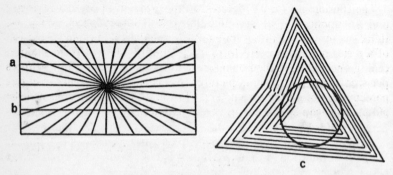

Fig. 22. Illusions of distortion

and you will find the lines to be straight and parallel, and the circle is perfect.

Illusion of Direction. Although they appear to be curved, all the vertical lines in Fig. 23 will be found to be straight and parallel.

Fig. 23. Zollner illusion of direction

While we have noted that habit and past experience are factors in creating these visual illusions, it would be incorrect to assume this to be the total answer. The nature of the stimuli in each case contributes to the perceptual error. For this reason they are seen in the same illusory manner by all viewers.

It would be a mistake to believe that such perceptual errors represent a sensory defect in any way. In practical applications, artists, decorators, sculptors, and architects must take into account such perceptual effects in carrying on their work. They often make allowances in their constructions by purposely curving some of the lines if it is desired that they be 'seen' as straight lines.

The Illusion in Cinema Pictures. In the creation of cinema films, we find an application of a similar universal illusory effect. What we think is a moving picture is in reality a presentation in rapid succession of a series of stationary pictures, each slightly different from the preceding one. When flashed on a screen at a rate of twenty-four pictures per second we see 'moving' pictures. Actually the movement is in our perception, not on the screen. This illusion of movement is termed the **phi-phenomenon** by the experimental psychologist.

PERCEPTION AND PERSONAL FEELINGS, ATTITUDES, DRIVES, ETC.

As we continue to explore the process of perception, it becomes more and more evident that it is not a simple mechanical process of receiving specific stimuli which produce specific results.

Psychology

The process of perception, whether it occurs as an illusion or yields a true perspective of external reality, is a two-way affair. It is like a reversible chemical formula. It is the result of action and reaction. Just as the 'setting', 'previous occurrence', and 'nature' of a *stimulus* affect perception, so do the 'background', 'setting', and 'nature' of the *individual* affect perception. Thus, any mental fact, emotional state, strong desire or attitude can be seen to have an influence on a perceptual response.

Perception and Emotion. It is a psychological truism to say that feelings and emotions will influence one's capacity for accurate or objective perceptions. It has been demonstrated time and again that descriptions of events by emotionally excited witnesses are highly unreliable. In courtroom murder trials where emotions run high, two or more witnesses with no reason to lie have been known to give completely contradictory testimony to identical events. By statute, neither a husband nor wife can be compelled to testify against one another because, among other considerations, it is felt that their emotional involvement makes it impossible for them to give reliable testimony. For the same reasons a judge will disqualify himself from a case in which members of his family are involved. Similarly, a psychotherapist generally refrains from treating his own family.

Effects of Enthusiasm on Perception. Even in situations of lesser emotional involvement it has been noted that a strong urge to win can interfere with accurate sensory perception.

As a youngster everyone has at one time or another been involved in an argument about 'where the ball bounced'. Two individuals, side by side, each having 20–20 vision, watch a ball bounce with reference to the 'service line'. One insists the ball bounced 'short' of the line; the other that it bounced over the line. Neither one is consciously lying nor desirous of cheating. One of the contestants is wrong. The retinal sensation of where the ball bounced was identical for both. One of them was committing an error of perception. This faulty interpretation was influenced by the enthusiasm to win a point. This kind of perceptual miscalculation is much more common in everyday experiences than we like to admit. It is the reason why in amateur boxing, for instance, two or more judges are asked to officiate.

Perceptual Distortions Due to Strong Drives. Psychological literature is replete with examples of situations in which individuals are prone to errors of perception when influenced by a strong drive or emotion. In a laboratory study on 'perceptual distortion', psychologists Gardner Murphy, Robert Levine, and Isidore Chein presented eighty different objects, one at a time, behind a ground-glass screen to a group of college students who had been deprived of food for varying periods of time. Through the ground-glass screen the students were able to see shadowy outlines of the objects. The study showed that as hunger increased the students tended more and more to interpret the indistinct forms as items of food. In real life situations of great stress, actions of this kind account for the fact that the desert traveller suffering from intense heat and parched throat sees the mirage of a thirst-quenching pool of water which turns out to be more sand.

Perception and Suggestion. Closely related to emotion and strong feeling, we find **suggestion** to be another factor in causing errors of perception. The late Professor Frederic Knight of Purdue University described a classroom experiment in which he uncorked a bottle which he stated contained a delicate perfume. He requested that the members of the class raise their hands as soon as they detected the odour. Although the content of the bottle was odourless, almost every student in the classroom had his hand raised within a few minutes.

The familiar 'rope trick' of India is reported to be a case of mass suggestion. Under the influence of the performer's vivid and persuasive description, the members of the audience 'see' a rope uncurl and stand upright, unsupported in space.

By suggestion, it is not too difficult to cause some persons to experience feelings of nausea or students in a comfortably heated classroom to feel chilled to the point of chattering teeth.

Some readers may recognize that these extremes of suggestion border on the effects of hypnosis. This is indeed the case. Preliminary to performing a hypnotic demonstration before a large group, a hypnotist will usually make some suggestion requiring a sensory or motor response and observe his audience carefully. Those who respond most readily and definitively to the suggestion are considered to be the best subjects for hypnosis.

In the phenomenon of **hypnotism,** as it is understood psychologically, we have innumerable situations in which our senses are deceived by what the mind is directed to see, feel or hear in an extreme state of suggestibility. Often we have witnessed hypnotic demonstrations in which it is suggested to a subject that an ordinary coin held in the hand is getting red hot. Immediately, the coin is dropped and the person says that he felt his fingers being burned. Such hypnotic influences of 'mind over matter' as they are called, are really commonplace psychological phenomena.

While we do not fully understand the mind effects that take place in hypnosis, it is generally agreed that hypnotic suggestibility can radically distort our perceptions regardless of whether they pertain to auditory, visual, political or philosophical events.

At its inception, hypnotism was used in a practical way to suggest to a person that he was insensitive to pain in some part of the body. In this way, it was employed successfully for surgical anaesthesia before the discovery of ether. Even today, hypnotism is still occasionally used instead of a chemical anaesthetic. Usually, the surgery is performed on external parts of the body, most often in amputation cases. However, hypnotism is sometimes used for abdominal surgery, such as the removal of the appendix. It has also been used in dentistry.

Sensory Deprivation. During the late 1950's and early 1960's a series of experiments investigated the effect of severely reduced sensory input on subjects. Subjects were required to do nothing but lie on a bed with eyes, ears and hands shielded to reduce to a minimum the sensory input from the environment. Few subjects were able to endure this task for long. Results suggested that the individual needs varying sensory stimulation from his environment.

Perception and Adjustment. It is apparent that perception plays an essential role in shaping our general adjustment. It is a premise of psychology that if more people were aware of the frailties and unreliability of our so-called powers of perception, we would all be less positive and more tolerant of each other's judgements and mistakes. With such a purpose in mind, the study of 'perception' from the earliest days of psychology as a science to the present has been one of the most important areas of investigation. As a result of innumerable studies in the field of perception, psychological research and analysis has helped us better to understand human behaviour by exploring the why and how by which we perceive the events, people and objects of our daily environment.

SUGGESTED FURTHER READING

Barber, P. J., and Legge, D., *Perception and Information*. Methuen: London, 1976.

Forgus, R. H., *Perception*. McGraw-Hill: New York, 1966.

Haber, R. N., and Hershenson, M., *The Psychology of Visual Perception*. Holt, Rinehart and Winston: New York, 1973.

Vernon, M. D., *The Psychology of Perception*. Penguin: London, 1962.

Vernon, M. D. (Ed.), *Experiments in Visual Perception*. Penguin: London, 1966.

Vernon, M. D., *Perception Through Experience*. Methuen: London, 1970.

4

LEARNING

In the preceding chapter it was shown how **perception** consists of the ways in which the brain interprets the sensations registered upon our sense mechanisms by stimuli. With this knowledge, we are now prepared to understand the processes of **learning, which consist of the ways in which we modify our responses to those stimuli that affect us.**

It may seem odd to connect the idea of learning with the idea of disturbance. However, a moment's thought will show that even the most impractical-seeming act of learning serves a practical, if sometimes obscure, purpose. Take so extreme a case as learning from a magazine article how to count to ten in the Mongolian language. This apparently useless deed can reassure us of our ability to understand and remember. Such reassurance would not be necessary if we were not occasionally troubled by doubts of our mental powers—doubts that would certainly upset us if confirmed.

Most acts of learning are more obviously related to a threatening situation. Sometimes the threat is physical: we may be pottering about in an unfamiliar cellar when the light bulb burns out and we must learn how to find our way back to the stairway in the dark. Sometimes the threat is emotional: we have offended our hostess and must soon apologize appropriately or lose her esteem and the social advantages that it permits. In either kind of situation, we must remember, discover or invent the proper thing to do. If we fail to come up with the solution, we shall suffer either a loss or actual pain.

In many problem situations, failure to arrive at a solution can result in more than mere discomfort. In some situations our very survival depends upon our ability to solve the problem posed to us. If we do not learn how to obtain water and food for our body demands, we will not long continue to live. We must attribute *survival* to our ability to learn how to adjust to situations of internal distress and external danger. To put it in to psychological language, we survive because we can **associate corrective responses with disturbing stimuli.**

How We Respond to Stimuli. You will recall from the chapter on sensation that **stimuli** are changes in our environment. Our eyes, our ears and our other sense organs are continuously bringing us messages of such changes. Some sensations come from stimuli **within the body.** They express our physical needs for air, water, food, warmth, and sleep, and our emotional needs for security, approval, and companionship. Other sensations come from stimuli in the **outer world** of objects and people. They communicate changes in material, spatial, climactic, as well as personal, social, business, and political conditions.

We saw that stimuli cause changes in behaviour called **responses.** The **species,** the **structure,** the **organic state,** and **past experiences** of an organism determine whether or not there will be a response to a given stimulus. Not every living element will respond to any stimulus. Germs do not react to music. A rabbit will flee a bone tossed to attract a dog. A sleeping man and a man suffering from nausea will each react differently to the smell of a sizzling steak than will a hungry man. A man who smiles with delight at the mention of the word 'parade' may have an otherwise identical twin brother who frowns at the memory called up by the word of a fatiguing march.

The smile and the frown just mentioned are examples of **muscular** responses to stimuli. Responses may also be **glandular,** as when we shed tears in sadness and salivate when hungry. Muscular and glandular responses that are readily observable like these are called **overt.** A person's responses are said to be **covert** when he reacts to stimuli with no activity that can be readily observed. While listening to music, we may say nothing and seem to do nothing. Nevertheless, we are responding to it, not only intellectually but emotionally and therefore physiologically and physically too. We may lift an eyebrow slightly, nod our heads a bit, or breathe a trifle more rapidly from time to time. If we think we are sitting absolutely still during so-called silent reading, delicate instruments would detect such subtle responses as inaudible movements of the larynx. These are examples of 'covert' responses. Although not readily observed, they are as specific as any which are 'overt'.

The point is that any stimulus able to register upon the brain is responded to in some way, however slight. Only a dead organism ignores *all* stimuli, whereas the entire behaviour of living organisms consists of making responses to stimuli. As we have seen, many of the stimuli in our inner and outer environments threaten to upset our self-esteem, happiness, or safety. **The process by which we come to make the responses that will overcome or counter the threatening stimuli is called learning.**

THE PREVALENCE OF LEARNING

Learning is certainly a universal experience. Everyone must always be learning, at every stage in life. Infants must learn to talk, to dress and feed themselves. Children must learn social habits acceptable to the community. Adults must learn how to perform their jobs, and how to meet the responsibilities of family life. Daily life is a succession of major and minor problems that have to be solved by learning.

If we reflect upon the examples of learning given above, we see that the words 'to learn' can have three different meanings. 'To learn' can mean: **to discover or invent; to commit to memory; to become efficient.** We intend the *first* meaning when we ask this question: 'Have you learned how to take this puzzle apart yet?' We intend the *second* meaning when we ask: 'Did you ever learn the words of "Twinkle Twinkle Little Star"?' We intend the *third* meaning when we say: 'Have you learned how to drive a car?'

Sometimes we intend all three meanings simultaneously, as when we say: 'Have you learned how to knot a tie without looking in a mirror?' In this example, we are really asking three questions. First, whether our friend has solved the problem for himself at all. Second, if he has, whether he has committed the steps of the process to memory. Third, whether he has developed any skill at performing the sequence of actions that makes up the solution to the problem.

Sometimes, of course, the best or even the only way to show that you remember a problem's solution is to perform it. It is certainly much easier to demonstrate how to tie a shoelace than it is to describe how to tie a shoelace. In such a case, the third step in the total learning process seems to include the second. You have committed the solution to memory by becoming efficient at performing it. You have, that is, **formed a habit.**

At other times, the solution may be said to consist of its description. This is the case of memorizing. Here, the proof of having learned consists of reproducing the words that supposedly express the problem-solving idea perfectly. In such a case, the second step in the total learning process seems to include the third. You have become efficient at reproducing the solution by committing it to memory. You have, that is, **memorized** it.

To summarize, the process of learning can consist of all, or some, or one of three steps: **inventing** an original solution to a problem, or **thinking; committing** a solution to memory, or **memorizing; becoming efficient** at applying the solution to a problem, or **forming a habit.**

Much is known about the laws that govern the performance of these steps, and about the distribution among human beings of the abilities to perform them. It will take *four* chapters to touch even briefly upon the important facts about these most important acts and qualities. In this chapter, we shall investigate the entire process of learning as it takes place in its most simple form, namely, in **animal learning.** In the next chapter, we shall cover the first step, **thinking,** as it occurs in human beings. In the chapter after that, we shall study human memorizing and habit forming, or **remembering.** In the chapter following that, we shall cover the abilities to think and to remember, or **intelligence and aptitudes.**

HOW ANIMALS SOLVE PROBLEMS

The first step in learning is **thinking, or the discovery of solutions to problems.** In so far as animals solve their problems, they can be said to think. Their *thinking* is very simple because they do not employ symbols and therefore they cannot be said to be *reasoning*. Because we can thus study learning in its most simple form and because animals are accessible and easy to handle, they have been used as subjects in many experiments in learning.

The modern, scientific study of animal learning or thinking may be said to have begun late in the last century. At that time, the English biologist LLOYD MORGAN watched his pet fox terrier Tony learn to open a garden gate by lifting a latch with its muzzle. The dog had been placed in a small yard that was enclosed by a picket fence. Apparently eager to get out, the dog kept pushing its nose into the spaces between the pickets, one space after another. The gate latch happened to be in one of those spaces. When Tony pushed its nose into that space, the latch was raised, the gate swung open, and the dog left the yard.

It ought to be pointed out that Tony had not previously seen the gate open or the latch manipulated. The dog, therefore, was not purposefully imitating human behaviour familiar to it. Could it have reasoned out the probability that a gate and a latch existed?

In commenting on the temptation to explain the dog's actions by attributing high intelligence to it, Morgan laid down a principle that has since come to be called in his honour **Lloyd Morgan's Canon.** In effect, it warns psychologists not to read human qualities into their animal subjects if animal behaviour can be sufficiently explained according to simpler, more humble qualities. To Morgan, such *personification* of animals seemed to be a modern throwback to primitive man's *anthropomorphism*, the savage's self-centred tendency to see human motives at work in every natural object, organism, and event. Morgan's terrier Tony was not to be thought of as motivated by the feelings animating Walt Disney's Pluto the Pup. All that one could legitimately say about the dog's solution of its problem was that it had learned to open the gate by a process that Morgan called '**varied trial-and-error, with the utilization of chance successes**'.

Acting on Morgan's clues, psychologists began a series of laboratory experiments on animal learning. Among the first systematic observations were those of the American psychologist, E. L. THORNDIKE, who started out by studying the **problem-solving behaviour** of cats. Before his death, Thorndike had become recognized as the foremost authority on studies of learning. He made significant early contributions to the field of study which we call **educational psychology.** In his early experiments with cats, Thorndike put a hungry cat in a puzzle box—a box that would open only if the cat pulled a certain string, stepped on a certain pedal, or worked whatever other device had been arranged to open the latch during the particular experiment. Then he put food outside the box, in plain view of the hungry cat. From the very first, the cat would scratch, leap, try to squeeze through the bars of the box, and generally engage in various vigorous responses. Sometime during this random activity, the cat would happen to work the particular escape device, the latch would open, and the cat would be freed.

TRIAL-AND-ERROR THINKING

From Morgan's observation and Thorndike's experiment, we can draw a general description of the course of what we shall now call **trial-and-error thinking.** A subject motivated towards a satisfaction (which may be the avoidance of discomfort) meets an obstacle in the course of attaining his goal. He shows varied and excess activity, until at last his responses come to include one or more that constitute the solution to the problem.

Let us cover the steps in this process more fully. The first factors to consider are the **motive** and the **obstacle.** Taken together, they constitute the problem to be solved. Some motive, or initial urge to activity, is necessary if one is to learn. As we have seen, one can be motivated by what appears to be a threat to one's real or ideal condition—by hunger, or the feeling of constriction. The cat in the puzzle box was hungry enough to want to get out. The subject must also recognize the obstacle as such and want to do something about it. To twist an old proverb, you can lead a subject to a problem but you can't make him think. He must have the desire to solve the problem. The cat was not too lazy, too tame, or too tired to try to get out.

The ability to react to an obstacle brings us to the next point—the necessity for many **random responses.** It is essential that the subject faced with a problem should engage in activity varied enough to include the correct action among the many unsuccessful responses. There will be no correct action among the many unsuccessful responses. There will be no progress towards the solution if one useless response is repeated again and again. The dog investigated every space in the fence; the cat did everything it could to escape. **Unceasing activity** led to success.

The point is not whether the cat and dog knew what they were doing—it seems certain they did not—but whether they came to know what they had done. Granted that, willy nilly, they had 'learned' (in the first sense of the word) to solve a problem. The question arises, did they 'learn' in the second and third senses too? Did they *remember* their solutions, and did they *become expert* in applying them to repetitions of the problems?

HOW ANIMALS REMEMBER SOLUTIONS TO PROBLEMS

Since animals cannot talk, the only way that they can show that they are aware of the solutions they have discovered is to repeat them when faced with the same problem again. Let us return to Morgan's dog and Thorndike's cat to see to what degree, if any, they memorized what they had discovered.

Confined again on the day after it had learned to open the gate by pushing its nose into the space where the latch happened to be, and confined for several days thereafter, the dog still began its daily attempts to escape by pushing its nose into many spaces. Each successive day, however, the dog began at a spot nearer the latch. Finally, it went directly to the right place and raised the latch at once. Similarly,

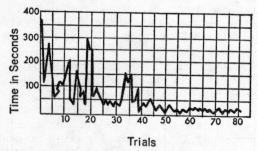

Fig. 24. An animal learning curve

Thorndike observed that the number of the cat's random movements decreased during repeated trials, until finally the correct response was made as soon as the cat was put into the puzzle box.

Fig. 24 reproduces a **learning curve** that Thorndike drew to show the changes in the time it took a cat to escape in each successive trial of a series that required the same solution.

Distances towards the right, along the bottom of the graph, represent the order of trials. Distances upward, along the side of the graph, represent the amount of time taken. Clearly, the cat responded with the correct solution more rapidly each time the trial was repeated, until at last it formed the **habit** of reacting to the stimulus situation with the correct response pattern.

We noted earlier that the response of an organism to a stimulus was determined by four factors: its species, structure, organic state, and past experiences. Here we have an example of the importance of **past**

experiences in the shaping of responses. Every act that an animal or human being performs creates a change so that it is not quite the same it was before. The resulting modifications of the nervous system show up in future behaviour. Each future response is modified because of the results of previous responses. Morgan's dog and Thorndike's cat gradually eliminated the unsuccessful responses from the many they had first made in their problem situations. Slowly but surely, they selected the right response. They were associating the act of escaping with the particular response that freed them.

Heeding Lloyd Morgan's Canon, we shall not claim that the cat and the dog abstracted the concept of escape and associated it with the correct response. For one thing, the fact that it took them many repetitions to fix the correct response argues against such a claim. For another thing, the more humble idea of **reinforcement** is adequate to explain their eventual efficiency.

Reinforcing a Desired Response. Reinforcement is the individual's involuntary judgement of his own activity. It is his check-up on results.

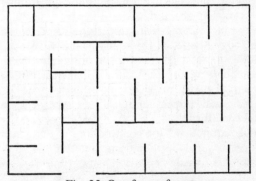

Fig. 25. One form of maze

Continual reinforcement of a response channels it, makes it the first choice in a repetition of the stimulus.

Certain experiments in **maze-learning** confirm the important part played by the attainment of the goal in reinforcing responses. A maze is a network of paths through which it is difficult to find the way to the goal. Fig. 25 reproduces one form of a maze.

A hungry animal placed at the entrance to a maze must learn to avoid blind alleys that do not lead to the food placed at the end of the maze. At first, all alleys are entered by chance. During a course of trial runs, the subject comes to make the correct turns more surely and to avoid the dead ends. At last it learns to run through the maze rapidly without error.

The interesting fact is that the first errors eliminated are those that are nearest the goal. Those more remote from the goal are harder to eliminate. In other words, the animal learns *backwards* from the goal. Considering the act of running the entire maze successfully and efficiently as a **series** of responses, we may say that of them all, the response learned quickest is the response most immediately and obviously successful. The last response of the correct series is the most vividly reinforced.

CONDITIONING

We have been discussing the way in which the correct response to a stimulus is selected from its many possible responses. Now we have to examine the way in which such a response comes to be made when evoked by a stimulus other than the original stimulus but one which is associated with it.

The most precise examples of this form of learning were furnished by the famous **conditioned response** experiments of the Russian physiologist, IVAN PAVLOV. He observed that just prior to being fed, his laboratory dogs drooled saliva from their mouths. In his first experiments, Dr. Pavlov served the dogs food at the same time or slightly after a bell was rung. After twenty to forty joint presentations of bell and food, the dogs salivated at the sound of the bell alone. The sound of the bell had come to substitute for the originally effective stimulus of food, so that the bell alone was able to make the dogs' saliva flow. In psychological language, the salivation response had become **conditioned** to the new bell-ringing stimulus. This type of learning is thus called **classical conditioning.**

The essential requirement for conditioning is that the two stimuli shall occur together. In laboratory practice, the two stimuli are presented either simultaneously or with the new stimulus slightly prior to the old one. No learning or very little learning occurs if the old stimulus is presented before the new one. This would be like the ineffective procedure of giving a child a reward before he had performed a task.

Generalization and Differentiation. A newly learned conditioned response is rather generalized, in both stimulus and response. A dog taught to salivate when a bell is rung at one musical pitch will salivate when a bell of a different pitch is rung. Also, he will react with other responses as well as salivation. By further practice, animals can be trained to differentiate between stimuli. If food is given only with a bell tone of a certain pitch, the animal will stop reacting to tones of other pitches.

Extinction and Reconditioning. Since many conditioned reactions are undesirable, as we have seen, it is fortunate that they can be done away with as well as learned. One way to abolish a conditioned response is to repeat the substitute stimulus with reinforcement. In the case of the dog, this would mean ringing the bell without giving food.

After a while, the dog would no longer salivate at the sound of the bell. The response would have become **extinct.** Extinction bears somewhat the same relationship to reinforcement that forgetting does to voluntary memorizing. **Like forgetting, extinction seems to be a temporary rather than a permanent loss of response, for an extinct response is much more quickly relearned than an altogether new habit.**

Extinction is best understood as an act of further learning. Again in the case of the dog, the stimulus of the ringing bell becomes associated with no food, and so becomes a signal not to salivate. In some cases, however, a conditioned response has been so firmly established that extinction cannot be accomplished by unreinforced repetition. The individual then has to be taught to make a response directly opposite to the undesirable response. This is known as **reconditioning.**

OPERANT LEARNING

The previous section has dealt with a kind of conditioning called classical conditioning. Another important type of conditioning is Operant Conditioning or, as it is often called, Operant Learning. It differs from classical conditioning in that there is no particular stimulus that will consistently elicit an operant response. B. F. SKINNER, **the dominant figure in the study of operant behaviour,** speaks of operant behaviour as being emitted by the organism rather than **elicited by** stimuli.

A central concept of operant learning is **reinforcement.** Behaviour which is reinforced is likely to be repeated. We can illustrate this by means of an experiment. A hungry pigeon is placed in a box which has a lighted button on the wall. The pigeon moves around the box pecking here and there. Eventually it will peck at the button and immediately a mechanism in the box feeds the bird with a little grain. The pigeon eats and then continues his movement around the box. Again it pecks the button and is **reinforced** with food. Eventually, the pigeon will cease the random behaviour and will simply peck the button to achieve food as required. **The pigeon has learned to peck the button to obtain food.**

Operant learning is by no means confined to the animal kingdom and the principles of learning new behaviour through reinforcement have been applied by Skinner and others to human beings. Examples of this application are diverse, ranging from teaching new material in schools by means of **programmed learning** (a method by which in each correct step the learner is reinforced by immediately being given the information that he has made a correct response) to **behaviour therapy** techniques for treating behaviourally disturbed children and adults. More will be said on this latter aspect in Chapter 16.

THE GESTALT APPROACH TO LEARNING

An example of what appears to be voluntary reconditioning on the part of an animal led to the founding of the influential **Gestalt** school of psychology.

In one experiment, WOLFGANG KÖHLER, a founder of the Gestalt school of psychology, put a chimpanzee named Sultan into a cage that contained two bamboo rods, one of larger diameter than the other. Outside the cage, and beyond the reach of Sultan's arms or either of the two rods, Köhler placed a banana. Sultan, who had already learned how to draw bananas into the cage with a single rod, tried unsuccessfully to obtain the banana with each of the two available rods. Then he lay one rod on the ground and pushed it with the other one until it touched the banana. This did not solve his problem, but did seem to give him a certain satisfaction, as if it were an achievement merely to establish contact with the banana. Then he drew both rods back into the cage and played idly with them until he happened to lay the end of one against the end of the other. At once he inserted one into the other, making a stick of adequate length, and immediately ran to the bars of the cage and drew in the banana.

The behaviour of Sultan certainly contrasts with the random scrabbling of the cats in the puzzle box. Sultan carried out the relevant associations involved in solving the task surely and at once. Sultan seems to have combined a memory image of 'drawing a banana into the cage' with a synthetic image made up of a memory image of 'extending a rod out of the cage' and a perception of a compound rod. In order to do this, Sultan had to recondition himself—he had to dissociate the image of 'drawing a banana into the cage' from the image of 'extending a single rod out of the cage' and associate it with the synthetic image of 'extending a compound rod'.

You may recall from the chapter on perception that there is a strong inclination to perceive incomplete patterns as wholes, and that items close together tend to be grouped. These are known as the laws of 'closure' and 'proximity'. In Sultan's case, it almost seems as if the principles of closure and proximity were at work to link the elements of the situation into the proper response. Sultan recombined past and present images in precisely the same way that human beings transpose algebraic symbols. Sultan was at a low level of the scale of symbolizing in which the highest level is represented by language, logic, and mathematics. In grasping the solution to this problem, the animal seemed to demonstrate what the psychologist calls a 'gestalt' understanding of the problem. In reporting his work Köhler suggests that before insight occurred Sultan engaged in thinking. As language was clearly absent here this poses an interesting question for the reader. How far can thinking take place in the absence of what we recognize as language?

DO ANIMALS FORM CONCEPTS?

Another human ability that some animals possess in crude and limited form is that of forming **concepts.** A concept is an awareness of a quality, formed by dissociating the quality from the various other qualities with which it is associated in the environment. 'Being at the extreme left' is a concept—and one that some animals can form. When presented with a series of groups of boxes, one of which always contains food, rats, cats, and pigs can learn to choose a given end box, and sometimes even alternate ends. Chimpanzees can solve problems involving the choice of the end, the next to the end, and the middle box. In the chapter on Perception, we saw that a chicken can master the concept of one subject 'lighter in colour' than another.

The fact that some animals are able to abstract the qualities of 'end' and 'middle' is merely another indication of the partial similarity of lower animal and man. By and large, animals form very few concepts. Moreover, they are utterly incapable of forming *propositions*, which are statements of relationships between concepts. The reason for this is the animals' inability to form verbal concepts. Only man uses conditioning to associate words with concepts, and only man forms concepts on a grand scale.

ANIMAL AND HUMAN LEARNING COMPARED

So far, we have been studying the principles of problem-solving common to both animal and human learning. The identities may have troubled any readers who would prefer that the animal nature of man not be emphasized. Other readers may be more interested in planned and purposeful human learning than in mechanical and uncomprehending animal learning.

Any account of problem-solving that failed to mention the similarities between some human and all animal thinking would be incomplete. On the other hand, it is certainly true that any account of problem-solving that did not go on from trial-and-error thinking to intelligent and purposeful reasoning would be even more incomplete.

A comparison of human and animal learning ability as found in the psychological laboratory points out the clear superiority of man. The main differences may be summarized as follows:

1 Man is more readily **motivated** towards a specific task. He responds to a wider range of incentives.

2 Man has better **control** of his emotions. He is less likely to become confused. He uses more deliberation and management in attacking a problem.

3 Man is a better **observer.** He sees many characteristics of things,

people and situations that lie beyond the animal's perceptual field. He is more likely than an animal to see relevant associations, and to discriminate between parts of a whole.

4 Through the use of **symbols**—language, numbers, maps, models—man is better able to weigh alternatives verbally without having to go through actual physical movements. To combine symbols is much easier than performing the operations that they stand for, therefore man can try out many more possibilities in a given time.

All four of the differences noted above enable man to learn more rapidly than the animal. But the last two are rather more important, in that they open up to man the opportunity to solve problems by a method that animals cannot employ—**reasoning.**

SUGGESTED FURTHER READING

Borger, R., and Seaborne, A. E. M., *The Psychology of Learning*. Penguin: London, 1966.

Cross, G. R., *The Psychology of Learning*. Pergamon Press: Oxford, 1974.

Davey, G. (Ed.), *Applications of Conditioning Theory*. Methuen: London, 1981.

Gagné, R. M., *The Conditions of Learning*. 3rd Edn, Holt, Rinehart and Winston: New York, 1977.

Houston, J. P., *Fundamentals of Learning and Memory*. Academic Press: New York, 1981.

Köhler, W., *The Mentality of Apes*. 2nd Edn, Routledge and Kegan Paul: London, 1927.

Medick, S. A., Pollio, H. R., and Loftus, E. R., *Learning*. Prentice-Hall: London, 1973.

Postman, L., and Keppel, G., *Verbal Learning and Memory*. Penguin: London, 1969.

Rachlin, H., *Introduction to Modern Behaviorism*. W. H. Freeman: San Francisco, 1970.

Skinner, B. F., *Science and Human Behavior*. The Free Press: New York, 1953.

Walker, S., *Learning and Reinforcement*. Methuen: London, 1975.

5

THINKING

It has been noted that animals cannot employ reasoning to help solve their problems. **Reasoning is that form of thinking in which the possible solutions are tried out symbolically. Since only human beings have adequate languages and systems of notation, only human beings reason.** Animals must try out their responses *physically*.

There is no generally accepted name for this animal kind of thinking as there is for reasoning. The basis for the lack of such a name can be found in the history of attitudes towards work. In most cultures, and in parts of our own, **symbolic thinking has usually been valued above non-symbolic thinking.** The mathematician has been honoured more than the scientist, the scientist more than the engineer, he more than the mechanic, and he more than the manual labourer—though each may have as successful a record as the others of solving problems in his particular field.

One cause of this familiar attitude stems from the fact that although reasoning proceeds much like physical thinking, it has a few refinements whose importance is out of proportion to their number. The mere invention of such symbols as words and numbers has actually made possible the creation of civilization.

Of course, human beings do not confine their problem-solving activities to reasoning.

Trial-and-Error Thinking. Frequently, unless prevented from acting freely, the person faced with a task of learning will start out in hit-or-miss fashion, varying his responses until he strikes upon the successful sequence of acts. People are most likely to engage in trial-and-error when faced with unfamiliar mechanical tasks, like solving a wire-puzzle, putting together the pieces of a jigsaw puzzle, untying a tangled knot, or—in the psychology laboratory—tracing a pattern they can see only in a mirror. In the last example, for instance, few people try to solve the problem by reasoning about the laws of reflections. Instead, most people will simply try moving the pencil in one direction, find that it doesn't work, and then try moving it in another direction, until at last they hit upon the right response.

Some people even seem to *prefer* trial-and-error thinking to reasoning. We may recall Thomas Edison's reply to a critic who chided his hit-or-miss method of seeking a substance that would serve as a filament in incandescent light bulbs. Said Edison, 'Now I know hundreds of things that don't work.' Even this famous inventor at times preferred trying hundreds of substances, one by one, to the more abstract approach of deducing the qualities required in the correct substance.

Thus people are apt to 'learn the hard way' by trying out potentially successful responses not symbolically in their imaginations but *physically*. In some situations, however, such trial-and-error thinking is the only kind practicable. It is certainly much less efficient to write out all of the possible solutions to a twisted-wire puzzle than it is to try them out with the puzzle in your hands.

In experiments with human subjects set to solve mechanical wire puzzles, the psychologist Ruger found that analysis of the solution came about *after* the solution was reached and not before. Understanding usually came in two steps. First the subject would perceive which part of the puzzle he had successfully manipulated. Then he would perceive what movements he had made. Each degree of understanding was arrived at quite suddenly. After fumbling blindly with the puzzle for several trials, the subject would suddenly 'see the light' and carry out the solution speedily. This abrupt attainment is called insight.

Insight, The 'Aha!' Experience. A classic account of a human reaction when such insight comes all at once is told about Archimedes. When the great physicist of the ancient Greek colony of Syracuse discovered the principle of specific gravity while in his bath, he jumped up crying 'EUREKA! I've found it!' and ran naked through the streets of the Sicilian town. He was so delighted with the solution to the problem that had been bothering him that he forgot he had no clothes on.

The anecdote expresses the force with which the sudden attainment of understanding can affect a person. Such abrupt insight into the structure of a problem usually moves even the most self-controlled person to some expression of satisfaction. It is therefore often called the **'Aha!' experience.**

If insight *precedes* rather than *follows* the solving of a problem, it will of course materially shorten the time needed to reach the solution. Such very rapid trial-and-error thinking was first studied by the German Gestalt school of psychology, as we have seen in the last chapter.

Trial-and-Error, Insight, and Reasoning. Perhaps the best way to demonstrate the nature and superiority of reasoning is to show three imaginary—but typical—subjects trying to solve a puzzle. Let us call them Tom, Dick, and Harry. We give each of them a set of the five little blocks shown in Fig. 26 and tell them that the five blocks are to be fitted together to make a perfect square with no gaps. Each of them attacks the problem in a different way.

Tom seems to have no overall view of the problem nor any guiding idea. He just keeps putting the blocks together in different ways, hoping that a certain amount of apparently useless activity will include the correct response. As Tom goes along with his trials and errors, he will probably observe certain characteristics of the pieces that may trigger a solution. It is quite possible, however, that if he hits upon the solution at all, it will be only by chance.

Dick notices at once that the projecting parts of the four similar pieces will fit into the four inner angles of the little cross. He has had what feels to him like insight. He even says 'Aha!', sure that he is

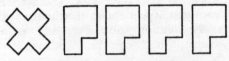

Fig. 26. A construction puzzle

on the right track. Whether he manipulates the pieces physically or mentally, he will end up with either a rectangle or a cross, but not with the required square. A little more pondering of the shapes of the parts of his undesired achievements and Dick may experience true insight into the modifications necessary to reach the solution. However, he may not have further insight. It cannot be depended upon.

Harry uses an indirect method of attack. He asks himself how large the final square is going to be. He finds that he can answer the question easily. The cross is divisible into five small imaginary squares, and, in a different way, so are all of the other pieces. Since the area of the final square will be twenty-five of these little squares, one side of the final square will be five times as long as one side of a little square. Harry then asks himself how to put the pieces together so that he will obtain straight edges of the required length. At once he sees how this is to be done and solves the problem.

Clearly, Harry's procedure is more rational than Tom's and Dick's. More than either of them, he keeps the goal before him while he explores the given material, so that his indirect method does not lead him off at a tangent but leads him around the obstacle.

Yerkes' Multiple-Choice Experiment. Let us turn from our imaginary puzzle to an historic experiment designed to reveal the nature of human problem-solving. The apparatus used is a box (devised by Yerkes) from which any of twelve keys may be extended towards the subject. On any given trial, only one of these keys is the 'correct' key. The subject must discover which it is (that is, in what *relation* it stands to the other keys). The correct key changes from trial to trial. The subject must determine by what rule the change is made (keeping in mind the relation of the correct key to the others). For example, in one series of trials, the general rule might be that the second key from the left is the correct one.

Other rules that have been used in this multiple-choice experiment are (1) the key at the left, (2) the middle key, (3) the third key from the right, (4) alternately the right-end key and the left-end key, (5) first key to the left of the middle, and (6) alternately to the left of the middle and to the right of it.

Human adults can succeed in all of these problems, but they find the last ones very difficult.

One such experiment (in Table II) proceeded as follows. The numbers under 'setting' show which keys were presented at each trial of the series. The numbers under 'responses' show the order in which the keys were pressed by the subject, the last one being the 'correct' key in each trial. The subject's 'observations' are perhaps the most important data.

Table II

Trial	Setting	Responses	Subject's Observations
1	3, 4, 5, 6, 7	3	'This is easy. It's the left-hand key.'
2	2, 4, 6, 8	2, 4, 6, 8	'No, it's not the left one—but it seems to be an end key.'
3	3, 5, 7, 9, 11	11, 3	'It must change from one end to the other.'
4	4, 5, 9, 12	12	'The correct key is alternately the left-hand and the right-hand keys.'

What we see happening in this experiment is the formation of abstract concepts through **generalization,** and their modification through **differentiation.** Let us define these concepts.

How We Form Concepts. As we said in the last chapter, a **concept is a general idea of a quality separated from its particular instances or concrete applications, given a name, and treated as an entity.** Qualities like hardness and greenness are typical concepts; forces like electricity and gravity are concepts; states like dread and joy are concepts.

In order to form a concept, you must be able to **abstract.** That is, you must be able to notice the **common characteristic of different individual objects.** All pairs of things, for instance, have in common the quality of duality, which we have named 'two'. It makes no difference to the 'twoness' of a pair whether it be a pair of shoes or a pair of stockings.

Having abstracted a common characteristic, you are in a position to **generalize** about the objects in question. You can make a general statement of the essential characteristic. If, in addition, you **discriminate** between the class of objects with the characteristic in question and those objects that share other characteristics with the members of the class, you have formed an **abstract concept.**

For instance, to form the abstract concept of 'triangle', one must recognize the characteristic of 'triangularity' common to all triangles. At the same time, one must differentiate triangles from other geometrical shapes.

There are several kinds of concepts. Some are based on **sensory qualities,** like 'red', 'bitter', and 'hard'. Others are based on **non-sensory qualities,** like 'friendly', 'safe', 'happy'. Perhaps the most important single concepts for reasoning are the **relations,** like 'identical', 'greater than', and 'smaller than'. In the Yerkes' multiple-choice experiment, the relationship of **alternation** was the concept to be found.

Let us return to the subject of that experiment. We want to see how he went about arriving at the correct concept.

You will recall that our subject began the first trial by resorting to random trial-and-error. Upon hitting the correct key, he made a generalization, abstracting the quality of 'left-endness'. The unsatisfactory result of his application of his rule in the next trial forced him to modify his original generalization, this time abstracting the quality of 'endness'. Again, another trial forced him to modify his generalization, this time abstracting the quality of 'alternate endness'. In this third form, his generalization was correct.

JOHN DEWEY'S ANALYSIS OF REASONING

An instance of thinking like that just described may be analysed according to the general scheme proposed as long ago as 1910 by JOHN DEWEY. In this scheme, reasoning is regarded as a series of steps that follow one another in an orderly way. These steps are:

1 **Obstacle.** The motivated person meets an obstacle.
2 **Diagnosis.** He locates the source of his problem and considers its structure. This is the realm of the analytical ability to abstract and form concepts.
3 **Hypothesis.** He makes one or more guesses. This is the realm of the creative imagination.
4 **Deduction.** He tries to work out a consequence of his guess that will be true if and only if his guess is true. This is the realm of logic and experience.
5 **Verification.** He checks such consequences against the facts. This is the realm of sampling and experiment.

Applying this five-fold scheme to the subject of our multiple-choice experiment, we can say that the test was the obstacle.

(It is interesting to note that many of the obstacles in life outside the experimental laboratory are as optional as this one was. People with great curiosity need to understand as much as possible about important matters, while other people find ignorance no obstacle to the attainment of great self-esteem.)

The subject made his first **hypothesis**—a random, trial-and-error hypothesis better called a **guess**—that the key on the left was the correct key, for the first trial. He knew, he did not have to **deduce,** that if it were the correct key he would be told that fact. He **verified** his hypothesis by selecting the key and learning that it was indeed the correct key.

Now the problem was to learn which quality of the left-hand key made it the correct one. On a trial-and-error basis again, the subject made the **hypothesis** that the essential quality was its left 'endness', deduced that the key to choose on the next trial was the left one, and put his conclusion to the test of experimental **verification.** This time, the extreme left key was incorrect.

Our subject now tried all of the keys until he found that the correct key was now the one at the extreme right end. Abstracting the quality of 'being at an end', he formed the concept of 'endness' and based on it a new hypothesis that the correct key for all trials was always at an end, though it was still uncertain exactly which end each time. He deduced that the only keys to press on the next trial would be those two at both ends. He verified his deduction, finding that the correct end key was not at the same end as the previous end key.

He now formed the concept of 'alternate endness' by abstracting and combining the qualities of alternation and termination. A final hypothesis—that the correct key was alternately at the extreme left and at the extreme right—implied that the only key to press on the next trial would be the key at the extreme right. Putting his conclusion to the test, he verified it.

CREATIVITY, THE THIRD STAGE OF REASONING

We have just seen that the subject of our multiple-choice experiment achieved success because of his ability to abstract qualities from the elements of his problem situation. Upon the concepts so formed he based hypotheses from which he drew conclusions that could be experimentally verified or disproved. Without the concepts, there would have been no hypotheses, conclusions, and experiments. How do theoretical concepts arise from material environments? What is the 'fluoroscopic' process that gives a glimpse of the skeleton of truth within the body of a problem?

Abstraction is the answer—the ability to ignore every quality of a factor but one at a time, the ability to perceive every quality in the first place, and finally the **ability to combine simple qualities into complex concepts.** Unfortunately, it seems that these abilities are never under much control. Creative thinkers agree that the creative process has at least one step that is not very responsive to intellectual discipline. This is the step called **incubation,** a period of seeming inactivity during which no apparent progress is made towards the goal. The entire creative process seems to consist of three steps:

Preparation during which facts are learned and observations made.
Incubation, described above.
Inspiration, the emergence of the concept.

Preparation for an act of creative thought may be voluntary or involuntary. The preparation of a research worker in science or a creative worker in the arts is apt to be voluntary, for the scientist must be a scholar and the artist must be a craftsman before they can contribute true originality. In everyday life, however, our continuous experience may be preparing us unwittingly with the facts or points of view that may in time come to be those needed to solve a problem.

Incubation is so called because the thinker's mind seems to be 'hatching' something. It is certainly not yet giving birth to insight. The thinker's ideas seem to him to be going around in circles. He may find himself pacing the floor or tapping his fingers; or, more commonly, he will be unaware of his bodily activity. He may be doing physical labour or he may be asleep. Sooner or later, an idea suddenly comes to him. He has experienced—

Inspiration, a sudden, joyful perceptual rearrangement of the problem that gives him some insight into its essential structure.

Several explanations have been proposed for the phenomenon of incubation-inspiration. One theory holds that 'unconscious' mental work goes on during incubation. Another theory claims that, during incubation, the abstract qualities of a problem's elements come to be symbolized by covert responses, and that inspiration is the sudden translation of the covert physical responses into language. Another explanation says that relaxation allows interfering unreinforced responses to become extinct, permitting the thinker to be reconditioned with the correct stimulus–response pattern. These explanations are not mutually exclusive. All may be true; they may even be equivalent.

A Check-list for Problem-Solvers. Though a frustrating period of incubation seems to be an almost inevitable experience even for creative geniuses, it can sometimes be shortened or at least made bearable by actively attacking the problem at hand. Here is a check-list of questions that it might be well to ask yourself about the elements of a problem situation. Any one of these or similar questions might lead you to an insight that can solve your problem.

What am I trying to accomplish?
Have I done this kind of thing before?
If so, how?
How have other people done this?
How about using something else?

What if I made it bigger?
Smaller?
What if I reversed it?
What could I combine it with?
How about using several?
What kind of people am I dealing with?
How near? How far? Which way?
How soon? How often? For how long?
How about doing the opposite?
What if I did nothing?

LOGIC, THE FOURTH STAGE OF REASONING

Having been inspired with a hypothesis, the thinker next makes **deductions** from it. Usually, these seem to be in the form of 'If A is true, then B is true'—as if all one had to do was then check whether B were true and, if it were true, proclaim the truth of A. It is not as simple as that. B might be true and A false. For instance, let A represent the proposition 'Tom committed suicide' and let B represent the proposition 'Tom was killed'. It is certainly true that, if A, then B; but it need not follow that if B, then A. To claim that it does would be to commit a **logical fallacy.**

We see that the implications we draw from our hypothesis must take the form 'If A then B and if B then A', or, more simply, 'B if and only if A'. How to be sure that this double implication holds true, so that we may safely infer A from B, requires a study of **formal logic** more thorough than we can undertake here. We merely point out that any statements that *can* be related in the double implication illustrated above permit one logically to infer either statement from the other.

Verification. Having drawn one or more deductions from his hypothesis, the thinker next puts them to the test of **experimental verification.** This act may be overt or symbolic. Physical scientists use overt experimentation. Mathematicians more often try to form a further deduction which is logical but false, thus showing the falsity of the hypothesis. That is, if the B is false in 'B if and only if A', then the A must be false too. Since the A is his inspired hypothesis, the thinker must then go through the entire process of reasoning again—a not uncommon experience, as we can all testify.

CONVERGENT AND DIVERGENT THINKING

In the early 1950s GUILFORD proposed his model of the intellect. The model postulated a number of cognitive operations and these included **convergent and divergent thinking. The person who is a convergent thinker shows an ability to cope with problems in which there is one**

correct solution which can be deduced from the information available.
Many intelligence tests contain problems of this kind. **The divergent
thinker is more at home in coping with problems where there may be
several equally acceptable solutions and where some originality of
approach is called for to reach the solutions.** Some psychologists correlate divergent thinking with creative thinking.

THE NATURE OF THINKING

We can now make a more comprehensive statement about the nature
of an act of thought. Our analysis of thinking has shown that the
process consists of the **origination, criticism, and acceptance or rejection
of hypotheses.** In non-symbolic problem-solving—say, in the solving
of puzzles—the suggestion and criticism of the hypotheses are carried
out simultaneously, in the overt manipulations of the trials and errors.
The responses are large muscle movements.

In symbolic problem-solving—reasoning—the suggestion of a
hypothesis is distinct from its criticism. The suggestion is always **symbolized,** and the criticism may be symbolized. If so, they are symbolized
by responses that differ only in degree from the responses made in
overt problem-solving. These covert responses may be sensations,
images, language sequences, or very slight incipient movements.

We conclude that people think not only with their **brains** but with
their **entire bodies.** Though the **nervous system** has the stellar role in
thinking because it integrates all of the other parts of the organism,
the **sense organs, muscles,** and **glands** also play important parts in
thinking. It will not surprise us, therefore, to find that the laws
governing memorization are identical with those governing the formation of habits. What those laws are, and how to apply them to practical
life, is the subject of the next chapter—on retaining what has been
learned.

THINKING AND LANGUAGE

Before moving on to Chapter 6 there is one further question which
we should ask and that is: **'What, if any, is the relationship between
thinking and language?'** Psychologists have not reached total agreement
on this issue and **at least three different views have been proposed.**

First there is the argument that the language which we use influences
and determines our thinking. This view is known as the **Sapir-Whorf
hypothesis.** A second view is that thought develops first and is itself
necessary for the development of language. Such a view is presented
in the **theory of cognitive development proposed by Jean Piaget.**

Finally, there is the argument that language and thought have
independent roots—that in very young children language and thought

are initially independent activities which gradually merge during the development of the child. This is the case presented by the psychologist, L. S. VYGOTSKY.

SUGGESTED FURTHER READING

Bruner, J., Goodnow, J., and Austin, G., *A Study of Thinking*. Wiley: London, 1956.

Burton, A., and Radford, J., *Thinking in Perspective*. Methuen: London, 1978.

George, F. H., *Models of Thinking*. Allen and Unwin: London, 1970.

Green, J., *Thinking and Language*. Methuen: London, 1978.

Hudson, L., *Contrary Imaginations*. Penguin: London, 1967.

Johnson-Laird, P. M., and Wason, P. C. (Eds.), *Thinking. Readings in Cognitive Science*. Cambridge University Press: Cambridge, 1977.

Thomson, R., *The Psychology of Thinking*. Penguin: London, 1959.

Vernon, P. E. (Ed.), *Creativity*. Penguin: London, 1970.

Wallach, N. A., and Kogan, N., *Modes of Thinking in Young Children: A Study of the Creativity–Intelligence Distinction*. Holt, Rinehart and Winston: New York, 1965.

Wertheimer, M., *Productive Thinking*. Tavistock Publications: London, 1961.

6

REMEMBERING

What do we mean when we say that a person has succeeded in learning something? At the very least, we mean that—whether or not he discovered the wonderful something by himself—he *remembers* it. **Memory** is the proof of his having learned.

All of us remember many things in the course of a day. Our behaviour is continually influenced by some past experience which is remembered.

Remembering can therefore be defined as **the present knowledge of a past experience.**

FOUR KINDS OF REMEMBERING

Remembering can occur in several forms. The simplest form is the remembering of something when it is presented to the senses. This form of remembering is called **recognition.** We recognize the faces of our friends, musical compositions, paintings—in short, patterns of physical arrangements which have previously registered on our sensory receptors.

Recall is a somewhat more difficult form of remembering, but not the most difficult. We are said to recall something when, without it being present to the senses we become aware of having experienced it in the past. For instance, we 'recall' the name of a book that we finished reading last week.

Still more difficult is remembering accurately enough to **reproduce** the material once learned. You may recognize the Ten Commandments and recall the experience of having once learned them, but can you reproduce them?

A fourth kind of remembering is the **performance** of habits so well learned that they are highly automatic.

However, whether we **recognize, recall, reproduce,** or **perform,** we must in every case have first acquired the material remembered. Acquiring is the first step in the complete process that culminates in remembering.

A particular form of acquiring is associated with each of the forms of remembering. In order to **recognize,** and **recall,** we must perceive. In order to reproduce, we must **memorize.** In order to **perform** a habit, we must **form** the habit.

As responsible adults, we are interested in learning how to learn—in learning how to memorize, how to develop skills, how to form good habits, and how to break bad habits.

The rules for successful studying and habit forming are based on the general principles of learning.

Since memorizing and habit forming are types of learning, the general principles of learning apply to both of them.

Memory *versus* **Habit.** All of the scientific data on **memories,** for instance, hold true of **habits,** and vice versa. In popular speech, the word 'habit' is distinguished from the word 'memory', as if they did not refer to the same kind of human function. Usually the word 'memory' is applied to the acquiring and retaining of words, symbols, and of conscious experiences, while the word 'habit' is used to refer to nonverbal acts. Actually, the distinction is more apparent than real. Many an act of muscular skill has been learned with the aid of verbal cues and instructions—for instance, driving a car, typewriting, playing golf—while almost all acts of remembering are based on muscular movements, if only of the vocal apparatus, as in taking an examination, calling to someone recognized in the street, or testifying in court.

In popular speech, the word 'habit' is usually applied only to **overt** learned responses, such as tying shoe-laces, knotting a necktie, typewriting, handwriting, driving, manners of eating, and so forth. In technical psychological discussions, the word 'habit' is also applied to **covert** patterns of responses. Thus, for instance, the silent speech in reading to oneself and in doing mental arithmetic is habitual. There are also habitual **emotional** reactions, like the fear of insects, snakes, and the dark. There are habitual ways of **attending** and **perceiving:** one bus passenger looks at the advertisements, another looks at his fellow passengers. **Attitudes** are habitual too, as when a man consistently despises members of races, religions, nations, or economic classes other than his own. The phenomenon of learning pervades all the topics of psychology. One cannot understand personality, individual development, thinking or remembering without studying the process of habit-formation.

Let us repeat that the idea of habit is not being arbitrarily extended from its everyday meaning of automatic, overt behaviour when it is made to include covert, conscious, and voluntary experience. From the procedural point of view—that is, in terms of what happens—memories are learned in exactly the same ways as muscular habits are learned; these are also the ways in which mental habits are learned. All are examples of the building of stimulus–response patterns or habits, the process known as learning. In order to give sets of rules for studying and habit-forming, we must look into the principles of purely human learning.

THE LAWS OF LEARNING

Over the years, experimental psychologists have discovered certain influences that help or hinder learning. Statements of these influences are commonly referred to as the **laws of learning.** They include the laws of: **intensity; organization; contiguity; exercise; effect; facilitation; interference.**

The **law of intensity** states that the rate of learning depends upon the strength of the response to the stimulus situation.

The **law of organization** states that learning is more rapid when material is organized into meaningful relationships.

The **law of contiguity**—which means 'nearness', here especially nearness in *time*—states that in order for association to occur, the associated events must fall within a certain time limit. In running a maze or in other sequential acts like memorizing poems, each part becomes connected to the part performed just before it, which is contiguous in time.

The **law of exercise** states that performance of an act, under conditions favourable to learning, tends to make subsequent performance of the act easier.

The **law of effect** states that a response leading to a satisfying result is likely to be learned, while a response leading to an annoying result is likely to be extinguished. The idea of satisfaction here goes beyond mere pleasure. To be satisfying, an act must fulfil some need or motive of the individual in the learning situation.

Some psychologists prefer the idea of **reinforcement** to the idea of effect, pointing out that unsatisfactory consequences can be as effective in response selection as satisfactory consequences if they are vivid, novel, or striking. For instance, everyone has learned the disagreeable sequence 'lightning followed by thunder' because it has been well reinforced.

The laws of **facilitation** and of **interference** state that one act of learning will assist another act of learning if some stimulus in the new situation needs a response already associated with it in the old situation, but will hinder the new act of learning if some stimulus which needed one response in the old situation needs a different response in the new situation. These two laws apply to conditioned learning.

Human Conditioning. The reader will recall our description of the famous experiments performed by Pavlov on conditioned learning with dogs.

Conditioned reactions occur in normal human learning, too.

Everyday examples of the process of stimulus substitution are innumerable. Our mouths water at the mention of a sizzling steak; a previously burned child shrinks back when he sees flames; the English-speaking student of German learns to say 'the dog' when he sees 'das

Hund' in print. In all of these cases, a response originally made to one stimulus has become associated with a substitute stimulus. The learning of a language is a process of conditioning, in which a word becomes a stimulus capable of causing a response originally evoked only by the real object. Fears of such relatively harmless objects as insects, snakes, and dogs are learned by conditioning. Sometimes conditioned-response learning is definitely maladaptive. A child who has come to associate doctors with pain will be extremely reluctant to undergo necessary medical examinations. A child that has been taught to fear all strangers may grow up to be an adult who is suspicious of all foreigners. If all unfamiliar people were dangerous, this adult habit of suspicion would be useful and adaptive; but since most unfamiliar people are harmless, the learned fear is unfortunate and an aspect of maladjustment.

Learning can also occur somewhat indirectly through a process known as **secondary or indirect conditioning.** If an unpleasant medicine is taken in orange juice, the sight of an orange may come to make the patient shudder. The sight of the orange, which is directly associated with the taste of the orange, has become indirectly associated with the unpleasant taste of the medicine. Human learning is so complex that such indirect conditionings, and even chains of indirect conditionings, are quite common. Two common examples of such learned response sequences are the driving of a car and the writing of a letter. Money, which has no intrinsic value, has value attached to it through indirect conditioning, as children learn that it will buy them what they want.

Generalization and **discrimination** of conditioned responses are quite common in everyday life. A baby learns to call a small furry animal a 'bunny', then **generalizes** the response to all small furry animals. After continually hearing the word 'bunny' in association only with rabbits, the baby learns to **discriminate**. Adults often generalize from one experience, pleasant or unpleasant. A truth learned about one member of a group will be asserted of all members of that group, usually inaccurately. Further experience with the other members of the group will cause the individual to discriminate. It is obviously one of the goals of education to teach students **to discriminate rather than to generalize.**

People, like animals, can also learn through **reconditioning**—that is, **through being taught to make a response directly opposite to an undesirable response.**

As an example, let us take the case of a child who had a conditioned fear of animals, generalized to such a degree that the child even feared fur coats. Over a period of days, several times a day, a kitten was brought into the room at some distance from the child shortly after the child was given chocolate. Each time the child enjoyed his chocolate, the kitten was moved closer and closer, until at last the child was playing with it. The child had been reconditioned; a fearful stimulus had become associated with a pleasant stimulus so often that the fear response became extinct. Finally, generalization of the reconditioning made the child unafraid of animals and their fur.

So far, we have met with but one principle—that of **organization**—that we might not have derived from animal experiments. Let us look into a famous experiment on purely human learning in which we shall see our general principles modified and amplified by the superior abilities of man, and his unique possession of language.

EBBINGHAUS'S EXPERIMENTS ON MEMORIZING

In 1885, the German psychologist EBBINGHAUS began a famous series of experiments to study the subject of memorizing. His technique required no other apparatus than a clock and a metronome. He was his own subject. The material he set himself to 'learn by heart' was a series of meaningless nonsense syllables like MOG, FID, TAZ and JUM. The syllables had been created by sandwiching a vowel between two consonants, all chosen by random methods. Ebbinghaus read the series of syllables over and over until he could reproduce them accurately. The score was the total time spent, reading at a standard rate set by the metronome beating 150 strokes per minute.

Throughout the learning period, Ebbinghaus kept the conditions of the experiment as constant as possible. He maintained his attitude of concentration. He controlled the objective conditions of his life to eliminate physiological irregularities. He avoided reading sense into the nonsense syllables, lest their resemblance to real words introduce chance disturbances. After learning a series, he always paused for exactly fifteen seconds.

Ebbinghaus was rewarded for his objectivity with discoveries that have been repeatedly confirmed by subsequent research. They are known as **Ebbinghaus's Principles of Economy in Acquiring.** We shall include with them additional principles discovered by later experimenters.

Distributed Practice is More Effective than Massed Practice. Ebbinghaus found that thirty-eight repetitions distributed over three days were just as effective as sixty-eight made on one day. Studies made since have confirmed his conclusion that distributed practice is more effective than massed practice. Two twenty-minute arithmetic drills are distinctly superior to one forty-minute drill. In subjects that require the student to 'warm up', however, study periods should not be so short that too great a part of the period is spent in the preliminary 'warming up'.

The principle of distributed practice explains why 'cramming' is so poor a method of study. Most students would learn more if the large amount of time devoted to last minute study were distributed throughout the term.

The principle must not be misunderstood to mean that it is more efficient to read half of a chapter at one sitting and the other half at another sitting. This would be a contradiction of the next principle of economy in acquiring.

Whole Learning is Usually Better than Part Learning. If one has to memorize a poem, a speech, or a part in a play, two methods of attack are possible. One, known as the **whole method,** is to read the material through from beginning to end at each repetition. The other, or **part method,** separates the material into a number of divisions and masters each division before going on to the next. Experimental comparisons of the efficiency of the two methods show that **most people learn fastest when using the whole method.** The minority who learn more effectively with the part method seem to be those who **divide the material into logical divisions.** They study by paragraphs or stanzas. Perhaps in such cases whatever inherent inefficiency the part method possesses is overcome by the beneficial effects of the presence of **meaning.**

Search for Meaning. Ebbinghaus used stanzas from Byron's epic poem *Don Juan* to determine whether meaningful material was memorized more easily than meaningless material. He found that the eighty syllables in an average stanza required eight or nine repetitions. The same number of nonsense syllables in a series required seventy to eighty repetitions. In other words, **meaningful material is nine times as easy to learn as rote, or meaningless, material.**

Thorndike has used the notion of **belongingness** to describe the relationship between two or more things that cause them to be integrated into a whole by the learner. In 1931 he performed an experiment in which series of sentences like the following were read to students:

Philip Barnes read slowly. Arthur Moore ran swiftly.
Michael Johnson argued heatedly.

The students were much more able to tell which word followed *Arthur* than they were able to tell which word came after *slowly*.

Clearly, a student does well to **seek for meaning** even in relatively meaningless material.

The Value of Reciting. Experiments have shown that if a student tries to recite a lesson to himself after having read it through several times, he will save time in fixing the lesson durably in his memory. One investigator who was practising a series of nonsense syllables tried out twelve different combinations of readings and recitings, prompting himself whenever he got stuck, and found that in his case at least the most economical method seemed to be the combination of six readings with fifteen recitations.

Of course, too early recitation wastes time. Too much prompting must be done. The material should be explored first, as in the whole method. The time for recitation is after one becomes familiar with the material.

Instruction. Certain simple experiments show the importance of definite instructions in learning. In one experiment, the words on a short list are shown to a subject one at a time. If the subject is told to learn the words on the list in the order of appearance, he has little trouble in doing so after repeated exposures. However, another subject who is not told to learn the words reports little or no learning, even after as many exposures as were given the first or instructed subject. When asked why, the uninstructed subject replies that he was not told to learn, and therefore merely looked.

In another experiment, subjects are shown pairs of words and are told to learn them well enough so that they will be able to give the second word when told the first. After testing their performance at this instructed task, their ability to give the first word when told the second is tested. The second score is usually about one-tenth as good as the first. As in the case of Thorndike's 'belongingness' experiment, the contiguity of the words paired was as high in one direction as in the other, but the subjects had been instructed to learn the association in one direction and not in the other.

Obviously, **we learn in accordance with the requirements of the task,** and not by a sort of photographic impression. **Repetition without reinforcement does not automatically teach us associations; we must actively participate in the learning process.**

Motives. Motives act as the spurs that prod the learner to activity. They start the learner off, and keep him going. Which motives will be effective in given instances depend upon the species, sex, age, intelligence, interests, and personality of the learner. A boy of nine learns the rules of baseball more readily than he learns the rules of grammar.

Motives are not always obvious, and they change from time to time. But some motive must be present, at least at the beginning of learning. Once learning has begun, pride in accomplishment or shame at failure may keep the activity going. Such social motives are called **derived motives.** They are important in maintaining the activities that lead to learning, and sometimes make the original motive lose importance.

Imitation. This requires careful observation of the model if the learner is to reproduce the right responses accurately. Animals are often said to learn by imitation, but experiments show that copy behaviour does not occur in more than 50 per cent of the cases involving monkeys. Apparently monkeys do not 'ape', in the sense of 'imitate', as much as is popularly believed. In animals lower than the monkey in the evolutionary scale—e.g. dogs and cats—there is no valid evidence of true imitation. Accurate reproduction of response patterns requires the high perceptual ability of man.

Of course, one does not learn by observation only; one must perform the imitated acts. But a demonstration can reduce the period of trial-and-error fumbling. A demonstration shows the best combination of movements immediately and enables the imitator to eliminate false and useless moves. Furthermore, a skilful teacher points out associations likely to be missed by the pupil, corrects errors before they have become fixed, and provides immediate reinforcement of correct responses by making practical applications in the area of the pupil's interest.

Knowledge of Results. Finding out just how well he is doing will offer the learner strong incentive to put forth extra effort. Schoolchildren will often work eagerly to surpass the record of another class or their own past records. If a student is timid or easily discouraged, it is often more desirable to have him work against his own past record rather than to vie with someone else. A shy learner is not so likely to be emotionally disturbed by his failure to exceed his own learning rate as he is by failure to exceed the record of some competitor.

Reward and Punishment. Praise, gifts, and such rewards act as **incentives** to learning when they provide **reinforcement** and are direct results of success. The learner's evaluation of the reward is important. For instance, a timid child lacking in self-confidence is reassured to a far greater degree by a word of praise than is a self-sufficient child.

Is reward more effective than punishment in reinforcing a given response? Experiments have shown that whenever punishment speeds up learning, it does so by forcing the learner to discard very quickly the responses that lead to punishment, and by making him more ready to accept responses that do not lead to punishment.

In general, however, **people learn more quickly when the right response is reinforced with a reward than when the wrong response is followed by punishment.**

The Effect of Punishment on Learning. The effect on learning of punishment depends upon its severity. In 1956, Dr. Percival M. Symonds, of Columbia University's Teachers' College, reported the results of years of study of this problem. Dr. Symonds, who was at the time president of the American Educational Research Association, declared that while mild punishment was found to have no effect, moderate punishment temporarily *inhibited* a child's ability to learn, and very severe punishment in some cases *permanently* affected the child's ability to absorb.

A child learns only when he responds to a situation. **Punishment has the effect of preventing a child from responding, and thus destroys the possibility of learning.** A punished child is not only damaged in his learning capacity; he also has his attention diverted by the punishment *from* the subject to be learned *to* the subject of his personal relations with the teacher. By making a child anxious, punishment loses its educational function, although it may have some values as a means of control.

However, Dr. Symonds notes that punishment, even as a means of classroom discipline, is not in the best interests of pupils because it is used by most teachers to foster their own needs, rather than as an instrument of learning. In any case, he points out, **acknowledging a child's correct responses is more effective for learning than publicizing his errors.**

HABIT FORMATION AND CONTROL

To many people, the word 'habit' has an unpleasant ring. It more often seems to signify injurious behaviour than useful behaviour. Most of us are often more concerned with the elimination of bad habits than we are with the formation of good habits. There are several psychologically valid rules for breaking involuntary habits and establishing new ones. They are all based on the laws and principles of learning discussed in this chapter.

However, the particular rules of successful **habit forming** differ in detail from the rules for memorizing because the muscles of the body play a larger role in habit forming than they do in the other forms of remembering.

Make an old involuntary habit voluntary. Deliberate exercise of a bad habit can give you control over the undesirable response, so that you can inhibit it at will. Typists, for example, often correct the bad habits of typing 'hte' for 'the' by consciously practising 'hte'.

Substitute a new response for the old one. The best way to overcome a bad habit is to replace it by a good one. A new response must be associated with a given stimulus by reconditioning. Smokers often replace the response chain of 'take, light, and smoke cigarette' by 'take, unwrap, and chew gum'.

Start the new habit with all possible initiative. Commit yourself publicly to your new course, so that fear of ridicule will strengthen your incentive.

Permit no return to the old habit.

Exercise the new habit voluntarily as often as possible. Repetition provides regular reinforcement. Unreinforced habits tend to become extinct.

There are some exceptions, however, to the old adage that says 'practice makes perfect'. Mechanical repetition may make a learner 'go stale'—that is, lose motivation. Also, rest periods may enable the learner to return to his tasks with renewed zest.

A TYPICAL LEARNING CURVE

Let us examine the behaviour of a man who has taught himself how to send and receive telegraphic messages in Morse code. How does his behaviour differ from what it was the first time he tried to achieve this feat? His current responses are now more *definite:* he makes almost no errors. His skill is now better *organized:* his performance is one smooth, quick, continuous action, no longer a stop-and-go series of trials and errors. It took him many hours of practice to reach this state of expert efficiency.

How much practice would it take to reach absolute perfection? More, perhaps, than he is physiologically capable of doing. We can only become as perfect as our bodies permit. Usually, however, we do not practise up to this limit. A graph of our learning curve would show that we had not stopped improving with practice.

Fig. 27 shows a typical learning curve, that of the telegrapher referred to. In contrast to the learning curve for Thorndike's cat (see Fig. 24), this graph uses the vertical distance along one side to represent efficiency, rather than inefficiency.

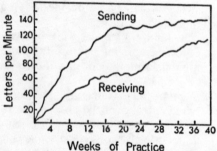

Fig. 27. A human learning curve

We see that the telegrapher's gain in speed was rapid at first and then progressively less rapid as practice continued. This deceleration of learning is very common, though not universal. We also see a long flat stretch in one of the curves. Such a stagnant period, if followed by more improvement, is called a **plateau.** Plateaus may be the result of weakening motivation and of inefficient methods. New incentives, and better ways of performing, can start the learning curve up towards its final plateau, or, more exactly, towards the level of a given learner's **physiological limit,** which is the upper limit of a person's ability to remember appropriate words and deeds.

Remembering in Images. Experiences may be remembered in **images,** as well as by words and deeds. An image is a subjective experience, resembling perception, in the absence of the original stimulus. For example, we can have visual images of colours and objects, or auditory images of music and voices. We can experience images in all of the other senses, too. Everyone can recall the taste of pineapple, the smell of burning rubber, the pain of a toothache, the feeling of nausea, the kinaesthetic feeling of standing on tiptoe, or the experience of being spun round. Many images are mixed, involving several senses at one time or in rapid succession.

Tests of imagery show that people vary considerably in their ability to experience images. Some people claim never to have images, while others have frequent, varied, and vivid ones. Though individual people tend to have one sense in which their images most frequently occur, almost everyone has images in more than one of the senses.

Visual imagery, the best-developed type, is nevertheless not especially useful for precise reproduction. Several experiments show this. If you happen to be a person who has vivid visual images, try the following three experiments.

1. Call up as clear a picture as possible of the building that stands across the street from the house in which you live. If you have never counted the number of windows in the wall facing the street, do so now—if you can.

2. Look at a blank piece of paper and call up the sharpest possible picture of the person you spoke to last. Now trace the image with a pencil. Do you get a recognizable portrait, or even a caricature? Most visualizers do not.

3. Stare at the following array of letters for one minute:

N W C
D R M
B T J

Now shut your eyes. Call up a picture of the letters in your mind's eye, and read off the letters in the array. Can you do it? If you can—and it is likely that you can—the odds are that you read them off in the order in which you learned them, probably left to right in lines from top to bottom, the normal scanning pattern. If so, shut your eyes and read them off from your image starting at the bottom right letter, going up the last column, down the middle column, and up the left column. Now can you do it? Almost no visualizers can. They must go back to where they started and painfully relearn the letters of the square in the new order. They do not really see the square as vividly as they suppose. They have really been acquiring by memorizing.

Retaining What Has Been Acquired. Having discussed the various facets of acquiring and remembering, we now come to **retaining**. Retaining is the word applied to the condition of the learner between the time he acquires and the time he remembers. Psychologists have not yet discovered the nature of the physical changes that presumably embody retaining—the so-called **memory traces** of the nervous system.

Since we cannot detect these infinitesimal rearrangements, we can only study retention by measuring the rate at which it declines.

Fig. 28 shows two typical **curves of forgetting.** As in the learning curve graphed earlier in this chapter, the vertical height stands for the amount of learning and the horizontal length represents the passage of time. Though one of the curves shows much slower forgetting than the other, both have the same general pattern: very rapid forgetting in the first few hours after learning, followed by more gradual forgetting.

Why Do We Forget? There are two major theories of forgetting: the **atrophy theory, based on metabolism,** and the **interference theory, based on behaviour.**

The **atrophy** theory holds that forgetting results from a progressive decay of memory traces in the brain and nervous system in much the same way as dents made in the skin by fingernails fade away. This common-sense view may account for some forgetting, particularly that found in certain diseases and in the senile condition of extreme age.

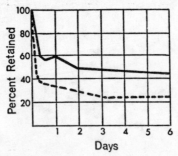

Fig. 28. Two typical forgetting curves

However, most of everyday forgetting is probably caused by the **interference** and confusion of the old with the new, rather than by a gradual fading away of old memory traces. In fact, some psychologists claim that nothing once learned is ever really forgotten, although it may be difficult to revive. There is much evidence for the interference theory:

1 The spontaneous recall of long-'forgotten' facts.

2 The invariably greater speed at which material can be *re*learned than newly learned.

3 The ability, when hypnotized, to recall long-'forgotten' facts and experiences.

4 The ability, after hypnosis, to carry out instructions given during hypnosis and now consciously 'forgotten'.

5 The fact that forgetting is slower during sleep—when almost no stimuli are evoking new responses—than during wakefulness, when a barrage of stimuli bombard the nervous system.

Of course, the fact that there is *some* forgetting even during peaceful sleep argues for *some* forgetting owing to 'fading'.

Inhibition and Transfer of Learning. The interference or confusion of present learning by subsequent learning is called **retroactive inhibition.** It is most noticeable when two learning situations involve similar associations—as when, for example, a player learning two similar games at the same time finds himself confusing the rules.

When, however, the learning in one situation is applicable in whole or part to other situations, we say that there is **transfer of training.** Modern psychologists have long since discarded the antique idea that the mere study of any one field will by itself cause an improvement in the study of any other field. Studying Latin does not improve the 'mind', nor will studying mathematics improve one's ability to reason logically—except in the field of mathematics. Studying Latin will merely teach one Latin, and the way to improve one's ability to reason logically is to study formal logic. Improvement from training occurs only when the same material or the same method can be used in the two situations.

The limited extent of transfer raises an interesting question about learning ability. Because there is no formal transfer, only transfer of material or transfer of method, is there no general intelligence? Is intelligence merely a collection of as many abilities as there are subjects? Such questions will be taken up in the next chapter, which will go on to cover other phases of the important abilities to think and remember which are aspects of intelligence and aptitudes.

SUGGESTED FURTHER READING

Baddeley, A. D., *The Psychology of Memory*. Basic Books: London, 1976.

Deutsch, J. A., *The Physiological Basis of Memory*. Academic Press: London, 1973.

Gregg, V., *Human Memory*. Methuen: London, 1975.

Gruneberg, M. M., and Morris, P. (Eds.), *Aspects of Memory*. Methuen: London, 1978.

Herriot, P., *Attributes of Memory*. Methuen: London, 1974.

Houston, J. P., *Fundamentals of Learning and Memory*. Academic Press: New York, 1981.

Hunter, I. M. L., *Memory*. Revised edn, Penguin: London, 1964.

Norman, D. A., *Memory and Attention*. Wiley: London, 1969.

7

INTELLIGENCE AND APTITUDES

Psychologists once believed that **intelligence** was a separate entity. They did not always agree on a scientific definition of intelligence. Some called it the **ability to learn.** Others called it the **ability to adapt adequately to the environment.** Still others called it **a general tendency towards achievement.** But all agreed that, like a flashlight, a person was as bright when focused on one subject as when focused on another.

Then some psychologists pointed out that there are people who seem to be more intelligent in some fields than in others. They put forth the theory that intelligence is a mixture of particular abilities called **aptitudes.**

Some psychologists tried to reconcile the two positions with the compromise suggestion that a person's **total ability** was the sum of his many **special abilities** and his general intelligence. Others put forth the idea that there are several kinds of general intelligence. One of the first to offer this theory was Professor E. L. Thorndike of puzzle-box fame, who suggested that intelligent behaviour might be roughly classified into three kinds: **mechanical, social,** and **abstract.**

By **mechanical intelligence,** Professor Thorndike meant skill in manipulating tools and gadgets and in managing the working of machines. **Social intelligence** covers the understanding of people and the ability to act wisely in human relationships. **Abstract intelligence** was the ability to handle symbols and ideas such as words, numbers, formulae, and scientific principles.

Believers in the aptitude theory replied that Thorndike did not go far enough in his classification. There occasionally seemed to be talents in each of his groups that exceeded others in the same group. Though abstract intelligence included both numerical and verbal talent, some linguists were poor calculators and some calculators were poor linguists. On the other hand, it was found that such instances were exceptions. A person's aptitudes within each of Thorndike's groups tend to be equal. In fact, a person talented in one group is more likely than not to be talented in the other two groups.

Progress in psychology has shown that there are **group factors** in between such specific aptitudes as the ability to detect errors when reading proof and the broad kind of groups suggested by Thorndike. These group factors include such capacities as the ability to understand words, the ability to handle numbers, and the ability to imagine spatial relationships.

In general, the modern conception of intelligence can be represented by this arrangement of factors:

(a) Very many particular **aptitudes**
(b) Many **group factors**
(c) Several **kinds** of intelligence
(d) **General intelligence**

There are tests for measuring intelligence at each of the levels of detail shown. But the four levels are more like points on a continuous scale than they are like discrete steps.

THE MEANINGS OF INTELLIGENCE

Each of the four levels of detail mentioned in the preceding paragraph can be understood in terms of the overall learning process that we discussed in the last three chapters. **General intelligence** can be thought of as a tendency to experience insight. The **kinds** of intelligence are the abilities to abstract different kinds of qualities, to form concepts of different parts of the environment. The **group factors** are habitual ways of thinking symbolically, or reasoning. **Aptitudes** are abilities to form habits efficiently.

It is fitting that intelligence would reveal itself in activities with so many qualities, since the problems recognized as solvable by man are numerous and intricate. However, inasmuch as all problems are similar, and the problem-solving method basically standard, it is permissible to speak of general intelligence, especially since this ability seems to lend itself to measurement.

Measuring General Intelligence. From the beginning of intelligence testing, there have been two parallel trends, one towards **performance tests** and the other towards **verbal tests**—tests in which the instructions are given in words and in which a good deal of the performance is in the form of words.

Performance tests can be given to people who do not know the language or who have not been to school. They are often given to people with poor vision and hearing, or to children whose handicaps seem more severe in verbal than in other areas.

In tests like these, the persons being examined might be asked to put blocks of various shapes into holes with corresponding shapes. They might have to trace a path through a maze, or be given a picture with some missing parts and asked to fill them in.

Naturally, the items in verbal tests are different from these. The emphasis is on verbal comprehension, especially in vocabulary tests.

One must know the language even when the quality being tested is the ability to reason by analogy, as in the test question 'What is related to grass as blue is related to sky?'

The first really workable test of general intelligence was devised at the beginning of the century by a French physician and psychologist, ALFRED BINET. It required the child to execute simple commands; to name familiar objects; to copy designs; to think of rhymes; to say what he would do in certain everyday situations; to define words; and so forth. It was both a verbal and a performance test.

Working with a French colleague by the name of SIMON, Binet revised his original test into a practical scale for testing the intelligence of children and adolescents from ages three to eighteen; it became known as the **Binet–Simon intelligence scale.** Below are some sample items from the original scale published in 1908 which indicates the kinds of abilities that were considered to be average for children at age levels three and seven.

AGE THREE

Ability to point to nose, eyes, mouth
Repeat two numbers
Ability to give last name
Name objects in a picture
Repeat sentences containing six syllables

AGE SEVEN

Ability to name what is missing in unfinished familiar pictures
Knowledge of numbers of fingers on each hand without counting
Ability to copy a diamond
Repeat five numbers
Count thirteen pennies
Knowledge of names of four common coins

The early Binet–Simon scale has since been revised by Professors TERMAN and MILES. Known as the **Stanford–Binet test of intelligence,** it needs to be administered by an experienced examiner, who sits opposite the person being tested. Only one person at a time can be tested with this scale in a period of one to two hours.

Since this beginning in intelligence testing, there have been devised many pencil and paper tests of intelligence for use with large groups of children or adults, which can be given by teachers or any instructed supervisor. These tests generally contain items requiring logical reasoning, original thinking, problem solving, deductive reasoning and other mental exercises, which are considered to be innate and which are not readily improved by practice. Below are some typical items to be found in pencil and paper group tests of intelligence:

1 Common-sense reasoning:

Gold is more suitable than iron for money because:
—gold is pretty
—iron rusts
—gold is scarcer and more valuable

2 Number series completion:

Decide how the numbers in each series go and then write the next two numbers

    1 3 5 7 —
    1 4 9 16 —

3 Comprehension of thought:

Explain the meaning of the following proverb:
A bird in the hand is worth two in the bush

4 Ingenuity of thought:

You wish to measure out exactly 4 l. of petrol from an open 100-l. drum. All you have is two cans, one a 3-l. can and the other a 5-l. can. How will you measure out exactly 4 l.?

5 Logical reasoning:

Tom runs faster than Jim
Jack runs faster than Jim
Which is the slowest of the three?

6 Reasoning by analogy:

sky is related to *blue* as *grass* is related to: table; green; warm; big.

Such tests may, however, give rise to problems of validity if the items in them reflect a particular culture.

The British Ability Scales. One of the most recent tests to be developed is known as the British Ability Scales and can be used to assess the intelligence of children up to the age of 17 years. This is a most versatile and effective measure and consists of 24 scales which are divided into tests covering a wide range of abilities. Such abilities covered include, for example, short-term memory, speed of problem-solving, reasoning, spatial imagery, fluency, and scholastic achievement.

Mental Maturity. If you were to give a child the same test twice—with enough time between the two testings for him to forget the questions—you would find that his scores would improve as he grew older. He would certainly do better at the age of eight than he would do at the age of four.

However, a time would eventually come when his ability to answer the test questions would no longer improve. You would then have to say that he had reached his **mental maturity.**

A person does not stop learning when he reaches mental maturity. He merely stops showing improvement in his ability to answer the general questions asked on intelligence tests. He can still continue to improve in his ability to answer questions in specific fields of study and business.

It's hard to tell exactly at what age a person reaches mental maturity—just as it's hard to tell exactly when a person stops growing in height. Psychologists agree that mental maturity is reached somewhere between the ages of **fourteen** and **eighteen.** The generally accepted figure is **fifteen.**

Mental Age. Imagine two mentally mature men (say, Smith and Jones) of the same age. Suppose that Smith could answer at the age of five questions that Jones could not answer until he was ten. And suppose that Jones has normal intelligence. Because Smith was as intelligent as a normal ten-year-old when he was only five years old, we say that Smith had a **mental age** of ten when he had a **chronological age** of five.

But what is normal intelligence? Binet and Simon considered that a child had normal intelligence if he could do something that half of the children of his age could do. For instance, half of all children three years old can point to their noses, eyes, and mouths; can repeat two numbers; can give their last names; can list certain objects in a picture; and can repeat a sentence of six syllables. Therefore Binet and Simon called a three-year-old normal or average if he could do these things.

The Intelligence Quotient, or **'I.Q.'.** It occurred to a German psychologist, Dr. William Stern, that you could easily get a number that would show how intelligent a person was by dividing his mental age by his chronological age. Professor Lewis M. Terman, an American psychologist who revised one of Binet's scales for American use, popularized the idea. Since the word for the result of a division is 'quotient', numbers arrived at in this way were called **intelligence quotients.** The phrase is often abbreviated to **I.Q.**

Actually, an I.Q. is not the quotient of the two ages. It is the product of that quotient multiplied by a hundred in order to get rid of the often inconvenient decimal point. The exact formula for calculating intelligence quotients is:

$$\text{Intelligence Quotient} = \frac{\text{Mental Age}}{\text{Chronological Age}} \times 100$$

or, abbreviated,

$$\text{I.Q.} = \frac{\text{M.A.}}{\text{C.A.}} \times 100$$

The concept of mental maturity raises an interesting problem. Think of a fifteen-year-old with a mental age of fifteen. Clearly, his I.Q. is 100, or normal. What happens five years later, when he is twenty years old? Since he is mentally mature, his mental age is still presumably fifteen. Therefore, if we stick to the formula, his I.Q. has sunk to $\frac{15}{20} \times 100$, or 75, which is decidedly inferior. This cannot be. In order to compute adult I.Q.s, we must take the denominator age as fifteen.

Another way to get around the difficulty is to assign people to their percentage category. That is, we can say that a given adult person is at a point where only 10 per cent of the population are more intelligent than he. Or we can say that a person is in the 'top 2 per cent' of the population. Or we can turn from the Binet method to such scales as the **Wechsler adult intelligence scale.** Here, the final score is not calculated from the mental age values of the tests passed by the person being examined, but from the total number of points made by him on all tests.

Intelligence Levels. We have used the term **normal** to describe I.Q.s of 100. Perhaps **average** is a better word.

Children with I.Q.s **markedly lower** than the norm for the population as a whole usually require special educational provision. Those with an I.Q. of approximately 50 or less are classified as **severely subnormal** and may be educated in special residential schools or in hospitals for the subnormal. At one time it was believed that such children were ineducable but it has since been shown that some are able to learn simple skills. Children whose I.Q. falls within the range of approximately 45–80 are termed **educationally subnormal.** Such children may be educated in special classes attached to primary or secondary schools or may attend schools which have been established especially to cater for the needs of educationally subnormal children.

The Intellectually Gifted. Towards the other extreme of the I.Q. scale stand the intellectually gifted. Most of those famous or eminent people who are not geniuses fall into this group. The vast majority of them showed their talent early and stood head and shoulders above their class-mates. Despite the exceptions that often get widely publicized, most of the gifted adjust better than average people do to the problems of life. Though they make up less than one per cent of the population more than 80 per cent of the individuals in this category go to university. They graduate with more honours, hold more degrees, hold more offices, have fewer divorces and fewer cases of illness or premature death. (With respect to fewer divorces many factors, including economic ones, may be of determining force.)

All this is even truer of the **genius.** His prowess appears at a very early age. He may learn to read at the age of two, for instance, and learn a foreign language at four. Mental derangement is not characteristic of a genius, but he may face special problems in his social and emotional development.

Helping the Gifted Child. Children with I.Q.s over 140 are not to be taken for granted. They offer serious problems, not to society in the sense of causing trouble, but rather to their parents and guardians, who want to help them find happiness. This is no easy task, because children with high I.Q.s are apt to find themselves intellectual giants in a world of medium-sized people.

It has been pointed out that intellectually gifted children make up a very small percentage of the population. Concern is often expressed that limited special provision is made for such children. Such lack of provision is in contrast to that made for children with severe learning difficulties. It is important that parents and teachers of intellectually gifted children ensure that their abilities are catered for and that, perhaps partly as a result of boredom or frustration, the child does not become socially or emotionally maladjusted.

The gifted child may thus face problems unique to those with his particular abilities. When young he may be bored by the games of his own age group but is yet too small to join the games of older boys and girls. In class he is likely to be wanting to cope intellectually with one or more subjects at a far more advanced level than his classmates.

Some False Beliefs About Great Intellect. There is a widespread belief that very bright people tend to be sickly and weak. Perhaps it arises from the fact that bright children are often advanced in their own class at school, and so come to be compared with older, larger children. In comparison with average children of their own age, bright children prove to be above average in size and to have better than average health.

Another general belief that has been proven false is that gifted people are less able to develop mechanical skills than are the less gifted. This false belief in the clumsiness of the gifted may be a face-saving rationalization on the part of parents of average children. It may also be based on the fact that bright children have many more interests than do average children and therefore may not give as much time to hobbies and projects that are only of mechanical interest. The belief is demonstrably false, for example, in the case of brain surgeons.

Still another mistaken belief about great intelligence is that it necessarily inhabits a large brain. Since men's brains are on the average larger than women's brains, this false notion seems to be a hidden claim that men are brighter than women, which according to the evidence of intelligence tests is equally false.

Can I.Q. Change? Early in the century, the psychologist ROBERT S. WOODWORTH summarized opinion on the variability of intellectual level by saying: 'Bright child, bright adult; dull child, dull adult. That is the rule and the exceptions are not numerous enough to shake it.'

Today, the exceptions are still not numerous enough to shake Woodworth's 'rule'. However, various studies do indicate that favourable and unfavourable environments can make the I.Q. fluctuate within a certain range. (Favourable environment here means a home in which there are love and culture; unfavourable means a household in which love or culture is absent.)

The exact extent of the dependence of I.Q. upon environment has not been determined. It seems to be at least plus or minus 15 points. That is, a person who would score an I.Q. of 100 if he were brought up in an average environment, might score as low as 85 if he were brought up instead in an unfavourable environment, and could score as high as 115 if he were brought up in a favourable environment.

Some of the variation found in these studies may be due to the imperfect **reliability** of even the best of modern intelligence tests. Given the same test three times, at suitable intervals, a person who scores 100 the first time may score 95 the second time and 105 the third.

The remainder of the variation found in these studies must be attributed to an effect upon intelligence of environment. However, no amount of diligent training will convert one of well below average intelligence into a person of normal intelligence, nor the normal person into a genius. **Any misguided attempt, no matter how well-meaning, to force an intellect beyond its ability may well result in frustration and misery for everyone concerned.**

What these studies really show is that **by affectionate cultivation a child can be helped to come closer to making full use of his potentialities.**

Qualities of a Good Test. We have just mentioned the concept of test reliability. Since it applies to all tests, including the aptitude tests we have yet to discuss, the concept is worth explaining more fully.

A method of measurement must agree with itself to be significant. Its results must not be accidental. We want to be sure that if we give a test to a person twice—with time enough between for him to forget the questions—he will do almost equally well both times. The extent to which the results agree is the measure of the test's **reliability.** Modern psychological tests of intelligence are about 95 per cent reliable—or, in statistical language, they have **reliability coefficients** of 0·95.

A good test must also be **valid.** That is, it ought to measure what it is intended to measure. To determine whether it does, we must compare it with a standard measure, or **criterion.** The criterion for validating the first intelligence tests was the estimate of children's school performance expressed in the marks that their teachers gave them. That there was no ultimate criterion beyond this opinion points up the inherent difficulty in validating all tests. **Validity coefficients,** therefore, are usually lower than reliability coefficients.

The rough tests of intelligence that laymen use have very low validity coefficients. Neither the ability to make money, the ability to memorize facts, nor the ability to endure years of schooling are very valid tests of intelligence. Evidence can be found to counter the validity of each of these. Thus Marie Curie, who would not apply for profitable patent rights on her discovery of radium and polonium, cannot be shown to have been intellectually inferior to Thomas Edison, who invariably commercialized his ingenious inventions. 'Walking encyclopaedias' do not always have the capacity for original thinking.

Using Intelligence Test Results. When intelligence tests were first developed, some people thought that at last there had been found a simple way to find everyone's natural and inevitable place in life. Of course this is not true. Human beings are far too complex and variable to be successfully and permanently classified by any simple system of measurements. Hard work and self-discipline will often overcome the handicap of a less than high I.Q.

Nevertheless, the results of intelligence tests can help to suggest how much and what kind of schooling people can be expected to benefit by, and what kind of jobs they can have reasonable hopes of succeeding at.

The situation is not as clear-cut in the field of vocational guidance as it is in educational guidance. A wide range of I.Q. scores has been found within each occupational group, with much overlapping of high and low scores between the different occupations. In general, however, professional men tend to have higher intelligence test scores than do men in retail and mercantile business and clerical positions. In turn, the latter tend on the average to have higher scores than skilled labourers, whose scores once again tend to be generally higher than those of unskilled labourers. But general intelligence is only one of a number of factors that determine vocational success.

APTITUDE TESTING

Tests have been developed to help people learn, before undergoing training in a particular line of work, whether or not they would be likely to succeed at it. Called **aptitude tests,** they are available for many fields, including the arts, sciences, and professions as well as the less highly skilled vocations.

A person who wants to determine his chances of success in mechanical work can take mechanical aptitude tests. Here are some questions typical of such tests. First, he might be asked to draw vertical lines through the cross-bars of capital H's as fast as he can. (The poorer his motor co-ordination, the more likely will he be to touch the sides of the H's.) Next, he might be asked to choose which tool of several shown he would use to do a certain job. (If he preferred to cut a board with a chisel, rather than a saw, he could not be expected to profit very much from mechanical training.) Then he might be asked to list certain illustrated parts in the order in which he would assemble them. (Here he can show his ability to understand mechanical drawings, and his mechanical judgement.) Tasks like these give some measure of one's specific interests, and are a measure of dexterity as well.

Group Factor Tests. If we set up tests for every conceivable manifestation of a person's abilities, we should soon be swamped with vast tables of correlations derived from them. What we often need are tests for a very limited number of human abilities that can be shown to be involved in most human achievements. These are the **group factors** mentioned at the beginning of the chapter. The many psychologists using factor analysis methods agree that the following group factors are fundamental abilities involved in all measured performances:

> **verbal** ability, as shown on vocabulary and analogy tests;
> **spatial** ability, shown in reading blueprints;
> **numerical** ability, shown in such simple arithmetical operations as adding, subtracting, etc.;
> **logical** ability, shown in detecting fallacies;
> **immediate memory** factor, demonstrated in recalling paired associates and nonsense syllables;
> **speed** factor, shown best on very simple materials that require few other abilities.

The nature of the duties involved in a career would determine which of these factors to test an applicant for, and how much weight to assign to the results. A potential engineer, for instance, would certainly be given one or more spatial aptitude tests, which measure the ability he must have as an engineer to visualize how parts would fit together even when they are not present.

He might, for example, be given the **Minnesota Spatial Relations Test.** This is administered with two boards, each of which has cutouts of different shapes and sizes. Most of the shapes have three sizes each. There are fifty-eight pieces. Each piece fits correctly into one cut-out. The potential engineer would have to place each piece into its appropriate cut-out as quickly as he could. His score would be the time it took him to fill in the two boards correctly. (A pencil and paper form of this test is extensively used in industry as one of the aptitude tests for design engineers, pattern makers, and other vocations requiring an ability for visualizing spatial relationships of geometric figures.)

Scoring Aptitude Tests. Tests like those described above have been given to thousands of people. Norms have been established. Sometimes they are expressed in terms of averages for different occupations. Thus someone who wants to become a welding operator will want to compare his scores on the battery of tests given him with the scores made by men who actually work with welding blowpipes and cutting torches.

Sometimes norms are expressed in a way that permits scores to be translated into letters like the marks given in schools: A, B, C, D, and E.

Sometimes norms are expressed in terms of what people of various chronological ages can do. Then, by dividing a person's **Mechanical Aptitude Age (M.A.A.),** for instance, by his **Chronological Age (C.A.),** we can derive his **Mechanical Aptitude Quotient (M.A.Q.),** just as we find an I.Q. by dividing M.A. by C.A.

CONCLUSION

Even very great gifts in any of these areas do not guarantee success, since much depends upon personal, social, or other qualifications for which the tests may be invalid. However, the wide variety of test data can help a person to see himself more clearly than he could before taking the tests. Therefore vocational and industrial counselling is decidedly worth while. Still, despite our ability to cut cross sections through the mind with general intelligence, aptitude, and group factor tests, we can never be sure that special incentives, stimulation, or great interests will not give dramatic expansion to powers that seem modest at the time of measurement.

SUGGESTED FURTHER READING

Akhurst, B. A., *Assessing Intellectual Ability*. English Universities Press: London, 1970.

Butcher, H. J., *Human Intelligence: Its Nature and Assessment*. Methuen: London, 1968.

Eysenck, H. J., *Race, Intelligence and Education*. Maurice Temple Smith: London, 1971.

Heim, A. W., *Psychological Testing*. Oxford University Press: London, 1975.

Kline, P., *Psychological Testing: The Measurement of Intelligence, Ability and Personality*. Malaby: London, 1976.

Pyle, D. W., *Intelligence: An Introduction*. Routledge and Kegan Paul: London, 1979.

Richardson, K., and Spears, D. (Eds.), *Race, Culture and Intelligence*. Penguin: London, 1972.

Savage, R. D., *Psychometric Assessment of the Individual Child*. Penguin: London, 1968.

Vernon, P. E., *Intelligence: Heredity and Environment*. Freeman: San Francisco, 1979.

Wiseman, S. (Ed.), *Intelligence and Ability*. 2nd Edn, Penguin: London, 1973.

8

HEREDITY AND ENVIRONMENT

The psychologist notes a vast difference among people in the way they react to events, their stature, mannerisms, talents, interests, intelligence, aptitudes, personality, and tendency for dying at a younger or older age.

Why are people so different from one another? Do they inherit their differences? Do their differences develop out of their environmental experience? Or are some differences the result of inherited and environmental factors interacting?

THE BASIS OF INDIVIDUAL DIFFERENCES

We have seen that the functions of the sensory organs and the way we put them to use determine the manner in which we adjust to the events of daily living. In the functioning of the senses, some of us are colour blind while others suffer from night blindness. A highly co-ordinated kinaesthetic sense characterizes the ballet dancer. A superior sense of taste is essential to the professional wine taster. Someone with an unusual capacity for pitch and tone discrimination might become a superior musician.

Whatever the nature, it is recognized that abilities, talents, and temperament are governed by essential sensory mechanisms. If the talents are displayed to a superlative degree, we find ourselves admiring an artistic genius, an intellectual giant, or a world champion. If they function at a low level, we feel we are in the presence of a social dullard, an athletic failure or an otherwise retarded member of the group. These sensory and perceptual capacities make us what we are. They limit our achievement, they extend our horizons, they account for the vast scope of individual differences that make up the human race.

'How do individual differences occur?'

'What is their basis?'

'How do the limitations operate?'

These are the questions the psychologist asks.

In effect, we have stated that the function of our sensory organs and powers of perception are responsible for the multitude of variations in our make-up and behaviour.

The psychologist then asks, 'What is the basis for the variation in the function of the senses and the perceptual powers?' The answer is threefold: **species, heredity,** and **environment.**

97

In other words we may say that (*a*) our sensory and perceptive powers are **confined to those functions within the range of the human species;** (*b*) they are limited by the **nature of the inheritance from the family line;** (*c*) they are modified by the **influences of the environmental experiences** brought to bear upon us. Let us look further into each of these three areas of limitation or influence.

LIMITATIONS BY SPECIES

In the discussion of the sensory mechanisms, it was pointed out that dogs were keener than humans in several respects. For example, a dog could respond to a sound frequency well above the maximum human range of 20,000 cycles. Bloodhounds and some other breeds of dogs can retain and recognize the spoor of an individual by an article of clothing which he had worn close to his body. These are functions distinctly beyond the range of human capacity.

Cats and dogs have been known to make their way to a completely strange place after having been abandoned by a family. Migrating birds unerringly find their way South with changing seasons. Trained aeroplane pilots would inevitably lose their way in a fog or dense cloud even on the most familiar route if they did not have the benefit of directional instruments.

Without the aid of a calendar, some migrating birds are known to arrive and depart on the same day each year, like the swallows at the Mission of San Juan, Capistrano. They are reported to leave on October 23rd and return regularly on March 19th.

These interesting aspects of animal behaviour used to be 'explained' by labelling them 'animal instincts'. Obviously, this was not an explanation of how the actions were accomplished. More recent observations and experimentation have indicated that the answers for many of these feats are to be found in the functions of the sensory mechanism of these animals. These are functions that can be duplicated by many other breeds of animals but not by members of the human species known as *homo sapiens*.

Rearing a Boy With a Monkey. We gain further insight into the question of species limitations from the account of an unusual psychological experiment in which a boy and a monkey were reared as if they were brother and sister.

Psychologist M. W. Kellog and his wife took into their Florida home a female chimpanzee, Gua, seven and a half months old at the time their son, Donald, was ten months. Their purpose was to learn what similarities and differences would develop between Donald and Gua if treated alike in every detail. The chimpanzee was dressed like an infant, in napkins and later in rompers. She was wheeled in a carriage, sat in a high chair, slept in a bed, and was kissed good night.

No special effort was made to teach Gua spectacular stunts but rather to teach her the same kinds of things a fond parent would do with a baby girl. The experiment was carried on with a careful day-by-day record of observations, films, and tests for a period of nine months.

It was found that the chimpanzee was able to take on many human ways. She wore shoes and walked upright. She was able to eat with a spoon, drink out of a glass, and open doors before the boy acquired these abilities. She imitated human gestures and ways of showing affection like hugging and kissing Donald as well as the parents. Like most children she made a fuss when the 'parents' went out and left them alone.

Gua's rate of development was much faster than the boy's, especially in the motor skills of climbing and jumping. She also learned to respond to a total of ninety-five words and phrases such as 'kiss Donald', 'shake hands', 'show me your nose'. She never could learn to utter words or phrases other than to make known her wishes through grunts and squeals. Her toilet training was appreciably slower than the control achieved by the boy.

Although the chimp progressed faster than the boy in the earliest stages, it became evident towards the end of the experiment that she was falling behind, especially 'in the matter of intellectual adaptation to human demands'. The early superiority is attributed to the fact that anthropoids in general mature much earlier than humans. A monkey reaches puberty at about four years, whereas humans reach puberty between twelve and fourteen on average, with girls generally reaching puberty before boys.

In the report of this experiment by Dr. Kellog and his wife it was indicated that a good deal of human socialization can be achieved by an animal through training and human association. But it also was noted that 'there are definite limits to the degree of humanization that can be achieved by a non-human species regardless of the amount of socializing and humanizing effects'.

HEREDITY

The influences of heredity upon our physical, mental, emotional, and social make-up are gross, yet difficult to define.

What is Heredity? Simply defined, **biological heredity is the transmission of traits from one generation to the next through the process of reproduction.**

We gain some insight into the process of human development and adjustment by an understanding of the mechanics of heredity.

The Mechanics of Heredity in Reproduction. Human reproduction takes place through the union of two specialized sex cells or **germ-line** cells, the 'egg cell' from the female and the 'sperm cell' from the male. These specialized germ-line cells are distinguished from the other tissue or **somatic** cells by their reduced number of chromosomes. The **chromosomes** are the all-important microscopic carriers of heredity which are contained within the nucleus of a cell.

In all higher plants and animals every somatic or body cell contains within its nucleus the unvarying number of chromosomes which is characteristic of a specie. In man this number is forty-six. No matter how many times a tissue cell divides to produce daughter cells, the number of these chromosomes remains constant. However, the germ-line or sex cells develop through a special process known as **reduction-division,** as a result of which each ovum and each sperm appears with only half the number of chromosomes characteristic of the species. Thus, when a male sperm cell and a female egg cell unite to form a new organism through the process of fertilization, the full number of chromosomes is restored. Here we see the biological mechanism whereby half of our inheritance is supplied by the mother (through the chromosomes of the ovum) and half by the father (through the chromosomes of the sperm). The inquiring reader then asks: how is it therefore possible for two red-haired parents to produce a child with black hair? The answer lies in the laws of heredity or the study of **genetics** as it is called.

The Role of the Genes. Genetics takes its name from the 'genes' which represent the unit determiners of hereditary traits. Previously we spoke of 'chromosomes' as the carriers of heredity. Actually, the chromosomes act as the housing elements for the fundamental carriers of hereditary traits, the **genes.**

The **gene** is the biologist's concept of the structure which is responsible for transmitting such traits as eye colour, hair colour, height, colour of skin, texture of hair, shape of the nose, etc. Although no one has ever photographed or isolated a gene even under the highest-powered microscope, there is sufficient evidence to assure us of their existence in numbers from twenty to several hundred in a single chromosome. It is estimated that any individual carries a minimum of 12,000 pairs of genes.

How Two Sexes Produce Variation. It is an odd circumstance that we think of 'heredity' as the means of reproducing likenesses. Yet in the very process of sexual reproduction whereby the hereditary traits are transmitted, there exists the basis for the infinite differences which distinguish human beings from each other.

With the union of an egg and a sperm, there takes place the pairing of two sets of chromosomes from two parents, both of whom have diverse hereditary backgrounds of their own. From this reshuffling of chromosome pairs there arises innumerable gene combinations. These show themselves in the endless chain of variables seen in the faces and bodies of men and woman.

Beginning with the number of sperms and the number of eggs

manufactured by the average human and multiplying this by the number of genes involved, Dr. Bentley Glass, author of *Genes and the Man*, computed the number of possible combinations resulting from the union of a human egg and sperm to be 281,474,967,710,656, or almost 300 trillion. From this he concludes, 'It is easy to see why no two individuals produced from separate fertilizations ever chance to be identical.'

Here we see the principal role of **sex** in the hereditary pattern; namely, to produce human variations. Were it not for reproduction by two sexes, every member of the human race would look like every other member, just as every muscle cell which is reproduced by cell division, looks like its neighbouring muscle cell. This assumption, of course, does not take into consideration the diverse effects of environment which exerts its own influence.

Having this knowledge of genes and chromosomes we are now ready to understand the laws of heredity as they determine similarities as well as differences between individuals.

THE LAWS OF HEREDITY

The average person, acquainted only in a general way with the concepts of heredity, expresses wonderment about the matter of individual differences when they ask: 'Why are Johnny and Jimmy so different even though they are brothers? They both come from the same parents and were brought up in the same home. Where's the influence of heredity?'

The answer here is in the same category as that of the black-haired child resulting from two red-haired parents. They are both explainable by our knowledge of hereditary determiners as first evolved from the experiments of that now immortal Austrian priest, GREGOR MENDEL. His work gave rise to what is generally referred to as the **'Mendelian laws of inheritance'.**

Gregor Mendel experimented for eight years with many varieties of garden peas. He cross-bred and inbred his varieties, always concentrating on pairs of contrasting traits. By manipulating the pollens of his plants he crossed tall peas with short peas, wrinkled peas with smooth peas, red flowers with white flowers, green seeds with yellow seeds, and many other combinations. His original experiments have since been repeated and expanded by many others. Such researchers as T. H. Morgan, J. B. S. Haldane, C. B. Bridges, and more recently F. H. C. Crick, J. D. Watson, and M. H. F. Wilkins are only a few of the more famous scientists who have so expanded our present knowledge of the science of genetics that it would take a lifetime of study to master the full significance of all their findings.

For our purposes in understanding the origin of certain human traits, the most elementary principles of the science of genetics will suffice. These are given as accurately in the original work of Mendel as is to be found in subsequent research.

Dominant *versus* Recessive Traits. Gregor Mendel observed that when he cross-bred his plants, certain traits were passed on without alteration from generation to generation. He also observed that some traits appeared more pronounced and more frequently than others. There was thus introduced the idea of **dominance** and **recessiveness** in traits.

For example, when Mendel crossed the tall strain of pea with the dwarf type of the same species, all of the products of this first cross-breeding showed up as *tall*. Then when this first generation of tall peas were self-fertilized, the resulting offspring showed a ratio of three tall peas to every one of the *dwarf* type. Tallness was thus designated as the **dominant** trait while the dwarf strain was considered to be a **recessive** character.

Dominance and Recessiveness of Human Traits. Making detailed observations on humans and following several generations of the same family by investigation and photographs, Dr. David Whitney of the University of Nebraska has compiled an extensive list of dominant and recessive inheritance as it applies to normal traits in humans. Concerning body structure he indicates that a round-shaped head is dominant over a long head, shortness is dominant over tallness, low arches are dominant over normal arches, and short fingers predominate over long fingers.

With reference to the eyes, brown is dominant over blue or grey, green is dominant to blue or grey, pigmented eyes are dominant over albino eyes. Astigmatism, long-sightedness, and short-sightedness are all dominant over normal sightedness. (Along with many other traits too numerous to include here, Dr. Whitney gives several of cosmetic interest to the ladies, such as drooping eyelids being dominant to non-drooping eyelids, freckles to an absence of freckles, dark skin to light skin, wavy hair to straight hair and long eyelashes to short eyelashes.)

Inheritance of Unit Characters. Returning to the experiments of Gregor Mendel we learn that when he interbred the recessive dwarf peas resulting from the second generation breeding, the offspring were all of the dwarf strain. Yet when the tall strain of this second generation were self-fertilized, only one-third of the number were tall. And these same arithmetic ratios held true whenever his experiments yielded enough offspring to give the laws of mathematical probabilities a chance to work. Thus it was that Mendel discovered not only the **law of dominance but also the principle of segregation of the genes.** That is, **'the unit characters contributed by each parent separate in an exact ratio in the germ cells of the offspring without having had any influence on each other'.** The tall and short traits, the smooth and wrinkled do *not* blend with each other, but rather remain independent as separate characteristics or **units** to reappear in future matings. Mendel's laws of dominance and unit characters may be illustrated by a convenient arithmetic presentation.

Let us cross a *grey* mouse with a true albino or *white* mouse. From previous experiments it has been observed that grey is dominant over white. Therefore, all the offspring of this mating of a grey mouse with a white mouse will appear *grey*. If we let the capital letter G represent the *dominant grey* and small w represent the *recessive white*, we have:

G plus $w = Gw$ and all these offspring appear grey.

Next, if we inbreed the offspring of this first mating, we are working with four unit traits. If we cross or multiply $G + w$ with $G + w$ we get $1\ GG + 2\ Gw + 1\ ww$.

$$
\begin{array}{r}
G + w \\
\text{times} \quad \underline{G + w} \\
GG + \quad Gw \\
\underline{\quad Gw + ww} \\
1\ GG + 2\ Gw + 1\ ww
\end{array}
$$

Thus, two mice which outwardly appear grey can breed one pure *white* mouse in every litter of four. The ratio is 1:2:1 or three grey-looking mice to one white mouse. From this bit of arithmetic it is seen that two red-haired parents can produce a black-haired child.

In the examples of Mendelian ratios there were included situations in which only one pair of genes was presumably operating. However, in determining the origin of traits in human beings or animals, this is seldom the case. Even the simplest feature will often depend upon several genes. Thus, if two pairs of genes are involved in a recessive trait, instead of a 3 to 1 ratio, it becomes a 16 to 1 chance that the trait will appear in the second generation or grandchildren.

We must remember that although the Mendelian principles of inheritance are mathematically sound, it will often be difficult to trace back human traits directly to one's lineage because of the complications of identifying the gene influences for any single trait. It should be kept in mind that many factors aside from those described by Mendel operate in determining certain characteristics of inheritance.

Blending of Traits. Aside from exhibiting dominance and recessiveness, certain traits appear to be inherited as a **blend** of two qualities. The best example of this appears to be 'skin colour' in human beings. This is thought to be due to either 'imperfect dominance' or the fact that two or more pairs of genes are involved in producing the characteristic traits.

In the mating of Negroes and whites, a true blend appears to operate in determining skin colour. From the resulting ratios, it is assumed that four genes in two pairs are involved, with none of them dominant or recessive. Thus, the first generation offspring of a Negro and white will all be mulattoes of an intermediate skin colour. If a male and female offspring of two such matings were to get together and produce enough progeny, the following ratio would result: one in sixteen would be pure negroid, one pure white, four dark-skinned mulattoes, four light-skinned mulattoes, and six in-between the dark and light-skinned mulattoes.

It is seen from this that the offspring of mulatto parents can produce either dark-skinned children or white-skinned children, depending upon the number of offspring and laws of chance.

Sex-linked Inheritance. In addition to 'blending' and 'dominance' as mechanisms of heredity, there are some traits that are known to be passed on in families in association with the sex of the individual. Thus, we speak of traits such as colour blindness and baldness which occur primarily in the male side of the family as having a **sex-linked hereditary basis.**

By 'sex-linkage' it is implied that the gene or genes that are responsible for a trait such as colour blindness, are carried in the same chromosome which is responsible for sex determination.

The chromosomes which presumably control sex determination in humans have been designated by the letters X and Y. When two X chromosomes unite, the result is a female. When an X chromosome unites with a Y chromosome, the result is a male. Certain conditions in humans such as baldness, haemophilia, and colour-blindness are considered to be **sex-linked hereditary traits.** This is deduced from the fact that these conditions prevail among the male and are relatively rare in the female.

According to the genetic theory of sex-linked traits, the genes responsible for those unique hereditary aspects are located in the X or sex determining chromosome. Therefore, when an X chromosome that carries a sex-linked disease, such as colour-blindness, comes together with a Y chromosome, the disease will show up in the resulting *male* offspring.

However, if that same disease-bearing, X chromosome unites with another X, then the tendency for *normalcy* present in the healthy X chromosome cancels out the disease and the resulting female offspring is not likely to show a sex-linked disease. The exception to this is the unusual coincidence of a female who inherits the disease-bearing tendency in both of her X chromosomes. In such cases, we find the rare instance of a colour-blind or bald female.

It follows from this explanation that in all males where the X chromosome happens to carry a sex-linked trait, the trait will appear in that individual, because the Y does not cancel it out. It may also be recognized that the female with a make-up of two *X* chromosomes is the prime carrier of such sex-linked traits as colour-blindness, haemophilia, and baldness which appear primarily in the male. In this we see why there are so many bald men and so few bald women.

Eugenics. The study of the application of such knowledge of heredity as we have about dominance and recessiveness, the blending of traits and the transmission of sex-linked traits is known as **eugenics.** It consists of scientific selection in the mating of individuals to bring out the best in the race. Horse breeders and dog breeders apply the science of eugenics in developing champion race-horses and pure-bred show dogs.

The average individual may apply his knowledge of heredity quite simply and realistically without resorting to scientific mating. It is immediately apparent that it would be almost surely fatal for close relatives to intermarry in a family carrying the gene for *haemophilia*.

This disease is characterized by an absence of blood-clotting platelets in the blood stream. Such an individual is apt to bleed to death on the occasion of any severance of a large artery. This situation is a matter of historical fact shown in the family history of the descendants of Queen Victoria of England who passed the disease down to a long line of Spanish rulers through her grandchild, Victoria-Eugénie, the wife of King Alphonso of Spain.

By intermingling their blood, this family gave rise to the male 'bleeders' and six female carriers of the disease. All ten of the royal princes were doomed to an early death.

In a more commonplace sphere, an individual worried about falling hair can assure himself of his fate and be protected against quacks who promise to grow hair on his bald head. He has merely to check his *maternal* heredity. If his mother's brothers were bald and also his mother's father, then there is little hope that he will escape baldness as he approaches middle age.

Such information about the hereditary determination of the origin of one's traits and characteristics gives the impression of predetermination in shaping the 'nature' of the individual. This, however, is not an accurate judgement of the total picture for it does not take into consideration the effects of **environment,** or **'nurture'** as it is called. To gain a fuller understanding of this aspect of human development, we shall examine more closely the relative influences of **heredity and environment** or **nature** *versus* **nurture.**

HEREDITY *VERSUS* ENVIRONMENT

Having defined heredity, we may clarify our definition of environment.

In the term **environment,** there is implied any and every influence with which an individual comes into contact after the hereditary pattern has been received through the germ plasma. It includes the effect of training, trial and error learning, influences of the home, school, neighbourhood, hospital, church, playground, climate, geographical location, and anything else that stimulates the senses in any way.

Where does the effect of heredity end and the influence of environment begin? What is the importance of each in any situation?

The answer is somewhat academic. We might say, **the relative influence of heredity and environment differs for each human trait or condition and from one individual to the next.**

Can Inherited Traits Be Changed? To illustrate the interaction of heredity and environment let us consider a trait such as body-build. Our knowledge of heredity tells us that the tendency to be slender or well built is a family matter derived primarily from the function of the endocrine glands. Diet and exercise, two environmental forces, are successfully employed by many persons to change their innate tendency to become stout.

This clearly represents an instance of environmental forces overcoming an hereditary tendency. On the other hand, it is a medical fact that many women and men are so constituted that no amount of diet and exercise will measurably reduce their tendency to obesity without serious injury to their general health.

Can we formulate an invariable rule about the relative influence of heredity *versus* environment with reference to physical traits? The answer apparently is 'No'.

A further illustration of this point of view is contained in an interesting experiment with animals described by psychologist Gardner Murphy. He cites these experiments in support of the idea that 'heredity does not necessarily refer to something foreordained'. Dr. Murphy states: 'After the time of birth, it is the outer environment that guides, releases, and gives expression to hereditary potentialities.'

Take this experiment with a species of white-furred Arctic rabbit. About the inheritance of his white fur there can be no doubt, for the stock breeds true. Nevertheless, in this species of rabbit, it is necessary only to change the light in the room in which the animal is reared and his coat colour turns out dark, rather than white. The potentiality for white can lead to an actual white coat colour if and only if the environment permits it. In the same way, some fish, like the flounder, which inherit a tendency to develop two eyes on the same side of the head, will if reared in water with a different salt content develop one eye on each side of the head like other fish. Thus what is 'inherited' in one environment is not 'inherited' in another. The environment makes a difference in the appearance of the hereditary disposition.

From evidence of this kind, it is seen that **heredity and environment are interdependent forces.** In some circumstances it will be easier than others to determine the effects of each. In some instances the influences of heredity will clearly predominate. In other cases, environment will be the dominant factor.

Inheritance of Physical Traits *versus* Environmental Influences. In the matter of physical traits, the influences of heredity are more easily recognized than for such factors as temperament, talents, and intelligence.

Many studies have provided convincing evidence that the size, shape, and appearance of our sensory organs are largely determined by hereditary factors. We could take each of the traditional five senses in order and show that their structural appearance is inherited according to Mendelian ratios.

The colour of the eyes and the shape of the eyes are inherited qualities. The size and shape of the nose is a fully recognized parental endowment and racial characteristic. Skin colour and texture is easily traced to parental lineage. The size of the mouth, shape of the lips, spacing of the teeth, and mould of the jaw are family characteristics. The size of the ears, the extent of their protrusion, their thickness, and the shape of the ear lobes have been shown to run according to family patterns.

Inherited Taste Abilities. About twenty years ago, an American chemist found, quite by accident, that some of his co-workers had no sense of taste for a substance called phenyl thiocarbamide. To those who could taste it, the substance was bitter. Geneticists learned of this odd situation, and saw that it could be used to test the inheritance of taste. Abbreviating the chemical term to P.T.C., they proceeded to test thousands of people with it.

The experimenters found that 70 per cent of the American population are P.T.C. 'tasters', and 30 per cent 'non-tasters'. Their studies further reveal that the inability to taste P.T.C. runs in families. Matings between 'non-taster' and 'non-taster' breed children who are invariably 'non-tasters'. Matings between two 'tasters', or between one 'taster' and one 'non-taster', give some children who are 'tasters' and some children who are not, in conformity to the Mendelian laws of heredity already described.

The Dionne quintuplets were given the P.T.C. taste test when they were about seven years old. Since the five Dionne girls were supposed to be identical—that is, to have developed from only one fertilized egg—their response ought to have been identical. Tested one by one by Norma Ford and Arnold Mason of the University of Toronto, each child expressed an opinion of the taste in some French phrase. Cecile said, *'Ce n'est pas bon.'* Annette said, *'Oui, c'est fort.'* Yvonne, Emilie, and Marie said, *'N'aime pas le gout du tout.'* ('It's no good'; 'Yes, it's strong'; and 'I don't like the taste at all.') Thus, all five Dionnes were seen to be P.T.C. 'tasters', as was their mother.

Inherited Smell Differences. People differ in their abilities to smell certain odours, as well as in their taste reactions. The differences range all the way from the person without any sense of smell at all—a condition called *anosmia*—to the smell expert who makes his living checking on the quality of perfume ingredients. The reader may test his own sense of smell with the flower called freesia. Some people deny that it has any fragrance at all. Others say that it has a pleasant odour. Still others claim that it stinks.

Stature Differences. In the matter of stature, we find that if both parents are tall, the children are bound to be tall. If both parents are short, the offspring are inclined to be short, with some exceptions who may be tall. When one parent is tall and one short, the tendency of the children will incline towards the shorter parent.

Although the influences of heredity are admittedly very great where physical traits are concerned, we cannot overlook the potential effects of environment. For example, it has been shown that Japanese brought up on the west coast of the United States are on the average 3 inches taller than Japanese reared in their native Japan. At the same time, these American-born Japanese are appreciably shorter than Americans as a group. Here again we see the interaction of heredity and environment.

Nature and Nurture of Internal Organs. It is not too difficult to demonstrate the basis for our information about the hereditary or environmental influences on physical or external traits. They can be confirmed by measurements or photographs. But when we consider internal organs, we are faced with a more complicated problem.

In the development of internal as well as external body structures, we know that genes are involved. There is little question that the brain, lungs, heart, kidneys, liver, and endocrine glands owe their nature in small part or large part to hereditary effects. But here we cannot readily see organic similarities or differences. The task is more complicated because we must judge in a second-hand way by their functions and effects.

Since the internal organs are so closely tied up with the functions that control such characteristics as temperament, talents, and intelligence, we end up by studying not the organs, but the influences of nature *versus* nurture in shaping these very components of our make-up. We therefore ask, to what extent are talents inherited? Are musical prodigies born or made? Is artistic genius inherited? How much of *temperament* is inherited? Is intelligence inherited? Are strong hearts inherited? Is long life inherited?

Is Musical Aptitude Inherited? In an effort to understand the origin of certain musical aptitudes, Professor Carl Seashore and his associates at the University of Iowa conducted some pioneering studies. They separated musical capacity into its elements of a sense of pitch, time, consonance, rhythm, and tonal memory. They then devised a series of gramophone records for testing these abilities individually. Their tests were given to thousands of competent musicians, mediocre musical aspirants, and a random sample of the general population.

Professor Seashore and his associates found that actual training in music did not affect the test results in these essential elements of music to any great degree. They concluded from their experiments that **inheritance is an important factor in the musical abilities shown by the most competent musicians.** They also showed that aptitudes in the specific musical elements were not necessarily correlated. One might have a good sense of pitch and a poor tonal memory. One might have a superior sense of rhythm accompanying a poor sense of pitch.

The Origin of Musical Genius. A study of this subject of the origin of musical talent was conducted by Amram Scheinfeld and reported in his book *You and Heredity*.

Mr. Scheinfeld took case histories of the most accomplished artists in the fields of instrumental and vocal music. His subjects included such virtuosi of world renown as Jascha Heifetz, José Iturbi, Arturo Toscanini, Arthur Rubenstein, Lili Pons, Kirsten Flagstad, Rosa Ponsell, Gladys Swarthout, and others, numbering seventy-two in all. Also included were fifty outstanding students of the Juilliard Graduate School of Music.

He sought answers to the following questions about these musical artists. At what age was musical talent revealed? Were the parents musically talented? Did the brothers and sisters show musical talent? Did their children show musical talent?

After compiling the answers to these questions for his total of 122 musical families, Scheinfeld reasoned as follows: 'If musical talent is produced by genes, this should be evident: where *both* parents are musical, we should expect a higher incidence of musical talent in their children than if only *one* parent is musical, and where one parent is talented, there should be more talented offspring than where neither parent is talented.' After reviewing the results of his statistical compilations Mr. Scheinfeld states: *'That is exactly what our figures reveal.'* They further showed the following facts:

> For the musicians, the average age at which talent was expressed was under five.
> The professional débuts were made at the average age of thirteen.
> Where both parents were talented, in most matings one-half to three-fourths of the children were talented.
> Where only one parent was talented, in most matings, one-half of the children were talented.
> Where neither parent was talented, the average of talented offspring was one-fourth or less.

These findings supply convincing evidence that heredity plays a **dominant role** in producing great musical talent. Mr. Scheinfeld was assisted in this work by Dr. Morton Schweitzer, research geneticist at Cornell University. Their own judgement about the conclusions of their research was quite definite. They stated: 'Upon reviewing all the data and opinions in this study of ours, we feel justified in leaving you with the conclusion that some unusual hereditary endowment is essential for great musical achievement.'

To state that 'hereditary endowment is necessary for musical greatness' does not mean that one's mother or father needs to be a musical virtuoso. The reader who has followed our discussion about how the laws of heredity operate has noted that a trait can be carried in the genes and passed on through a second or even third generation and in such small ratios that it will appear in one out of sixteen offspring. Recognizing this fact, it is then understandable that Yehudi Menuhin, the renowned violinist, *inherited* his potential for musical greatness although neither his mother nor father had any marked musical ability. In the same circumstance we learn that Arthur Rubinstein, the famous pianist, came from a home in which no member of the family played a musical instrument.

Is Athletic Genius Inherited? The discussion on the subject of 'talent and heredity' has centred about musical traits up to this point. What can be said about other performing talents?

World-famed professional athletes, Olympic stars, and circus performers also tend to display unusual abilities at an early age. They have family histories of similar achievements. In the backgrounds of these performing geniuses there is found the unmistakable influence of heredity in contributing to their greatness. However, it is pointed out that the long lines of family artistry among these performers are not to be misinterpreted. While they indicate biological hereditary transmission, they also give evidence of **environmental influences.** There can be little doubt that family traditions, parental dictates, and the lure of fame and glamour are powerful factors in getting circus offspring and other professional performers to follow in their parents' footsteps. These family associations ensure early training, expert teaching and high promise of a job.

As for the **hereditary factors,** it must be noted that what great athletes, dancers, and gymnasts inherit is the nature of their sensory structure which makes possible the heights they attain. The performance abilities themselves are not inherited. The form they take is due primarily to practice and training—or 'environment', as it might be called.

In the same way that an inherited capacity for a perfect sense of pitch contributes to the making of a virtuoso, an inherited capacity for a superior sense of balance contributes to the development of a great gymnast. However, neither the musician nor the acrobat could achieve greatness without untold hours of practice and training. It was said of Ignace Paderewski, the famous pianist, that he would often spend eight hours a day of practice on one page of piano composition. And it has been related that from her childhood, Sonja Henie frequently practised figure skating for seven hours a day. Both performers were known as 'child prodigies' in their field. Was their greatness due to heredity or training? The best answer is—again—a combination of heredity and training.

Inheritance of Great Artistic, Mathematical, and Literary Talent. Similar empirical studies, employing a biographical approach, have yielded the same kinds of conclusions about outstanding individuals in the world of art, letters, and mathematics. The biographies of many famous painters such as Michelangelo, Leonardo Da Vinci and, in our own time, Max Ernst have indicated that they very early exhibited a remarkable degree of artistic ability which could not be solely the result of training. The same has been shown to be the case with great mathematicians like Isaac Newton and the Bernoulli family, who were largely responsible for developing the study of calculus. In the world of letters the pattern is repeated in the classic examples of such men as John Stuart Mill, Thomas Macauley, and Goethe, each of whom gave evidence of their future literary greatness while they were children.

No Greatness Without Industry. In all scientific discussions about individuals of great talent who attain world renown it is almost always pointed out that along with the hereditary endowments there is evidence of an unusual amount of application—sheer hard work. These represent the contributions of training or environmental influences, without which their greatness would not have been achieved. We see, therefore, that while **heredity supplies the potential talent, favourable environmental influences are needed to bring it out.**

Influences on Temperament. It was previously noted that the visceral organs gave rise to the bodily sensations of hunger, thirst, fatigue, nausea and sexual desire. These represent internal tensions which affect attitude and behaviour. They are variously referred to by psychologists as 'motivating forces', 'urges', and 'basic drives'.

We know that people differ with reference to these internal impulses which combine to produce what may be called **temperament or disposition.** In popular expressions we speak of one man as having 'the appetite of a horse' and another of having 'the sex drive of a bull'. Originating from bodily organs, it is the view of many that such basic drives are influenced by heredity. However, experience has indicated that these patterns are also very much subject to the influences of the home, school, church, and playground. It is maintained that external influences during early developments may be so great as to overshadow the effects of heredity. We therefore ask: **'To what extent is temperament shaped by heredity and/or environment?'**

Again, there is no definite answer. To quote Professor Ross Stagner:

'Studies of the hereditary nature of emotional behaviour have been especially prolific in producing controversies, if not understanding, in the area.'

The most illuminating information on this question of the relative influences of heredity and environment in shaping temperament has been gathered through studies of twins.

Comprehensive studies of twins have been carried out by Professors Freeman, H. Newman, and K. Holzinger, who gathered essential data on nineteen sets of identical twins who had been separated early in life and reared in different homes. In contrast to this, they made observations on fifty sets of identical twins brought up together. They administered personality and intelligence tests and collected detailed notes on their observations of all sixty-nine twin pairs. They compared the results of their findings for the two groups.

While there were found to exist varied differences in temperament between the individuals, the authors were surprised to find *similar test results* on a group basis, for the measures of temperament in comparing the twins reared apart with those brought up together. They concluded from this result that **'heredity and environment are about equally effective in shaping the temperament of the sixty-nine pairs of twins'.**

The differences in temperament that were found to exist between pairs of twins were attributed to influences of environment. The fact that the differences between the separated pairs were *not greater* than those found among unseparated pairs was considered to be due to the effects of heredity.

In an effort to confirm their surprising findings, Professors Freeman, Newman, and Holzinger made additional observations on pairs of brothers and sisters (**siblings** is the term used by the psychologists). They employed two groups. One group was composed of siblings brought up together; the other group was made up of brothers and sisters reared apart. Their first important result with the new data showed **that the differences in temperament between the siblings were significantly greater than those existing between the twins.** This further confirmed a degree of hereditary influence in shaping differences of temperament.

However, the measured differences in temperament between the brothers and sisters reared in the same home were as great as the differences between the brothers and sisters brought up separately in foster homes. Here again, the results from the study of siblings were the same as they had found from their investigation of twins. They again concluded that **heredity and environment are equally important in determining temperament and emotion.**

Is Intelligence Inherited or Developed? Regarding 'intelligence', the question of nature *versus* nurture is more than academic. If heredity is the prime force in fixing the intellectual level, it can be of practical value in guiding the parent or the teacher. If, on the other hand, intelligence levels are a product of the environment and can be measurably influenced by home, school, and social surroundings, this too is valuable information. Many studies and various approaches have been employed by psychologists and sociologists to provide answers to these very vital questions.

One of the earliest inquiries on the inheritance of intelligence was conducted by SIR FRANCIS GALTON in England and dates back to 1869. He studied the family tree of all persons directly related to a family of superior intellect. He concluded that in a family of genius there are many others of eminence—and that 'average' individuals could expect to have few relatives that would achieve renown.

At the lower end of the scale of intelligence, we have what is now the famous study of a family called the **Kallikaks.** In this study there was traced a long line of what was then termed feeble-mindedness, delinquency, and prostitution. It was reported that out of 470 descendants of the illicit mating of Martin Kallikak with a normal woman only 5 per cent of 496 descendants were shown to be below normal.

Another early investigation of again, what was then called feeblemindedness concerns the equally well-known and infamous **Jukes** family studied by the psychologist R. L. Dugdale. In five generations, out of 540 descendants, more than half were in the category of low intellect, vagabonds, and paupers.

These comprise the best-known and earliest studies relating to the inheritance of that quality which we call 'intelligence'. They used to be cited as proof positive of the hereditary nature of mental deficiency. However, the data of these studies have been criticized as being 'impressionistic'. It has been further pointed out that 'the negative home environments of the defective Jukes and Kallikaks could easily have contributed to their lowered status'.

From a psychological point of view, it is now generally conceded that the unwholesome environment of those born into a 'defective' family would contribute to their lowered status as measured by tests and other criteria. It is unlikely, although not out of the question, that an extremely impoverished environment would result in high I.Q.s. There is little question that one can raise measured intelligence levels of any group of individuals by improved surroundings and increased educational opportunities. But it is equally true that the amount of such measured increases of intelligence on a group basis is rarely more than 10 to 15 per cent. In view of these facts plus all other evidence from psychological researches, it must be concluded that **intelligence levels are largely inherited.** If asked to make a quantitative estimate, some argue that **at least 75 per cent of our demonstrable intelligence can be attributed to hereditary influence.** However, we must note that to some extent the answer to this question remains a moot point.

At the higher end of the intelligence scale, the evidence tends to support hereditary influence. The early study of Sir Francis Galton was adequately confirmed by the widely publicized treatise of Drs. Terman, Cox, and Hollingworth on their study of 1,300 cases of genius and gifted children. They too concluded that 'the predominant influence of heredity was evident in offspring with high I.Q.s'.

An interesting finding of this study by Dr. Terman and his associates was the fact that among this group of persons of genius and gifted intellect, five of their offspring were of very low intelligence. Oddly enough, this is further proof of the hereditary nature of very low intelligence. Such children, born and reared in homes with other children of normal intellect and parents of high I.Q., cannot be the product of environment. Therefore, they must be due to germ plasm and the result of the intricate mathematics of the laws of heredity as previously outlined.

Finally, we obtain our best evidence on the status of hereditary influence in intelligence from the previously described twin studies by Drs. Freeman and Holzinger. They compared identical twins brought up together with identical twins reared apart and fraternal twins brought up together. With this approach they held heredity constant while varying the environment. Their result on I.Q.s conclusively favoured the influences of heredity. It was shown that, whether brought up together or apart, the identical twins were much more alike in their resulting intelligence than the sibling twins who were reared in the same home. Here again the evidence conclusively favoured the influence of heredity in determining levels of intelligence.

SUMMARY OF VIEWS ON HEREDITY *VERSUS* ENVIRONMENTAL INFLUENCES

In reviewing the total picture of the relative influences of heredity and environment, it may be seen that the psychological findings for the shaping of temperament, artistic and intellectual talents, and intelligence are quite similar to the findings in the investigation of musical, athletic, and performing talents. Once again, it is found that **heredity lays down the essential foundations while environment can alter these foundations for better or worse.** Stated differently, we might conclude as follows: **heredity determines what can be the possible limits of accomplishments for any individual in any given situation while environment determines how close to these limits of performance any individual will come in any given situation.** Thus we frequently need to think in terms of heredity and environment interacting.

SUGGESTED FURTHER READING

Barrass, R., *Modern Biology Made Simple*. Heinemann: London, 1979.

Carstairs, G. M., *This Island Now: The Surge of Social Change in the Twentieth Century*. Penguin: London, 1964.

Carter, C. O., *Human Heredity*. Penguin: London, 1962.

Krech, D., Crutchfield, R., and Ballachey, E., *Individual in Society: A Text-Book of Social Psychology*. McGraw-Hill: London, 1962.

Lorenz, K., *On Aggression*. Methuen: London, 1966.

Tinbergen, N., *The Study of Instinct*. Oxford University Press: London, 1951.

Wright, D. S., *et al., Introducing Psychology. An Experimental Approach*. Penguin: London, 1970.

9

THE PSYCHOLOGY OF INFANCY

The study of how we mature is an important branch of psychology. There are two reasons for its importance. One is simply the great *length of time* that it takes us to come of age. Nine months of prenatal development are followed by eighteen years of growing up. This period of almost nineteen years is between a *third* and a *quarter* of our normal life expectancy.

The other reason why child psychology is so important is that **adult personality has its roots in childhood. What we are and what we do as adults is largely determined by the ways in which we were allowed to experience the inevitable events of childhood.** ('Childhood' in this sense refers to the entire period between conception and maturity.)

During this long period of development, the major problems faced by the growing child and his guardians depend upon his age. Up to the age of about three, the problems are mostly those of physical development. The child must learn to gain control of his body. We shall call this period **infancy.**

Prenatal Life. Physically, life begins at the moment of conception, when a sperm fertilizes the ovum. At once, the complete cell so formed divides into two complete cells, and they divide into four, and so on until the embryonic organism consists of about a trillion cells. This period of very rapid growth lasts about 280 days. At the end of it, the once microscopic organism weighs about seven pounds.

When the mother-to-be can first detect motion in her womb it is termed that the embryo 'quickens'.

Psychologically, life begins no later than birth and possibly before it. Man has long believed that the pregnant woman can somehow mark her baby by her thought, experiences, or emotions. Some traditions say that if the period of pregnancy is a happy one for the mother, the child will have a cheerful temperament. Likewise, a worrisome or fearful prenatal period will supposedly give the baby a morbid personality. At the present time, there is not enough scientific knowledge to prove or disprove this belief. If the emotional experiences of the mother do influence the developing foetus, it must be through the glandular changes that take place in her body during the prenatal period. There is no *direct* connexion between the mother and the foetus.

The Birth Experience. Psychologically speaking, then, life can be said to begin at birth. The only psychological importance of prenatal life is the contrast it makes with postnatal life. Before birth, the child is literally a 'parasite' enjoying continuous nourishment within the shelter of the mother's body. Within the womb, there is no need to perceive, to think, but simple conditioned responses can be learned.

It is sometimes said that the Utopias and Gardens of Eden written about so wistfully are based on vague memories of perfect parasitical prenatal life. If any memories at all lie beneath imaginary Golden Ages, Happy Isles, and Never-Lands, they are more likely to be memories of early infancy than memories of foetal life. As pointed out before, neural connexions in the foetal brain are too few for much, if any, prenatal retention.

It is even doubtful that the newborn infant remembers being born, violent though birth is. Poetical philosophers are apt to claim that the birth cry is an indignant shriek of rage and regret. Actually, it is a **reflex act** to establish breathing. Air is drawn in over the vocal chords, causing them to vibrate.

Reflex Acts. Reflex acts are unlearned. They require no thought. They cannot be controlled by the will. You can stimulate a newborn infant to make several of these automatic responses.

Place your finger in an infant's palm. He will grasp it tightly— sometimes tightly enough for you to lift him. This is known as the **grasping reflex.** It normally disappears after the age of about four months.

The **pupillary reflex** will cause the pupil of an infant's eye to contract if a beam of light is shone into his eye. It can be found in all infants with normal vision as soon as the second day of life.

If you tickle the soles of their feet, most infants will curl their toes and extend their big toes. This **plantar reflex** normally changes after a year or two. Thus, a two-year-old whose sole is tickled will flex his toes.

Tapping the patellar tendon just below the kneecap will usually cause a kicking of the foot; however, this response is normally absent in a small percentage of the population. The response is called the **knee jerk** or **patellar reflex.** The newborn child starts life with a variety of other abilities. Observe an hour-old infant. His body squirms, twists, rolls, and bends. His back arches. His hips sway. His head rolls from side to side, or is thrown back. His arms slash vigorously. His legs are kicked in exaggerated thrusts, or are flexed at the ankles, knees, and hips.

A baby does still more on its first day. He cries, sucks, swallows, hiccoughs, grunts, vomits, urinates, defaecates, blinks, and stretches.

From the presence or absence of such reflexes, the trained expert can tell whether or not nerve and muscle connexions are developing normally. This progress-according-to-schedule is called **maturation.** It is the psychologist's extension of our everyday word 'maturity'.

Maturation. If an infant develops normally, we can expect certain of his abilities to **mature** at ages that are roughly the same for all children. Such abilities—the ones that depend upon age—need little or no help to appear, nor can they be made to appear before the time is ripe for them to do so. Experiments show that teaching and training *must* await the process of development, or it will fail.

For example, the muscle and nerve connexions for bladder and rectal control must be sufficiently developed before a child can be trained not to wet or soil himself. Until such time parents cannot expect their training to be effective.

For another example, children come to walk chiefly through maturation. From birth, they show a regular sequence of progress towards walking. Table III lists the approximate ages at which the various stages of motor development occur in children. This developmental process is graphically illustrated in Fig. 29. These stages almost always occur in the order shown, although the ages can vary widely.

Table III. Stages of motor development

Age (*Months*)	Stage
1	Chin up
2	Chest up
3	Reach and miss
4	Sit with support
5	Sit on lap and grasp object
6	Sit on high chair and grasp dangling object
7	Sit alone
8	Stand with help
9	Stand holding furniture
10	Crawl
11	Walk when led
12	Pull to stand by furniture
13	Climb up stair steps
14	Stand alone
15	Walk alone

This regular sequence of improvements accompanying a gradual increase of age is typical of maturation. The same *kind* of pattern can be found in the development of a child's ability to talk, dress, reason, and so forth.

Talking. Children learn to speak largely by imitating the sounds they hear. If they hear no sounds during the years when the ability and the drive to mimic are greatest, they will be unable to speak.

Thus, children who are deaf but not dumb utter no language. They have never heard human speech.

Children whose hearing is normal and who are brought up among talkative people usually utter their first word at about the age of ten months. At one year, they have three words; at fifteen months, they are in command of nineteen words; at eighteen months, their vocabulary extends to twenty-two words; and by two years, it is 272 words.

tal sture		sit with support		stand with help		pull to stand by furniture	
۱o.		4 mo.		8 mo.		12 mo.	
n up		sit on lap grasp object		stand holding furniture		climb stairs	
۱o.		5 mo.		9 mo.		13 mo.	
est up		sit on high chair grasp dangling object		crawl		stand alone	
۱o.				10 mo.			
ch and ss		6 mo.		walk when led		14 mo.	
۱o.		sit alone		11 mo.		walk alone	
		7 mo.				15 mo.	

Fig. 29. Stages of motor development

It is important to note that the rate of development differs from child to child, and that the figures given in this and subsequent sections are merely group averages.

Toilet Training. An infant cannot gain control of his bladder or his bowel until the nerves and muscles that regulate these organs are matured or developed. On the other hand, a child will not be able to exercise control unless he has been properly trained. Thus, the child's mastery of bladder and bowel depends upon development and training.

The wise mother matches nature with nurture. She is aware that all sorts of nervous tensions may be caused in a child by training that is too early, sudden, or rigid. She knows that, like the child's ability to walk alone, his ability to control his bladder and bowel develops from helplessness to independence.

Bowel control takes at least two years of maturation. During the first few weeks of an infant's life, bowel movements occur haphazardly from four to six times a day. By the second month, there are about two bowel movements a day, which may follow feeding periods. A semblance of regularity appears at about the fourth month. Training at this time will appear to be successful, but the success will be brief. Growth changes are taking place in the child.

At six to seven months, movements become irregular in pattern. At ten months, some regularity returns. When walking starts at about a year, faecal 'accidents' recur. At fifteen months, the child learns verbal signals. At eighteen months, only a few mishaps occur. By the age of two, bowel control is well established in the average child.

At the age of two and a half to three, a child may suffer mild constipation. Later, about the time that school begins, the tension, anxiety, and emotional excitement may cause loose bowels.

This description is very general. Variations are to be expected, as well as stool smearing and dabbling with faeces. This innocent mal-behaviour can be easily overcome by providing the child with Plas-ticene or modelling clay, a socially acceptable substitute.

Daytime bladder control is established in the average child by the age of two, if training has begun near the end of the first year. For the most part, such training consists of getting the child to make mental associations. He must be taught to associate his feeling of internal pressure with a signal to his mother.

Even after control is established, there will be frequent urinary lapses. Cold weather, or the onset of head cold, may cause temporary loss of control, as may teething, illness, emotional upsets, and the drinking of too much liquid.

Lapses occur more often in the night than in the day. Nocturnal control is generally established from six months to a year later than daytime control. With proper training and normal physical condition, day and night dryness is established in the average child by the age of three. Some children, past the age of three and a half to four, continue to wet their beds. The condition is called **enuresis.**

About 10 per cent of cases of enuresis have physical causes. Allergists have traced many cases of bed-wetting in older children to food sensitivities. The bed-wetting stops when the responsible food is removed from the diet.

Most cases of enuresis, however, result from psychological disturbance or poor training procedures. Punishment, scolding, and excitement exaggerate the enuresis. Punishment causes the child to become obsessed with the fear that he will wet himself, and the fear causes him to wet himself.

Feeding. A child is ready to try to manipulate a spoon before he is a year old. He normally has enough control at two and a half to feed himself. Between the ages of one and five, children normally refuse certain foods. Their dislike may be genuine, it may be a temporary mood, or it may be an imitation of some other member of the family. There are few real feeding-problem cases. They are created by parental tactics of forcing, coaxing, and bribing children to eat. A normal hungry child will eat enough food, if it is at all palatable. Experiments show that, left to themselves, children will eventually select the foods needed to make and keep them healthy.

The Choice of Foods. Dr. Clara M. Davis experimented with children in hospital whose ages varied from those newly weaned to those of four years. They were offered a variety of foods on a tray, and could take or get whatever they wanted or pointed to. They ate as much or as little as they desired. They were also allowed to use any style of eating they preferred, with utensils, hands, or face in the plate. In her report, Dr. Davis notes that 'all the children chose meals of such a nature that they were excellently nourished. They showed great glee when the food was brought in. They ate eagerly and their appetites were good.'

Dr. Curt Richter of the Johns Hopkins Hospital reported the case of a three-year-old child who was addicted to eating huge amounts of salt. The child died before proper treatment could be given. Autopsy showed that the child was suffering from an adrenal gland disorder and was unwittingly trying to keep himself alive with his enormous salt intake.

Thumb-sucking. Like food refusal, thumb-sucking is another child problem created by parents. It is normal for even a well-fed child to place his thumb in his mouth. In fact, marks on the thumbs of some newborn infants indicate that they sucked their thumbs before birth.

Thumb-sucking relieves an infant's tensions and stimulates the sensitive membranes of the mouth pleasantly. In this respect the thumb is to the infant what the cigarette is to the adult. When children are over-tired, sleepy, hungry, sick, or teething, their finger-sucking increases.

Thumb-sucking will not cause 'buck' teeth or facial deformity if the habit stops before the age of six. Scolding a child for thumb-sucking will make him feel guilt, which he will try to relieve by more thumb-sucking. It is more effective to keep him well fed and to provide him with adequate toys to occupy his hands and fingers.

The Importance of Play. Play is any activity indulged in for the pleasure it gives and not for some end result. The person plays for play's own sake. Play differs from work, which a person engages in because he wants the end result which it can achieve.

Play is so great a part of child life that people often overlook its important role in child development. Play is important in several ways:

Physically, play helps develop the child's growing muscles. It also lets out nervous energy which if not expressed makes children tense and irritable.

Socially, play leads children to behave in a social manner. Without it, the child becomes selfish and domineering. From his play with others, he learns to share, to co-operate, and to make friends.

Educationally, play teaches young children to perceive shapes, colours, sizes, and textures.

The play of little children passes from simple motor activities with toys to socialized play with other little children, and then to dramatic and constructive play. The fifteen-month-old child, for instance, likes to put objects into receptacles. The two-year-old likes to play beside but not with another child. The three-year-old will play with a few other children in co-operative projects like building bridges and buildings out of blocks. The four-year-old prefers playing with other children in complex dramatic play. The five-year-old will work on projects that last more than a day, and likes to go on excursions with his friends.

Masturbation. Almost all infants discover that manipulating their sex organs arouses pleasant sensations. The practice is normal, in the sense that the majority of children practice it. They make no attempt to conceal play with their sex organs and show no guilt or shame when observed. If scolded or punished, they do not stop the habit but begin to practise it in secret, developing feelings of guilt and anxiety.

Tying the child's hands, and other forms of corporal punishment, are not only ineffective but psychologically harmful. Since irritation of the genitals focuses the child's attention on them, one can often divert the child's attention from his sex organs by dressing him in loose clothing, seeing to it that the organs are clean, and providing toys to occupy his idle hands.

The Child's Morality. Babies are neither moral nor immoral. They are not moral because they do not guide their behaviour by standards of right and wrong. Still, they are not immoral, because they are not consciously flouting known standards of right and wrong. They are *non*-moral. They simply do not have a moral code. Their deeds are guided by **impulse.** They judge right and wrong in terms of **pleasure and pain.**

By the age of three or four, however, the child whose discipline has been consistent knows what is acceptable and what is disapproved. Whenever the child can understand, he must be told the reason *why* certain deeds are *right* while others are *wrong*.

The Child's Understanding. As William James wrote in 1890, the infant is probably conscious of his environment as a 'big, booming, buzzing confusion'. As he matures and learns, the child begins to perceive objects, and then to abstract qualities. Old experiences become more meaningful as he associates new meanings with them. *Orange*, for instance, which he first knows only as a fruit, comes to mean a colour, a tree, a juice, and a flower as well. His concept of *orange* is expanded and he has a precedent for suspecting that other complexities lie hidden behind simple-sounding words.

Because of the baby's limited experience and knowledge, he does not distinguish between living and inanimate objects. Like primitive people, he believes that all objects are alive. **Animism,** the tendency to attribute life to all lifeless things, is characteristic of pre-school children.

THE DEVELOPMENT OF THE SELF

We can almost certainly say that the newborn infant has no idea of himself as an entity distinct from his environment. When awake, he seems to be conscious only of feelings, and these are of only two kinds, very unpleasant and very pleasant.

In studying how personality develops, we can divide the basic drives into those whose satisfaction tends to make the infant **dependent,** and those that tend to make him **independent.**

The hunger drive and the sensory drives for warmth and skin contact can be satisfied only by the infant's parents. The baby cannot successfully gratify those all by himself. All he can do is to react emotionally. Someone else must feed and fondle, clean and clothe him for quite a while. It is inevitable that the baby will occasionally have to wait before these drives are satisfied. No baby can escape *some* frustration. Therefore, when his nervous system matures to the point at which retention begins, the infant acquires memories of both frustration and gratification. Later, when the nervous system matures still further, to the point at which abstraction begins, the child associates these similar memories into the conception of a continuous, identical sufferer, the **self,** or the **ego** as it is sometimes called.

The Psychological Effect of a Name. There is another factor at work to strengthen the child's growing awareness of himself as a separate entity. This is his given name. Having a name makes him a being, a thing. (At this age, children consider all things to be alive, so that 'being' and 'thing' are identical in their minds.) It confirms his **distinct existence.**

(It might be argued therefore that boys who are given their father's first names are at somewhat of a disadvantage because they are deprived of this additional help towards feeling independent, unless a diminutive nickname is used.)

The Desire for Love and Esteem. Being aware of himself as a person enables the child to see a meaning in his parents' attitudes towards his drives. Giving him food and body contact becomes a sign of **love.** Praising his deeds becomes a sign of **esteem.** Love and esteem become very valuable to the child, because they result in gratification. As his grasp of the idea of time improves, love and esteem become more important because they promise future gratification to console him for current frustrations. Eventually, love and esteem become valuable in their own right. That is, **psychological** motives for love and esteem come to parallel **physiological** drives for gratification.

These motives can come to be as strong or stronger than the basic drives, if they are developed by giving the child love and approval. Eventually, he becomes **socialized** by means of them. That is, he will learn to endure some frustration of his drives in order to experience satisfaction of his motives for love and esteem.

Sometimes little children seem to express a feeling of not yet being 'integrated'. A child of two or three can be heard to refer to himself in the first, second, and third person all at once. He may say something like: 'Now listen, Johnnie wants you to be careful, or I'll get hurt!' The 'you' in such a sentence would symbolize the child's independence drives, the 'I' his self, and 'Johnnie' the ideal little boy that he wishes he could be, in order to please his parents.

Freudian Theory About Infant Development. No discussion of the psychological development of pre-school children would be complete without some mention of the theories of SIGMUND FREUD.

Freud's major idea about infantile sexuality was that all infants go through certain stages. The first of these stages, according to Freudian theory, is the **oral erotic.** While at this stage, the infant obtains sexual satisfactions by way of the mouth. Oral sexual pleasure is first derived in nursing, then in thumb-sucking, nail-biting, chewing, and speaking.

The next stage is the **anal erotic.** In this, sexual pleasure is derived from the eliminative functions—first from expelling, then from retaining the contents of the bowel.

The final stage is the **genital erotic,** in which sexual pleasure is obtained from manipulation of the sex organs.

At about the age of three to four, the so-called **Oedipus Complex** develops. (The phrase refers to Oedipus, the legendary Greek hero who killed his father and married his mother without knowing they were his parents.) The child wants to replace the parent of the same sex in the affections of the parent of the other sex. That is, a boy wants his father to disappear, a girl wants her mother to disappear. Both desires conflict with the children's love for the envied parent and with the teachings of morality. Normally, the conflict is resolved by identification with the parent of the same sex and through maturation. The child invests more of his energy in friends, teachers, and pets, so that the two conflicting drives involving parents weaken in relative importance.

Associated with the Oedipus complex is the **castration complex.** The little boy who believes that his father can read his thoughts, fears that his father will retaliate by depriving him of his penis. The little girl, on the other hand, comes to believe that she has been cheated or deprived of a penis (this Freud called 'penis envy') that she once had or ought to have had. She blames her lack on her mother.

This Freudian theory of infant development is not, of course, accepted by all psychologists; many disagree with all or part of it.

Questions About Life and Sex. The best time to guide and teach children in matters of sex is when they ask questions about them. The answers should of course be fitted to the child's capacity to understand. In all cases, however, the proper anatomical terms should be used. The male organ should be called the *penis* and the female organ *vagina*. Other parts of the body that are often avoided or given fanciful names include the breast, nipple, navel, belly, foreskin, scrotum, testicle, buttock, and rectum. No feeling of nastiness or naughtiness should be attached to any mention of these parts of the body.

Some children, however, are intelligent and sensitive enough to feel the uneasiness that sexual and anatomical matters arouse. They become ashamed to ask questions about them. Such children should not be left in ignorance of vital information. The subjects should be broached at the proper times in the development of the children. Most children go through a definite sequence of sexual attitudes.

The one- and two-year-old infant needs to exchange affection with its mother. Cuddling the infant in the arms and singing lullabies gives the child a much-needed feeling of security. The 'love-life' of the child consists of just such fondling, caressing, and rocking. Such motherlove has caused amazing cures of apparent stupidity and loss of appetite in orphans who were receiving 'proper' training and food but no personal attention.

At about the age of two and a half, the child becomes curious about anatomy. The answers to questions about sex organs should be given as calmly as replies pertaining to parts of the face.

Three-year-olds begin to ask, *Why?* Such questions deserve to be treated seriously, in the sense that the answers should not be given in a mocking tone. However, the adult ought not to become self-conscious, but should assume a straightforward, casual attitude.

At about the age of four, children want to know where babies come from. The child's curiosity is intellectual, not sexual, and merits a simple but true answer, based on the biological truth that all life comes from life. He will be satisfied to know that babies grow in their mother's body.

At five or six, the same question will be repeated. Now the answer should include the information that two parents are necessary for producing life.

The same question will be repeated many times. Answering simply and calmly will lead the child to trust his parents. He will not feel shame or hesitation about discussing sexual matters with them.

Emotional Growth. A newborn infant's birth-cry, as we saw, is a **reflex act** to establish breathing. After this first cry, an infant's cries have emotional meaning. They express his displeasure with being hungry, wet, cold, hurt, restrained, or alone.

If his wants are satisfied, the baby is capable of shifting his reactions immediately. He will turn from anger to smiles instantly, and will laugh through his tears. This does not mean that the infant feels any less deeply then the adult. It means, instead, that the child discharges his emotion by expressing it completely. He is uninhibited.

An infant reacts emotionally to any stimulus with his whole body. His response is bewildered and confused. As the child develops, his emotions become more refined. His emotional reaction is applied more directly to the particular cause. This emotional refinement, like the rest of his behaviour, depends not only upon maturation but also upon environmental experiences. Learning and training can and do influence the course of natural development. Thus, one parent may curb and punish every outburst of rage. Another may succumb to the child's temper tantrums. A third may permit a child to display an appropriate amount of emotion before teaching him that mere display of emotion is a futile means for gaining his end.

Anger is a natural reaction to frustration. There is nothing unworthy in anger itself. It can be used to motivate wholesome attempts to overcome obstructions that lie in the way of some goal. A child can be taught positive ways of gaining the ends over which he has his tantrums. To do this, the cause of his tantrum must be found. Obviously, the cause cannot be found if the tantrum itself is either suppressed entirely or entirely ignored.

Parents who pretend to overlook temper tantrums are likely to pamper their children in other ways. They give them too much affection of the wrong kind. Their children are kept from growing up. Such children come to depend too much upon the devotion they receive at home. They grow up with a certain lack of self-confidence.

The parent who stifles all emotional expression may well develop a **repressed** child whose emotions will be diverted into some unwholesome substitute for normal emotional expression. On the other hand, the parent who permits a child to get whatever he wants by threatening or actually throwing a temper tantrum probably will develop a child with little or no emotional control, and with little or no respect for parental authority. The parent who lets an upset child give some vent to his emotional upheaval and who then helps him to see that temper alone will not get him what he wants will develop a child with a good chance to grow into an emotional adult.

Acceptance by Parents. It is the parents' duty to help, or at least permit, the growing infant to learn how to satisfy his dependent tendencies by means of habits that are motivated by his independent tendencies. Parents do just that when they teach a baby to feed himself, to walk, to talk, to dress himself, and to solve his minor frustrations.

Beyond the *practical* benefit to the baby and the family in learning how to take care of himself is the psychological benefit of the praise given for making attempts and for succeeding. The praise makes the baby confident of his own abilities. It makes one child feel as good as the next child.

If, too, the baby's dependence drives have been lovingly satisfied, there will be a vital psychological benefit vastly more important than the practical benefit of immediate relief from crying and tension. The baby will feel loved and safe. He will feel that the environment is a generous, comfortable, friendly kind of place.

These feelings of **self-confidence and security** are the two most important gifts that parents can present to their children. Without the feeling of self-confidence, the most talented person in the world will feel inferior. Without the feeling of security, the most powerful man in the world will be anxious and fearful.

Experience has shown that the feelings about himself and his environment that a baby has at the time he first becomes aware of himself and his environment, are usually the attitudes he keeps through life.

Clearly, the parental attitude that will develop optimistic feelings in a child is **acceptance.** By no means does acceptance mean neutrality. One does not accept by ignoring. One accepts by liking. Parents who like their child as he is, for *what* he is, remembering that what he is will change as he matures, will have a brave and generous child.

Parental acceptance will have an obvious effect upon the child's **emotional readiness to learn.** Being confident of his ability's worth, and feeling secure in his parents' affection even if he fails to attain perfection, the child will be willing to undertake the learning of morality and other tasks. the odds are high that such a child will be well adjusted, to the full limits of his inherited abilities.

Dominance by Parents. Needless to say, not everybody enters childhood feeling sufficiently love-worthy and praise-worthy in a pleasant enough world. Most children are at least a bit anxious about their security and competence. To some extent, they share the feeling that the poet A. E. Housman expressed in one of his last works:

> *And how am I to face the odds*
> *Of man's bedevilment, and God's?*
> *I a stranger and afraid*
> *In a world I never made.*

The reason is that many parents dominate their children, in a belief that a 'well-brought-up' child is one whose spirit has been broken, who is timid rather than brave, helpless rather than self-confident. In the interests of discipline, they ignore the natural rhythm of the child's dependence drives, satisfying them according to some arbitrary schedule. They ignore the maturation of the abilities that satisfy the child's independence drives, forcing the child to learn when and how they please, discouraging his native bents.

The external result is what is known as a 'good child', obedient, orderly, and submissive, with a well-developed conscience. If one were to ask the parents of such a child certain questions about his subjective life, they might well paraphrase these lines from a poem by W. H. Auden:

> *Was he happy? Was he free? The question is absurd;*
> *If anything were wrong, we should certainly have heard.*

To which one could truthfully reply that the neuroses and other forms of maladjustment are the means by which such children eventually let society 'hear' of their inner misery.

The Effects of Deprivation. Let us first consider the effects of the inevitable deprivations that the dominant parent will force his child to undergo. There may be no deliberate cruelty involved in letting a hungry infant scream for an hour because it isn't time for his next bottle, nor in withholding caresses when he is afraid, lest he be spoiled. Nevertheless, the result is the same as if the parents intentionally subjected their child to terror—which, of course, sometimes also happens. The child is permitted to experience the horror of emotional panic. Remember that an infant is emotionally uninhibited. He reacts totally. It is several years before he reacts somewhat more proportionally to the amount of pain or discomfort.

Emotional excitement is not pleasant when one is utterly helpless. Even when the child is better able to take care of himself, the feeling of helplessness persists. The world seems hostile, and his parents— those potent giants—violent monsters.

Should the child attempt to soothe himself by sucking his thumb, or fondling his genitals, punishment and threats follow. He is made to feel guilty, and threatened with total loss of loving care, or so it seems to his undeveloped judgement.

Should the child rebel against the strict rules that frustrate him, he is punished again, and made to feel even more helpless and alone than ever.

To assure himself of some approval and love, the child will do anything. He agrees to whatever he is told, at first on the surface, later in his own mind. He is never sure that he is doing the right thing, however, so he becomes emotionally anxious—that is, always a little afraid, on edge, tense. The world becomes a hostile place, people seem untrustworthy and not sources of affection and ease.

To bolster his feeling of fearful helplessness, the child may determine to become powerful and dominant himself. He will bully inferiors, or work very hard to earn money or glory. These motives for mastery are more rigid and joyless than those which evolve from the enjoyment of an aptitude or talent.

Frustration of the Drives for Independence. Meanwhile, the dominant parent is also frustrating the independence drives of the growing child.

Such frustration often begins soon after birth, when the infant is so tightly swaddled that he can move almost nothing but his eyes. What effect, if any, this restraint has upon the child's personality is still a matter for debate. The initial excitement that it causes—as found by Watson's experiments on emotion—soon passes away, as utter passivity becomes one of the child's facts of life. Also, it does satisfy the child's dependence drives for warmth and body contact, even though it frustrates his motor drives.

Even if the child is not swaddled, his natural maturation is ignored by the dominant parent who wants him to control his bladder and bowel long before he is able to do so. The guilt and inferiority feelings caused by his failures and reprimands are not easily forgotten. The parent is convinced that something is wrong with the child, and eventually the child comes to believe this wholeheartedly.

When the child does manage to succeed at something, his achievement is either ignored or disparaged. He receives little of the approval that helps him to overlook his failures.

As a result of his continued frustration, the child becomes **aggressive.** He wants to hurt back, as he has been hurt. However, aggression frightens him, for several reasons. One is that rage is emotionally as unpleasant as the helpless fear suffered during deprivation. More important, he quickly learns that to express himself threatens him with loss of whatever approval and love he does get. In addition, he had been taught to believe that aggression is morally wrong. His outraged ideals—the voices of his dominant parents—speak up through his conscience.

Therefore he turns his anger against himself. He feels not only inferior but guilty. He becomes depressed. He tries at all costs not to display the violence within him, until at last he succeeds in burying it apparently for good, and conformity becomes his second nature. These motives are often mistaken for signs of a true spirit of co-operation. They are quite different, however, from such spirit. They never result in a desire for responsibility or leadership. They do not stem from a feeling of equality but from a feeling of inferiority.

However, it is unfounded pessimism to view the emotional mishaps of ages two and three as the *inevitable* basis for adult neurosis. It is equally arbitrary to think of the pre-school years as the period in which the adult personality is *permanently* fixed.

This is a good time to remind the reader that stress upon the psychological effects of various parental attitudes towards their children does not discount the importance of heredity, temperament, physique, glands, society, and all of the other factors that shape personality. If people could not continue to grow and learn despite their childhood experiences, ours would be a world made up largely of neurotics and psychotics plus a few normals.

We know that this is hardly the case. Indeed, there are far more people between the extremes of perfect adjustment and utter maladjustment than there are at those extremes.

We shall cover the subject more fully in our chapters on adjustment. Now, however, we continue with our description of child development.

SUGGESTED FURTHER READING

Bowlby, J., *Attachment*. Penguin: London, 1971.

Bowlby, J., *Child Care and the Growth of Love*. Penguin: London, 1953.

Bowlby, J., *The Making and Breaking of Affectional Bonds*. Tavistock Publications Ltd.: London, 1979.

Clarke, A. M., and Clarke, A. D. B., *Early Experience*. Open Books: Eastbourne, 1976.

Millar, S., *The Psychology of Play*. Penguin: London, 1968.

Mussen, P., *The Psychological Development of the Child*. Prentice-Hall: London, 1973.

Richards, M., *Infancy*. Harper and Row: London, 1980.

Rutter, M., *Maternal Deprivation Re-assessed*. Penguin: London, 1972.

Winnicott, D. W., *The Child, the Family, and the Outside World*. Penguin: London, 1964.

10

THE PSYCHOLOGY OF CHILDHOOD

In legal usage, the word 'child'—and even the word 'infant'—is applied to any person who has not yet reached his eighteenth birthday.

In everyday speech, the word 'child' is usually applied to any person whose adolescence has not yet begun.

In psychological language, the word 'child' often has the legal meaning, especially when used in the title of a book. It often has the everyday meaning, too. Strictly speaking, however, **childhood is the period between infancy and adolescence.** It therefore begins at about the third birthday and ends at about the eleventh. This is the time-span with which we shall concern ourselves in this chapter.

During childhood, the major problems facing the child and his guardians are **interpersonal.** He must realize that other people exist in the same way that he exists. He must develop a sense of right and wrong. He will form his first friendships. He will be reacting emotionally to the other members of his family. He will be thrown into relationships with teachers, who are the first adults other than doctors whom he will have to obey besides his parents and grandparents. Once in school, he will have to compete and co-operate with his classmates.

EARLY SOCIAL BEHAVIOUR

In early childhood, children begin to behave socially in crude ways that preshadow their later social behaviour. Most of these show an excess of qualities that are virtues when held in moderation. The child has not yet learned the proper amounts and styles of these acts and attitudes.

Negativism is a form of behaviour in which the child resists adult authority. Called 'stubbornness' or 'contrariness', it makes a young child hard to manage. It is at its peak at the age of three, the so-called 'no, no' stage, when it is so common that it must be regarded as normal. **Negativism is the product of adult intolerance** towards babyish behaviour on the part of children whose increasing fluency of speech makes adults forget how childish the child still is. The child reacts to aggressive suggestion by refusing to comply with adult requests. Negativism declines after the fourth year. By then, the adults in the child's environment have come to respect his individuality and the child has learned that it is more rewarding for him to comply.

Rivalry is another form of early social behaviour. At three, he is interested only in the toys themselves. At four, however, he becomes jealous towards any child of the same age who shows interest in his toys, and at five he is envious of the praise given for high or speedy output of drawings, buildings, etc. By six, his competitive spirit is well developed.

Teasing and bullying are aggressive forms of behaviour. Teasing is an attempt to anger a person by reminding him of his faults. It is appropriate only when used against hypocrites and liars, but children use it almost for its own sake. Bullying is a physical attack upon a weaker person with the intent to inflict pain. It is never excusable. The children who engage in these forms of aggression frequently have feelings of inferiority or insecurity. Feeling themselves to be the 'butts' of still older children, or even of adults, they crudely or symbolically imitate their supposed tormentors, and discomfit still more helpless children or animals.

Jealousy is an almost universal emotional experience in young children. It is an attitude of resentment, different from **envy.** One is envious of something that someone else has but one is jealous of something that one has been having oneself.

Jealousy usually starts at the birth of a younger **sibling.** ('Sibling' is a generic term meaning 'either brother or sister'.) The older child does not want to share its mother with the new arrival. Pre-school children show jealousy towards younger siblings in several ways. They may attack him bodily. They may ignore his presence. They may deny his existence. Sometimes they make none of these obvious signs of jealousy towards the sibling. Instead, their general personality changes. They may revert to such infantile behaviour as bed-wetting and thumb-sucking. They may refuse to eat, or become generally naughty. By pretending to be ill or afraid, they bid for the mother's attention, which they want to continue to monopolize.

The peak of jealousy comes between three and four years of age. Statistics indicate that out of three jealous children two are girls. There is more jealousy in children of higher intelligence than in those of lower intelligence. Jealousy is most apt to occur when the age difference between the siblings lies between one and a half and three and a half years. The oldest child in the family is more often jealous than his later-born siblings. He was once the centre of attention, but the later-born have always had an older sibling, and are more resigned to sharing the parents' love. Even the oldest child's jealousy, however, need not develop.

There is a popular belief that the attitude of a child to his newborn sibling can be avoided by preparing him for the birth. Psychological experiments seem to indicate that preparation is not a determining factor in such jealousy.

Many young children show jealousy towards members of the family other than younger siblings. Because a child constantly associates with his mother, he sometimes comes to feel that she belongs to him. As a result, he resents her affection for his father, and shows jealousy towards him. At other times, a younger sibling will resent the privileges given to older children in the family. He develops envy, especially if the parents nag him by comparing him to an older sibling.

Jealousy decreases at about the age of five, as the child begins to develop interests outside the home.

STUTTERING AND STAMMERING

Stuttering is the involuntary repetition of a sound, syllable, or word. **Stammering** is the inability to utter even one complete word. Stammering is a severe form of stuttering. Both are serious but curable speech disorders.

More than a half of those who stutter begin at the age of four or five. Most stuttering has a psychological origin. It is a symptom of social maladjustment and develops because of fear, self-consciousness, a feeling of inferiority, thwartings, or too much parental supervision.

Though possible, it is not easy to cure stuttering. Patient handling and intelligent understanding are required. Psychologists offer the families of stutterers the following simple rules:

1 Don't nag a favourite child.
2 Don't call attention to the child's speech.
3 Don't insist that the child say things in a certain way.
4 Don't interfere with the child's descriptions and reports.
5 Don't upset him by requiring him to preface every request with 'please'.
6 Do try to help the child adjust to his fears or feelings of inadequacy.
7 Give the child self-confidence.
8 Get him to pay less attention to himself by listening to what he says, rather than how he says it.

Children whose stuttering habit is firmly established can be sent to speech-therapy clinics. At such institutions, a thorough examination is made of the patient and his unstable voice. He practises the most difficult sounds. He is given lessons in correct speech and help in dealing with his emotional life. His parents are interviewed and helped in understanding his difficulties.

THE YOUNG CHILD'S MORALITY

The moral laws of the child's cultural group ought to be established in him between the ages of three and six. It does little good at this age to tell the child why certain behaviour is prohibited. His understanding is still too immature to comprehend the reason for prohibitions. He should merely be told how to act, rewarded if he obeys, and reproached if he disobeys.

Rewards need not be exaggerated. A small gift, a word of praise, or even a smile will do. Likewise, punishment does not have to be over-severe. However, it must be consistent, and its severity must be in proportion to the seriousness of the prohibited act.

In all cases it should be made clear to the child that not he but his act is bad. In this way he can **learn to discriminate between the concept of his self and his deeds.** Such discrimination enables him to become conscious of his intentions. This then permits him to consider them beforehand rather than to become aware of them only after plunging thoughtlessly into the acts that carry them out.

The child conforms to standards of conduct to gain approval and to avoid disapproval. He does what is right without actually knowing why. Still, he does not yet question the fairness of the rules, as he will come to in later childhood. His acts of disobedience are not based on a sense of injustice. If he tries to 'get away with' forbidden acts, he does so to test the authority and consistency of the adults in his environment, or because the rules are irksome in themselves, not as symbols of oppression. The idea that the rules may be invalid does not arise until later.

Though he accepts the rightness of punishment, the young child does not feel guilty when he disobeys. Only if *caught* will he become afraid, and rationalize by giving acceptable reasons for the act. In short, the young child does not yet have a conscience.

The Child's Conscience. The body of ideals by which a person guides his actions is called his **conscience.** It is the person he would like to be. Whenever he does something that conflicts with this ideal self, he feels what is popularly called a 'twinge or pang of conscience'. At first, this ideal self is a portrait of the parent of the same sex. Later, the growing child learns other ideals, from his friends, his teachers, and from books. Some of these—teachers, counsellors, characters in books—become substitute ideals. From each such hero, he seeks a form of love and approval. He will thus learn self-control primarily for the reward of such love and approval.

If the child feels **accepted**—that is, feels loved for his own sake, and approved 'as is'—he will trust his parents' judgement in the matter of deprivation. If their prohibitions are mild and consistent, and delivered matter-of-factly rather than excitedly, the child will learn to obey them with a minimum of resistance. If the learning of these moral and aesthetic ideals is praised and rewarded, the child will make the ideals his own.

PLAY

Real and Imaginary Companions. All that a young child requires of a companion is that he play with him. This requirement is usually best met by a child of about the same age. Unlike adults, another child will play with him in the way he wishes to play—childishly. The sex of the companion makes no difference, nor does race, nationality, religion, and social status. The only important question is: will his companion join in his activities?

Because his environment is limited, he must seek for acceptable companions among the children in the immediate neighbourhood. If none seems to fit his requirement, he may create **imaginary companions** who will play with him as he wishes.

To the young child, an imaginary companion is real. It has a name, physical features, and a personality. The child talks to it and takes it with him. In these journeys, the real child is always the leader. The imaginary playmate is always a submissive follower.

Once accustomed to playing with an utterly docile and agreeable playmate, the child forms the habit of domination. Later, in the company of real children, the child usually must change his domineering ways or run the risk of losing the friendship of his real companions.

Psychological Importance of Toys and Games. Toys play an important part in the life of the child. Children need toys that can be moved, changed, and manipulated. Not only does toy-play help develop **precision** and **agility,** toys reinforce the concept of **property.** Toys also let the child feel that there are at least some parts of his environment that he can master as thoroughly as he pleases. To be of psychological value, **toys should require the active involvement of the child in their use.** Toys that are too automatic or too complete leave nothing for him to do.

After the age of about eight, toy-play takes less and less of children's time, for two reasons. First, few toys are complex enough in form to challenge the level of intelligence the child has reached by that time. Second, his play interests change. To toy-play he begins to add games, sports, collections, reading, and other more mature types of entertainment that involve him in relationships with people and the outer world. This addition of new play activities to the old ones leads to so wide a range of play activities that late childhood is often called the **play age.**

The new kinds of play begin to be added at about the age of five. The child becomes interested in **neighbourhood** games, played with the children next door. Ring games, hide-and-seek, cops and robbers, advancing statues, and blind-man's-buff are typical games of this sort. Games in which any number can play give way to **pair** or **team** games. At first, the child is not a good team player. He wants to dominate the play. Gradually, he learns to limit his efforts to his own role. He finds that there can be as much enjoyment in co-operation as in domination.

Parents should therefore welcome the participation of their children in communal play activities. The children are learning valuable lessons in equality and in law-abiding adherences to rules.

LEARNING IN SCHOOL

We are now at the time in the child's life when he moves into the environment of the school. The child of five or six brings to school more than an untutored mind and a limited set of skills. He brings a dynamic personality studded with all sorts of attitudes, habits, and ideas about every aspect of his life. These emotional and social qualities influence his ability to learn just as his I.Q. does.

If he has been given the love and training that he needed he will now be genuinely eager to learn. He will have outgrown his babyhood, with its self-centredness and its all-or-nothing emotional behaviour. He will have become sufficiently interested in other people, and stable enough, to co-operate with his teacher in the joint enterprise of learning.

If, however, his parents have failed to give him the amount and kind of love he needed, he is likely to fail as a student. A pampered child, for instance, is not likely to make the efforts needed to succeed as a pupil. Another child, already burdened with his parents' wishes for him, may find the additional load of schoolwork more than he can bear. The youngster whose parents have ignored him presents still another kind of learning problem.

Of course, failure is not *necessarily* harmful. It can sometimes produce a sense of reality about one's limitations in a particular field. Adequate guidance will then lead the failing child to an area in which he can succeed. Again, a properly interpreted failure may stimulate a child to greater effort.

In general, though, the memory of previous failures makes a student enter a new learning situation with diminished eagerness and hope. If the course of study is graded so that a child can succeed at each step, he will be encouraged to persevere at the still harder tasks ahead.

THE MENTAL DEVELOPMENT OF THE CHILD

This area of development has been extensively studied by **Professor Jean Piaget** (1896–1980) and is referred to as a **cognitive-developmental approach.** In the early stages of infancy the child will have passed through the period of **sensori-motor** development which is usually completed by the age of **two.** This stage is characterized by an increasing co-ordination of sensory perceptions and motor movements. Following the sensori-motor period is the period of **pre-conceptual thought** or, as it is sometimes termed, **pre-operational thought.** At this stage the child begins to produce mental images of his activities—**he is beginning to be able to use symbols** and is **thinking** as we generally understand the term. Usually at around the time a child begins school he reaches what Piaget terms the stage of **intuitive thought.** This leads on to the **period of concrete operations** which often begins around the age of seven years. Here he is moving to a genuine reasoning process and logical thinking is beginning to evolve.

When at school the teacher should be aware of the stage of cognitive development reached by the children in the class and plan and organize work appropriate to that stage of development.

THE GANG AGE

At about the age of nine or ten, children find more and more pleasure in being with small groups of children of their own sex. No longer does the child look forward to going out with the family. He now wants to spend most of his time with 'the gang'. Being away from the other members of the gang, set, or crowd, makes him fretful and unhappy. The gang dominates his life. It sets the styles in clothing, play, and ideas of right and wrong.

The most important psychological trait developed in the child by participating in a gang is **sensitivity to the approval of his peers.** He strives constantly to win it. In any conflict between gang and home standards, he may side with the gang.

This loyalty makes the child highly liable to suggestions of the gang's leader. He may accept almost without question whatever plans the leader makes.

The Gang Leader. During the gang age, the ideal of the group is represented by its **leader.** The gang leaders tend to excel over their fellow gang members in most characteristics. Usually the gang leader is the oldest, largest, most skilful, and cleverest member of the group.

Wise parents do well not to antagonize the leader of the gang to which their children belong. Otherwise, they may force their child to endure an uncomfortable conflict of loyalty. Furthermore, they may expose him to teasing and even bullying on the part of the threatened leader.

Psychological Effect of the Gang. At about the time that the nine- or ten-year-old is most open to suggestions by the leader of his gang, he begins to act like a three-year-old again, doing the exact opposite of what he is told to do by adults. This spirit of contradiction, coupled with his gang loyalty, may result in petty **juvenile delinquency.** To show that he is not afraid, he will commit misdemeanours like pilfering, exhibitionism, and minor acts of arson.

Other bad activities that result from gang membership include the taking of physical risks, the use of obscenity and profanity, lying, truancy, and acts of contempt for adult values.

In addition, members of a gang often develop the attitude that only their fellows are all right, while anyone not a member of their particular gang is inferior. This **in-group snobbery** is similar to adult snobbery towards people who are different in the various possible ways.

At the same time, the gang favours the development of certain good traits. The gang member develops courage, self-control, loyalty, obedience, fidelity, and fair play—if only within the gang. When parents and teachers can find it in themselves to welcome these qualities, even if privately regretting the group upon which these qualities seem to be wasted, the child eventually finds it easier to expand his world to take the tolerant adults in.

Competition and Co-operation. Rivalry is a recognized feature of much of our school procedure. It happens at all levels and in various forms. It may be between pupil and pupil, or between two rows of pupils, or between the sexes. One class may be set to compete against another class, even school against school, as in athletic contests and debates.

The psychological effect on children of excessive competition has been widely studied. Their reactions seem to depend mostly upon their rate of learning. Slow learners experience discouragement and despair. Average pupils tend either to excessive emotional stress or to a 'just get by' attitude. Fast learners develop an over high and optimistic opinion of their abilities. *All* pupils develop indifference to the fate and welfare of other pupils. It also includes strong fear of losing 'face' or status, if one should fail to maintain his expected position in the class.

When children are put into learning situations that call for genuine co-operative effort, their behaviour tends to show the following features:

They pool their experiences of problems similar to the one before them. This is good practice in communication, as well as an exchange of actual information.

They distribute tasks according to desires, which are usually based on aptitudes. When a child's desires are not based on true aptitudes, he finds out sooner that his true interests lie elsewhere.

The effort and responsibility for an adequate solution is shared. Each child feels responsible. In addition, he has the example and the urging of his mates to strengthen his motivation to contribute.

There is common credit for success and common blame for failure. The child is guaranteed a share of the reward, or, on the other hand, has the company that misery is truly said to love.

In short, **the competitive pattern stimulates intense struggles for reward and status.** It calls into play the emotions of **aggressiveness, and fear and anger if frustrated.** It tends to emphasize **indifference at the expense of sympathy.**

In contrast, the co-operative method emphasizes sympathy, not indifference. What the proportion ought to be between these two traits is a question beyond the scope of the science of psychology. Psychologists merely point out that those children who fail to make good in harshly competitive activity are reduced to less acceptable roles, and suffer otherwise at the hands of their fellows, teachers, parents, and others in the community.

Those children whose failure to do well stems from physical disability or intellectual inferiority may seek revenge for the injustice of their handicaps. Perhaps worse, they may become convinced that they are worthless, and give up 'the pursuit of happiness'.

If emotional problems cause their failure, they are less likely to solve those problems when discouraged by the failure.

The Reason for the Gang. We are now in a better position to understand the psychological attractions that the gang holds for the school-age child. Within the gang, the child need not compete—or rather, need not fear loss of status if he fails. There are only two grades: 'success' and 'perfection' (the leader's). Any failures on his part are not considered real because they are not recorded and do not affect his membership. His fellows teach him what he needs to know in terms that he understands.

We see that the gang results from the child's need for a society in which he can be himself with the minimum possible amount of criticism and comparison. The gang gives him freedom. Its ideals seem to balance those of the school and of the adult world. The current trend in education is towards more co-operativeness. Whether the values and ideals of the typical gang will change as a result is an interesting question. Adults may be able to make an accurate prediction by asking themselves whether the quality of their own social life is related to the quality of their professional life.

The Older Child's Morality. Unlike the younger child, the child old enough to have joined a gang has a strong sense of injustice. Adult-made rules are 'unfair'.

What seems to irk the older child is not the content of the rules but their origin. A curfew rule that he would obey if it were established by referendum of the gang, he will rail against if laid down by his parents. He is a passionate democrat.

The gang member has other passionate convictions, all based on his resentment of his inferior status in the home, school, and world. He has a strong sense of honour. He believes that it is wrong to lie (to another member of his gang), to betray (another gang member), to abuse the weak (gang members), and to steal (from his gang's members).

If an adult breaks any of the rules of adult morality, the older child is convinced of the utter moral hypocrisy of the adult, and sometimes of all adults. It is vital, then, if parents want to keep the respect of their children, that they be scrupulously honest and just, especially to their gang-age children. Otherwise the children will become cynical, if only for a time, and there will be a temporary estrangement between parents and children.

The older child is *rigid* in his morality. He tends to be literal about the letter of the law, ignoring its spirit and intention. In fact, he has many of the supposed qualities of the pedant, or sophist. He quibbles, he quotes, he does anything to avoid true communication.

This dread of admitting his failure to behave in conformity to adult ideals is actually a *hopeful* sign. It shows that he has developed a conscience. Like all new possessions, his conscience is not yet under much control. It stings him terribly, continually reminding him that he is not yet adult, since his acts prove that he lacks adult motives. To silence his conscience, he pretends—to the point where he believes—that ritual *conformity* and not *intent* is the sign of virtue.

The best that parents can do to preserve a reputation for integrity is to *have* integrity. They must not only practise what they preach. They must also be convinced in their own hearts that only self-discipline earns a person the right to require discipline in others. If in addition they temper such justice with mercy, their children will be helped to realize that the strict moral code of the gang lacks an ideal found only in their wise parents. That ideal is tolerance of human weakness.

Permitted to be weak themselves, they will become more lenient towards their parents' human weakness. They will then have taken the first step towards realizing that the proper heroes to admire are not imaginary perfect men but all real men who are merely good.

SUGGESTED FURTHER READING

Boden, M. A., *Piaget*. Fontana: London, 1979.

Bruner, J., Jolly, A., and Sylva, K., *Play: Its Role in Development and Evolution*. Penguin: London, 1976.

Freud, Anna, *Normality and Pathology in Childhood: Assessments of Development*. Hogarth Press: London, 1966.

Gabriel, J., *Children Growing Up*. University of London Press: London, 1964.

Maier, H. W., *Three Theories of Child Development*. Harper and Row: London, 1966.

Millar, S., *The Psychology of Play*. Penguin: London, 1968.

Mussen, P., Conger, J., and Kagan, J., *Child Development and Personality*. 4th Edn, Harper and Row: London, 1974.

Mussen, P., *The Psychological Development of the Child*. Prentice-Hall: London, 1973.

Oates, J. (Ed.), *Early Cognitive Development*. Croom Helm: London, 1979.

Piaget, J., *The Origin of Intelligence in the Child*. Routledge and Kegan Paul: London, 1953.

Piaget, J., *The Child's Construction of Reality*. Routledge and Kegan Paul: London, 1955.

Piaget, J., *The Child's Conception of Movement and Speed*. Routledge and Kegan Paul: London, 1970.

Winnicott, D. W., *The Child, the Family and the Outside World*. Penguin: London, 1964.

Wright, D., *The Psychology of Moral Behaviour*. Penguin: London, 1971.

11

THE PSYCHOLOGY OF ADOLESCENCE

Adolescence is the period of transition from childhood to adulthood. It is generally thought to begin with the onset of puberty but an individual can be adolescent without being pubescent and vice versa.

A century ago, only the sons of rich families had the leisure to enjoy a decade of adolescence. Most young people finished their schooling at the age of twelve or thirteen, went right to work, married at any age after sixteen, and were self-supporting by eighteen.

In our time, however, education has been extended and marriage postponed beyond the age of sexual maturity. A long period of adolescence has become a normal experience for the youth of all social classes.

How Adolescence is Studied. Psychologists gather information from and about adolescents in many ways:

Direct Obervation of individuals and groups.

Genetic Case Studies of one person over a long period of time.

Attitude Scales, on which adolescents rate their reactions to listed items or phrases.

Non-directive Interviews in which the adolescent is free to discuss what he pleases.

Standardized Interviews, which use a fixed set of questions.

Projective Techniques that interpret the imaginative responses of adolescents to test situations.

Adult Recollections, which seem more likely to be true accounts of adolescence than do the reports of adolescents, but which are subject to forgetting and emotional colouring.

Adolescent Diaries, always a good source of information about activities and feelings, and also usually written by the more intelligent adolescents.

Questionnaires, signed or unsigned by the adolescent.

Anecdotes told about particular adolescents by their peers and superiors.

Not all of these methods are suitable for every study, and their reliability and validity vary from one method to the next. However, by putting together the results obtained with all of them, a reasonably clear picture of adolescent development can be obtained.

Adolescent Phases. In their volume *Youth: The Years from Ten to Sixteen*, Dr. ARNOLD GESELL and his collaborators reported the results of their search for the laws of adolescent development. A few quotations will show the kind of phases they have found American adolescents to go through. The authors point out that the pattern of growth that emerges is not invariable, and must often be qualified with the words: 'some', 'a majority', 'a few'.

Ten not only likes to listen to stories but likes to tell his own about something he has seen or heard or read about. He can talk on and on and run what he is talking about 'into the ground'. Talking can indeed be one of his favourite activities.

A horse, a dog, and a farm—these are still the paramount wishes of many **Eleven**-year-olds, especially eleven-year-old girls. The main difference from Ten is that Eleven wants a stable *full* of horses.

Twelve adores double meanings . . . When a teacher decides against letting a boy and girl sit next to each other and says she is going to separate them, some Twelve is sure to say: 'I didn't know they were married.'

Perhaps it is because **Thirteen** is so touchy that he is constantly annoyed by his younger siblings, especially those in the six- to eleven-year range. He himself may be able to explain it by saying, 'I'm going through a stage when everything bothers me.' But all too often, 'It's hard to explain.'

When **Fourteen**-year-old girls cannot meet, the telephone brings them together. This is the peak age for interminable phone communications, gay, serious, and hushed. The conversations are punctuated with giggles, gossip, and all sorts of apparent trivia, which, however, are charged with meaning for the young persons on the line. How much time is spent at the phone? 'As much as mother can stand.'

Some **Fifteen**-year-olds can be very faddish about their clothes. They often follow the group blindly; shifts in style may be made every week or two.

Sixteen's happiness is very real but not exuberant. He doesn't go to extremes. 'Perfectly content' describes the pervasive quality of his happiness. He has his sad moments but these are infrequent. As one Sixteen asks, 'Why be sad?'

PUBERTY

The essence of puberty is the maturation of the sex glands. In girls, this is signified by the first menstrual period. In boys, the maturation must be deduced from the secondary sex characteristics, such as the change of voice and the growth of pubic hair. Physical growth is accelerated among boys by the onset of puberty. However, the advent of menstruation marks the end of rapid growth for girls.

The age at which young people mature sexually varies between males and females and within each sex. For girls, it ranges from nine to eighteen; for boys, from eleven to eighteen. Table IV shows what percentage of all boys and girls have become sexually mature at each age in this range.

Table IV. Ages of sexual maturation

Age	Per cent Mature	
	Boys	Girls
8	0	0
9	0	1
10	0	2
11	2	10
12	5	38
13	14	72
14	48	82
15	78	94
16	93	97
17	98	99
18	100	100

It is apparent from Table IV that girls generally mature two years earlier than boys, and that the boys do not draw even with them until the end of adolescence.

Sexual maturity is very important to adolescents. Their reactions to it vary. Some are embarrassed, or so secretive that they try to pretend that no change has taken place. Others anticipate and meet each change with dread. Still others are quite proud of each new development. In almost every case, the adolescent cannot ignore his changing body but is fascinated by its growth.

Sexual Maturity in Boys. The onset of puberty can be very upsetting to a boy. His sexual organs grow rapidly and seem independent of his will in reacting to stimulation and suggestion. At night, he may be distressed by erotic dreams, and embarrassed or even frightened by nocturnal emissions. The researches of Dr. Alfred C. Kinsey and his group of scientists have shown that the height of male sexual vitality is reached in the teens.

To relieve his sexual tension, the adolescent boy will often masturbate. Since it is widespread, it can be regarded as a normal development, to be expected during adolescence if not earlier.

As puberty comes on, a boy watches changes in himself quite anxiously. The attainment of masculinity has great prestige value among boys. Pubic and facial hair, potency, and change of voice are taken as signs of manhood. Not all sex characteristics appear in boys at the same time, though thirteen seems to be the age at which they all most commonly appear, with a distribution range for each characteristic from ten to sixteen years. Table V shows the percentage of each age group that has begun to experience the characteristics listed below.

Table V. Percentage of each age group first experiencing certain sexual characteristics

Age	Ejaculation	Nocturnal Emission	Pubic Hair	Voice Change
10	1·8	0·3	0·3	0·3
11	6·9	3·7	8·4	5·6
12	14·1	5·3	27·1	20·5
13	33·6	17·4	36·1	40·0
14	30·9	12·9	23·8	26·0
15	7·8	13·9	3·3	5·5
16	4·9	16·0	1·0	2·0

As a boy becomes sexually mature his attitudes and interests change. The relationship between emotional reactions and physical development can actually be measured. The more male sex hormones a boy passes in his urine, the higher will his maturity be ranked on a scale for measuring emotional age in terms of attitudes and interests.

Sexual Maturity in Girls. The age at which menstruation begins is related to height, weight, and skeletal age. That is, girls who are taller, heavier, and more advanced in skeletal development mature earliest.

Whether or not a girl anticipates her first menstrual discharge, she may be considerably alarmed by its arrival, since a haemorrhage that cannot be stopped is always terrifying. The association of unpleasantness with bleeding in general may prevent a girl from ever disassociating this unfavourable emotional tone from menstruation. The relatively few girls with some abnormal physical condition may actually experience pain. For the majority, pain is slight or non-existent, although there may be some digestive disturbance and a general feeling of lassitude.

Until the menstrual periods are established, their recurrence taken for granted, and any initial discomfort forgotten, some girls are embarrassed by menstruation. To those girls who react with more than embarrassment, menstrual bleeding may be found to have an unconscious symbolic meaning. It may, for instance, seem to confirm the never-quite-forgotten belief of many children that girls are really boys who have lost their penises by accident or through punishment. An adolescent girl who as a child bitterly resented the loss of her imagined penis may be very disturbed emotionally when the onset of her menses reminds her unconscious mind of the supposed amputation. She may

try in a variety of ways to deny her femininity, which she associates
with inferiority.

The main secondary sex characteristics for adolescent girls are the
widening of the hips, the development of the breasts, the growth of
pubic hair, hair in the armpits, a light down on the forearms and
upper lip, and a partial lowering of the voice. Though the widening of
the hips is likely to inspire attempts to diet, on the mistaken assumption that fat and not bone is the cause, only the breasts give rise to
much real embarrassment, since, like the boy's sex organs, a girl's
breasts are external, can move, and can show through clothing.

ADOLESCENT PROBLEMS

Except in rare cases of severe biological abnormality, boys and girls
achieve sexual maturity early in adolescence, and physical maturity by
the end of it. Each of these invariable processes of maturation is
independent of personal control; therefore **the real problems of the
adolescent lie in the area of social, emotional, moral, and economic
maturity.** Some maturing in these fields is inevitable, too, since the sex
hormones play a part in determining the maturity of adolescent interests and attitudes. To a large extent, however, it is up to the adolescent
himself, his family, his friends, his school, and his society to determine
whether or not he is to become fully adult.

The remainder of this chapter will describe adolescent progress in
satisfying the seven criteria of adulthood listed below:

Independence of Family. The adolescent should gradually emanci-
pate himself from his attachment to and dependence upon his parents'
home.

Emotional Maturity. The adolescent should emerge from childish
into adult forms of emotional expression. He should learn not to flee
from reality. He should substitute rational for emotional reactions—
at least in situations that recur.

Social Maturity. The adolescent should get along with and work
well with others. He ought to develop self-reliance in matters of taste.
He ought to develop tolerance of human differences.

Economic Independence. The adolescent should select work for
which he is fitted. Then he should if possible train for it.

Intellectual Adulthood. The adolescent ought to learn to require evidence for statements. He should desire explanations.

Use of Leisure. The adolescent ought to develop interests that re-
create but do not exhaust his energies. He should learn to read well,
and to explore the possibilities of culture for useful leisure.

Philosophy of Life. The adolescent must begin to develop an attitude
towards experience that will give his life meaning. He should develop
a set of ideals to guide him towards his goals.

During the period when the adolescent is becoming aware of and beginning to react to these demands, he is undergoing physical changes that weaken his sense of continuous identity. Adolescence can often be a time of 'storm and stress'.

Adolescent Masturbation. Questionnaires on the prevalence of masturbation among teenage boys and girls show that it is quite common. Studies by Dr. Alfred C. Kinsey and other scientists indicate that from 70 to 90 per cent of males admit to having masturbated during adolescence. In females the reported percentage is lower, ranging in various studies from 30 to 70 per cent.

Organically, there is no difference between masturbation and sexual intercourse. The glands and organs do not differentiate between different sources of the stimuli that produce orgasm. Masturbation therefore has no unique physical effects on the mind or body. It does not fatigue a person any more than an equivalent act of intercourse. It neither causes nor cures pimples. The adolescent masturbator will not lose his virility, become a pervert, or lose his intellect because of this practice. These are myths which have the effect of terrifying young people. They can serve no useful purpose.

Becoming Independent of the Family. No matter how old people are they are still emotionally children as long as they continue to run only to their parents for assistance and understanding. To be truly adult, one must be free of the parental rule. That does not mean that grown-ups who are callous and indifferent to their parents are mature. Such people are actually still adolescent, since they are behaving in a way which is normal during adolescence but a sign of immaturity after it. The true adult loves his parents, considers their desires, yet makes his own decisions, and lives his own life.

For an adolescent to become free of his childhood's attachment to parental authority, parents must learn to give up the control that they have been maintaining for a dozen or so years. Attempts to continue it will produce either childish or rebellious adults.

There are three main areas in which parents can help their adolescent children to progress towards mature independence:

They can refrain from trying to pick his friends for him.

As far as possible, they can let him get out of difficulties by himself.

Finally, they must let him choose his own mate. When a permanent attachment is made, the time for parental control has passed.

Attaining Emotional Maturity. Some people never grow up. Those who have grown up are people who do not run away from reality, who do not 'take things personally', and who do not become angry in trivial social situations. They have outgrown childish expressions of anger and fear.

Each of these emotions has different causes at different ages. In early childhood, anger results more often from conflicts over daily routine and possessions. The causes of adolescent anger are mostly social. An adolescent gets angry in situations that make him feel annoyed, offended, ridiculous, or embarrassed. A mature adult seems to become angry only when his sense of abstract justice is offended.

Childhood fears are usually of material things, like snakes, dogs, the dark, storms, high places, and strange noises. Some of these fears may persist into adolescence and even into adulthood. Usually, however, they are replaced by new subjects. Thus, early in adolescence, both sexes worry most about family and school conditions, then about personal adequacy, economic problems, and health problems. In middle adolescence, the ten most frequently mentioned subjects of anxiety are school life, home life, boy and girl relationships, recreation, friends, vocational choice, religion, health, clothes, and money. In late adolescence, the four most common worries are not being successful, hurting other people's feelings, the impression made on others, and not working hard enough—all questions of personal inadequacy. Then follow worries about religion, physical defects, lateness, familial obligations, friends, and vocational success.

Changes in the expression of emotions have been recorded. **Timidity,** for instance, increases during pre- and early adolescence, then declines after thirteen or fourteen. **Fighting** declines rapidly from its peak at seven and eight. However, **impertinence** and **sulkiness** increase during adolescence. Among adults, the verbal expression of emotion almost completely replaces the other forms of expression.

Several psychologists have worked out tests for measuring emotional maturity and expressing it in terms of **emotional age.** Dividing emotional age by chronological age gives an **emotional quotient.** The measurement of emotional maturity gives a clue to the behaviour of **juvenile delinquents.** They are almost always found to have low emotional quotients, coupled with intelligence quotients that are more likely to be low than to be high.

Social Maturity. The adolescent boy and girl are acutely aware of social relationships and pressures. This sensitivity makes them want to conform to the taste of the group. They react faster to prestige within their own group than they do to most forms of adult approval. They are intensely loyal to the other members of their own group and highly critical of all outsiders.

This group is not the **gang** of late childhood—that social unit made up of members of one sex, whose object is to seek excitement in adventure. The adolescent's group is his 'crowd' or 'set', made up usually of couples, whose unconscious object is the establishment of normal social relationships between the two sexes. The positive values gained from membership in this small select group include experience in getting along with other people, experience in social skills, practice in evaluating other people, the feeling of loyalty, and experience in limited and controlled love-making. The only negative result seems to be the growth of antagonism towards other sets. On the whole, the set seems to be a socially valuable unit of society. It may do more to accomplish normal social development than parents and teachers together.

Table VI describes the normal course of social development from the onset of puberty through the years of adolescence.

Table VI. Social growth

Growth From	Towards
Variety and instability of interests.	Fewer and deeper interests.
Talkative, noisy, daring behaviour with a great amount of any kind of activity.	More dignified, controlled masculine and feminine adult behaviour.
Seeking peer status with high respect for peer standards.	Reflecting of adult culture patterns.
Desire for identification with the crowd of boys and girls.	Identification with small select group.
Making family status an unimportant factor in the choice of associates.	Making it an important factor in choosing associates.
Informal social activities, such as parties.	Social activities of a more formal nature, such as dances.
Rare dating.	Frequent dates and going steady.
Emphasis on building relationships with boys and girls.	Increasing concern with preparation for own family life.
Temporary friendships.	Lasting friendships.
Many friendships.	Fewer but deeper friendships.
Willingness to accept activities that provide chances for social relationships.	Desire for activities in line with talent development, vocation, academic interest, or hobby.
Little insight into behaviour.	Increasing insight.
Accepting the provision of reasonable adult rules.	Making own rules with definite purpose in view.
Ambivalence towards adults.	Seeking equality with adults.

Economic Independence. Choosing an occupation, training for it, finding a job, and adapting to the conditions of employment are problems of middle and late adolescence. Only people who have solved them are economically adult. Work is the adult's chief business in life. Vocationally childish people either hate all work or their particular work, change jobs constantly, have no interest in what they are doing, and are never satisfied with their salary, hours, or working conditions.

The adolescent frequently considers permanent employment an

imposition. He quits any job that bores him, which any job available to him is likely to do. An adolescent may become vocationally maladjusted for any one or more of a number of reasons:

Attempting to enter a line of work for which he does not have the necessary vitality or endurance.

Trying to enter occupations unsuitable to his type of personality.

Entering work either much below or much above his mental level.

Entering a vocation which requires some special talent which he lacks and cannot or will not acquire.

Entering an occupation in which he will need some academic skill he lacks or will not get.

Idealizing some vocation in such a way that he is blind to its true nature.

Doing work that emphasizes some characteristic in him that needs elimination.

Choosing a vocation for which there is little or no demand while one is young.

Choosing lines of work for which there is no present demand.

Entering training he will not be able to afford finishing.

If a girl, persuading herself that she wants a career when she really wants to be a housewife.

Fulfilling the thwarted ambitions of his parents.

Having no vocational objective at all.

The kind of help required to avoid this baker's dozen of reasons for vocational maladjustment can best be obtained from trained vocational guidance counsellors. Such counsellors will probably administer aptitude tests of the kind described in Chapter 7.

Intellectual Adulthood. During the years of adolescence, boys are most interested in travel, sports, cinema, television, and radio. Pets, collections, the family, reading, and school come next, followed by painting, writing, music, social relationships, and extra-curricular activities. Church and Sunday School come last.

Except that home and social activities have somewhat more fascination for girls, and sports somewhat less, the same general order holds true for girls.

Many of these adolescent interests become the bases for lifelong interests. Some develop into occupations. Otherwise, the typically adolescent activities not only fail to interest but actually come to bore the intellectual adult.

At the same time that the adolescent's interests are changing, his mental capacities are growing. With increased intellectual maturity in the middle teens, he is more likely to develop intellectual independence. He will tend to require evidence for claims, and to demand explanations.

Intellectual Development. In the previous chapter we traced Piaget's views of intellectual development as far as the period of concrete operational thought. Some adolescents do not progress beyond this period but the majority move on to the final phase of cognitive development during the early years of adolescence. This final stage has been termed by Piaget the phase of **formal operations.** With this stage comes a new capacity for **abstraction** and **generalization.** A main difference between this and the previous stage has been pointed out by **Professor Peel,** who stated that the child at the stage of concrete operational thought **describes** a situation whereas the adolescent with formal operations **explains** it.

A Mature Philosophy of Life. The modern adolescent wants to feel secure and to enjoy emotional satisfaction. Some find these satisfactions in traditional religion. Others are blocked from accepting religion by its apparent incompatibility with science, which adolescents hold in high esteem.

There are many reasons why science fascinates adolescents. To some, scientific investigation into the dark secrets of Nature is an acceptable expression of their long-thwarted sexual and anatomical curiosity. To those who are suspicious or even cynical of the motives of the adult world, science seems all that is trustworthy. Others 'desert' to its authority merely to spite parental and religious authority. A few, of course, have the intellectual aptitudes of the true scientist.

Some adolescents adopt radical social and political positions. Reforming the world seems so much easier than reforming oneself. Themselves not yet accepted as equals by their parents, adolescents easily sympathize and even identify with the victims of intolerance. The adult regards prejudice as a fact which one cannot ignore, even if one cannot accept. However true in some cases, it would be a grievous error to regard zealous egalitarianism as a psychological aberration. In fact, the more moderate attitudes of the adult may be, in this instance at least, morally inferior to the enthusiasms of the adolescent.

Some adolescents assert their individuality by adopting unpopular and reactionary positions. They hope to claim adulthood by being more conservative than even conservative adults. Another motive enters their adolescent desire to keep the world just as it has been or even to go back to the supposed Utopia of yesterday. This unconscious motive is the desire to remain a child.

More modest adolescents face the complex universe with an attitude of perplexity. They think that there is one simple answer to the question, what does it all mean? Their search for a unified philosophy may lead them to accept the same rigid systems that the revolutionaries adopt. They are more likely to leave it for another, perhaps religious, system—equally rigid.

The emotionally mature adult can face up to the complexity and evil of the world. He can bear knowing that he is ignorant. He is content to achieve that which is within reach. What is possible contents him, even when it falls short of the apparent ideal. No longer so sure of all the answers, or even whether there are answers, he is too busy working to achieve his reasonable goals to torment himself with over-whelming questions. We must be grateful, however, that some people cannot escape asking such questions, and seeking answers, for the results of those enterprises have sometimes been great literature, philosophy, theology—to our immeasurable profit.

SUGGESTED FURTHER READING

Conger, C., *Adolescence*. Harper and Row: London, 1979.
Conger, J. J., *Adolescence and Youth*. Harper and Row: London, 1973.
Rutter, M., *Helping Troubled Children*. Penguin: London, 1975.

12

EMOTIONS AND PERSONALITY DEVELOPMENT

Emotion has been variously defined as **'a state of agitation'; 'disturbance of equilibrium'; 'an intense, random, and disorganized response to a stimulus'.**

Although the state of calmness is supposedly the 'normal' condition, emotional states in modern living seem to be more characteristic of individuals than any absence of emotion. In the modern tempo of life, emotions demand greater understanding because of their pervasive effects on behaviour, personality, and health.

Emotional Feelings. Whenever we experience an emotion, the most striking aspect is the **feeling** it produces. An experience of fear, anger, gloom, or glee yields a vivid, immediate sensation.

The number of such different emotional feelings seem to be countless. The well-known psychologist, Professor G. W. ALLPORT, found roughly two thousand words in Webster's unabridged dictionary that named emotional states of feeling, each of them having its own particular quality. Yet when asked to describe an emotional feeling, we often find it difficult to do more than give the feeling a name.

Other Aspects of Emotion. There are other aspects of emotion to investigate besides subjective feelings. To the objective observer, the most notable aspects of emotion are the changes they cause in immediate behaviour—overt acts like fighting, fleeing, sulking, laughing, crying, and their verbal equivalents. A person who manages to control such gross behaviour may still betray his feelings by facial expressions. Even if he maintains a 'poker face' like a veteran gambler or diplomat, he nonetheless experiences certain bodily sensations, such as a lump in the throat, buzzing in the ears, a dry mouth, or cold sweat. These sensations express only some of the many internal changes that occur in response to stimuli which provoke an emotional state.

THEORIES OF EMOTION

To understand fully the various aspects of emotion, it is necessary to know something of their relationship to one another and to the stimuli which produce them. The true significance of the many features of emotional arousal depends upon the part they play in the overall emotional pattern.

The best way to present what modern psychology knows about

emotion is to show how that knowledge was derived by putting old armchair theories of emotion to experimental test.

William James's Instinct Theory of Emotion. In the early days of psychology (in the 1880s) William James first put forth what was to become a controversial theory about the relationship between emotional stimuli and responses. James claimed that emotional responses were **instinctive.** According to James, the feeling, sensations, and behaviour appropriate to the emotions were inborn reactions to the particular stimuli. He compiled long lists of the stimuli that had been found to arouse the emotions. Fear, for instance, was supposedly an *inborn* reaction to certain noises, strange men, strange animals, solitude, darkness, and high places.

Are Emotions Inborn or Learned? JOHN B. WATSON, the founder of the **Behavourist School of Psychology,** put James's list of fear-provoking stimuli to experimental test. Babies four to six months old were shown a black cat, a pigeon, a rabbit, a rat, and a large dog—all strange animals. The infants displayed a total lack of emotional reactions. They also revealed no fear of fire, high places, or of darkness.

These children were not abnormal unemotional. They showed definite fearful reactions to other stimuli, namely, loud sounds, pain, and loss of support. To the stimuli on James' list, however, they were emotionally neutral. Through extensive experiments of this type with children of varying ages, it was shown that the fear responses reported by William James were acquired and *not* instinctive.

Inborn Emotional Responses. The stimuli that Watson found always caused a fearful reaction were loud sounds, pain, and loss of support. The behaviour reactions to these stimuli were of various kinds including reflex responses, a startle pattern and various facial grimaces and body movements.

Reflex Responses. A reflex act in an infant is an **automatic, unlearned, muscular response to a stimulus.** Reflexes usually consist of some movement that tends to protect the body against injury. In the evolutionary struggle for existence, animals that were equipped with the best reflexes survived.

Human beings have inherited many reflexes from the lower forms of animal life, some of which seem to serve no practical purpose. Pinch a toe and the foot will withdraw. Press the toe, however, and the foot will push. One reflex removes the foot from harm, the other thrusts it towards balance. Prehistoric men who lacked either or both of these reflexes were at a disadvantage in the struggle for survival.

The Crying Reflex. Only a limited number of stimuli provoke reflexes and only a few of these are involved in emotion. The best known is the **reflex of crying.** It is first provoked by pain, usually the pain of a slap on the buttocks after birth. Crying is useful not only to start the vital breathing process, but also as a signal of distress. The newborn infant can do absolutely nothing for himself. Crying alerts the mother, and is therefore a useful response in a helpless infant.

Unfortunately, the success of crying as a signal causes the infant to retain it as a response to difficult situations. In other words, a child can **learn** to remain emotional through the reinforcing effect of parental protection. Even when at later stages of development the individual becomes better able to overcome the source of his frustrations by himself, he may retain the infantile manner of appealing for help by crying.

Obviously, parents should give a child no more help than is really needed. The amount and nature of this help will be determined by the degree to which the child's various abilities have matured.

The Startle Response. Not all stimuli provoke specific reflexes. Some arouse **patterns** of behaviour, involving several muscles, rather than one, as in a reflex.

The most important inborn emotional pattern of behaviour is called the **startle response.** Immediately after a sensory stimulation that is intense or sudden—such as a flash of light, or a gunshot—one reacts with a response that involves muscles of the face and almost the entire body. The *facial* part of the pattern begins with a blinking of the eyes, then a stretching of the mouth and a jerking forward of the head. Meanwhile, the *bodily* responses occur. The shoulders hunch forward, the elbows bend, the fingers flex, the knees bend, and the abdomen contracts.

This 'startle' pattern is found in some lower animals, monkeys, and apes, and in all human beings, infant or adult. It is never completely overcome by training. Even policemen with many years of experience on pistol ranges cannot inhibit the response entirely. It is a kind of protective shrinking of the entire body.

Are Facial Expressions Inborn? Some facial expressions do seem to be learned during infancy. Shaking the head from side to side, by which we express our disagreement or unwillingness, dates back to the time when it was the only possible way to avoid unwanted foods. Crying, as we have seen, is *unlearned*, though it may be modified by learning into saying 'Ouch!' when hurt or 'Mama!' when frightened.

CHARLES DARWIN, who was responsible for our 'laws of evolution', suggested that the other unlearned facial expressions were inherited from ancestors whose survival had been helped by having these responses in their repertoire of abilities. He claimed that **snarling** dates back to a prehuman stage of animal development. Those animals that bared their teeth to prepare for a fight often scared their enemies away. This made the fight unnecessary, and increased the chances that these animals would survive to parenthood. The response continued to be transmitted through the generations—even to us, who now attack less with our teeth than with our tongues.

Darwin tried to show that other facial expressions were also acts that had once been useful. The **set lips** of determination, according to him, are residues of the stopped windpipe and rigid chest that help great muscular effort. The **wrinkling of the nose** in disgust supposedly was once a defensive movement that sealed the nostrils against bad smells.

Even laughing can be explained this way, as an act that once helped to release the extra oxygen inhaled during the emotional tension that preceded the laughter. When situations that threatened to be unpleasant turned out safely or even pleasantly, those of our ancestors who could quickly return their inner conditions to normal by laughing were a bit more likely to survive than those who remained unnecessarily keyed up.

Facial Expression in Emotion. It has just been shown that there is at least a *tendency* for certain muscles or muscle groups to be involved in one emotion that are not involved in another. Crying, smiling, snarling, wrinkling the nose, shaking the head from side to side, compressing the lips—all of these emotional responses can reveal the presence of *particular* feelings in a person. There is obviously *some* truth to the popular belief that every emotion has its own particular facial expression.

However, facial expressions are not altogether dependable as indicators of emotion. One reason is that they can be too easily **suppressed or exaggerated** with or without a real stimulus. Another reason is that adult facial expressions are largely modified by learning. Thus, a person of one culture may express a particular emotion with a grimace that has a different meaning in another culture. Still another reason for putting little reliance on facial expressions as clues to emotion is the close resemblance of certain expressions, particularly in violent emotions. Great joy is hard to tell from great grief by facial expressions alone. In fact we speak of one who 'laughs so hard the tears flow'.

Judging Emotion by Behaviour. Just as facial expressions are not altogether reliable as indicators of emotion, behavioural responses are also difficult to take at face value, even though the most important results of emotions are the acts they cause.

Any classification of external responses is somewhat arbitrary. We cannot always be sure that similar acts have the same meaning. However, psychologists have found it helpful to consider emotional behaviour in four categories, according to the **direction of activity.** In analysing the grossly maladjusted individual, psychiatrists are particularly interested in knowing whether a person directs his emotional energies **against, towards, away from** people, or **inward** against himself. The feelings usually associated with these four responses are rage, love, fear, and depression. In rage, one moves against the source of one's frustration. In fear, one moves away from it. In love, one moves towards the source of pleasure. In depression, one stops making overt responses and turns the emotion inward against oneself.

John B. Watson reported finding three of these four emotional responses in infant behaviour; namely, fear, rage, and love. We have already seen that Watson's infant subjects seemed to withdraw from pain, loud noises, and loss of support. He found two other 'stimuli' to which the infants invariably made emotional responses. Restraining them so that they could not move made the infants tense and seem to show anger. Petting them made them stop crying, smile, coo, and extend their arms.

Watson gave the names of **fear, rage,** and **love** to the three emotional reactions he found in the infants that he observed under test conditions. He claimed that these three emotions were basic, the building-blocks from which the many complex adult emotions were ultimately constructed.

Later critics said that Watson committed an experimental error in his original study. According to them, the muscular movements of the 'angry' children were different from the muscular movements of the 'fearful' children precisely because the 'angry' children were *restrained* from making the same responses made by the falling 'fearful' children.

To show that knowing the stimulus biases the judgement of the response, the psychologist Mandel Sherman tested the ability of student nurses, doctors, and psychologists to name the emotions shown by infants subjected to various annoyances. The observers showed little agreement or accuracy. The infants' responses to hunger, restraint, pain, and falling were all called 'anger' at one time or another. Only four out of thirty-one judges called an infant's reaction to falling 'fear' when the act of falling was concealed, but twenty-seven out of the thirty-one called it 'fear' when they saw the baby dropped. It is obviously difficult to distinguish infantile rage from infantile fear, on the basis of *overt* responses.

As a result, fear and rage came to be thought of as different forms of one emotion, best called **'excitement'.** Subsequent research has given further evidence that fear and rage are physiologically equivalent. The marked internal changes that occur in a person who has been frightened are indistinguishable from those that occur in a person who has been angered.

Internal Changes in Emotion. During strong emotion, many changes occur in the organs of the body. These changes are interesting and help to explain many of the varied reactions that the emotionally aroused person displays.

The pupil of the **eye** dilates. The eyelid lifts unusually wide, and the eyeball protrudes.

The speed and strength of **heartbeat** increases.

Blood pressure increases. The volume of blood in the extremities also goes up, as the large arteries of the trunk contract, driving blood outward towards the skin. The resulting flush is one of the surest signs of emotion.

The **hair** tends to stand on end, causing 'goose flesh'.

The rate and depth of **breathing** changes, though not in any predictable pattern. Sometimes breathing speeds up, sometimes it slows down. It may also become deeper or shallower, or more irregular in rhythm.

There is, nevertheless, one constant pattern that can be found in the disturbed breathing. This is the relationship of the time taken to inhale to the time taken to exhale. This ratio of inspiration to expiration, or **I/E ratio,** *increases* in emotional states. That is, inhalation is slower than normal and exhalation is quicker.

Lung bronchioles dilate, so that a person can consume more oxygen than normally. The gain may go as high as 25 per cent.

The secretions of **duct glands** are affected. The liver pours out more sugar for the muscles.

The **sweat glands** of the skin secrete excessive amounts of perspiration—the well-known 'cold sweat'. The additional acid changes the **galvanic** or electrical response of the skin, by which the rate of excess secretion is measured.

Unlike the sweat glands, the **salivary** glands are inhibited by emotion. The stoppage of saliva produces the so-called 'dry mouth' feeling.

Secretion of **gastric fluids** is also inhibited by emotion. This is only part of the effect of emotion on the digestive system. Emotion also stops the digestive movements of the stomach and intestines, by withdrawing blood from the viscera.

One of the ductless glands (which we shall discuss more fully when the time comes to examine **temperament**) also reacts to emotional experiences. The adrenals secrete the hormone **adrenalin** into the blood. This chemical substance has several effects, as can be shown by artificially raising the adrenalin level of the blood by injection. Adrenalin makes the heart beat faster, makes the liver release sugar into the blood for muscular energy, and increases the ability of the blood to clot quickly. In fact, it reinforces almost all of the other effects.

The 'Lie Detector'. Excepting respiration, none of these bodily functions which occur in the grip of a strong emotional state can be controlled by the will, unless the claims made for yogis are true. Unfortunately, scientists have not tested the supposed ability of yogis to control circulation and digestion. In any event, it is safe to say that the vast majority of people cannot control their inner bodily functions. Therefore the body changes are the most reliable sign of an emotional state.

To measure these bodily changes accurately, Prof. John A. Larsen devised a machine sensitive enough to detect the slightest variation in blood pressure, pulse rate, breathing rate, and skin electricity. Prof. Leonard Keeler, who improved the machine, called it a **'polygraph',** because it plotted a graph of each of these varying measurements.

The ability of the polygraph to detect even mild degrees of emotion has made it famous as a 'lie detector'. Of course, it does not actually detect lies. It detects the bodily changes that usually accompany the telling of lies. We say 'usually' because most people who tell lies do so out of fear. We cannot say 'always' because a few people, the **psychopathic personalities** whom we shall study in Chapter 17, may not feel guilty about either lying or law-breaking.

Identity of Fear and Rage. The results of the polygraph show that fear and rage cannot be distinguished by involuntary responses. In both emotions, the heart beats stronger and faster, adrenalin is secreted into the blood, the skin flushes, digestion stops, the skin sweats, the mouth goes dry, and the blood pressure rises in the limbs and head. In effect, the pattern of bodily changes that is typical of fear is also typical of rage.

Further evidence of their identity may be found in the occasionally undecided behaviour of startled adults. Excited by the threatening stimulus, they waver between attack and flight, with only muscular changes as they shift from one attitude to the other.

CANNON'S 'EMERGENCY' THEORY

The renowed Harvard University physiologist Walter B. Cannon pointed out that these internal changes are useful to people who must either fight or flee.

The stopping of digestion, the increase in pulse rate, and the expanding of the blood vessels shown by flushing, all provide more blood for the muscles of the arms and legs. As noted previously the adrenalin secreted at such times not only accelerates heart action and decreases muscular fatigue, but also promotes the clotting of the blood. These are beneficial changes in a man faced with an emergency in which he must exert himself and in which he may be wounded.

The first thing that one notices in the behaviour of an emotionally aroused person is the exaggeration of his energy. He does not speak, he shouts; he does not close the door, he slams it shut; he does not sit or stand still, he jumps up, he gesticulates, or he strides about.

In some situations, this extra energy can be useful. A man whose house is on fire will find himself able to carry burdens which in normal times he is hardly able to budge. Emotion not only *raises strength* to its maximum, but also *prolongs the time* a person is able to continue his efforts. A man will run for his life not only faster but longer than he will for a less important cause.

A third effect of emotional arousal is the temporary anaesthesia it bestows upon the aroused person. Enthusiastic football players, for instance, can remain oblivious to injuries as serious as broken bones until their wounded bodies collapse. More clearly beneficial is the fact that people who are seriously wounded in accidents, and in battle, are often able to help themselves and others in such emergencies. Only when nothing more is to be done do they finally collapse from the effects of their injuries.

Cannon's theory is that since emotional excitement prepares a man for coping with emergencies, those primitive men who made the response tended to survive in the evolutionary struggle for existence.

THE ANATOMY OF EMOTION

Anatomical research has confirmed the idea that there is one basic emotion, **'excitement', opposed to the state of calm.** It has been found that the brain controls the inner organs through one or the other of two sets of nerves that are antagonistic to each other. One set, the **sympathetic** nerves, runs the body on an emergency basis; the other set, the **parasympathetic** nerves, keeps it in normal running order.

All of the ordinary vital functions are carried out by the parasympathetic nerves. They protect the eye from bright light by contracting the pupil. They focus the lens of the eye for near vision. Digestion of food, its passage along the alimentary canal, and the final elimination of waste products are all controlled by parasympathetic nerves. This system also suffuses the genitals with a richer supply of blood during sexual excitement.

In certain unusual conditions, however, the brain sends motor impulses to the body along a different set of autonomic nerves called the **sympathetic.**

The sympathetic nerves are known to take over under four conditions:

When life is threatened by extreme **cold;**
during continuous **pain;**
during **violent exercise or effort;** and
during **fear** and **rage;** that is, whenever the person *expects* to undergo any of the previous three stimuli.

In Cannon's view, therefore, the parasympathetic set of nerves is the 'drudge' that carries on the everyday work of life and meets the minor emergencies. The sympathetic system is the standby 'troubleshooter' that takes charge in a real emergency.

Antagonism of the Nerves. Most of the organs of the chest and abdomen receive nerves from both systems. Where this happens, the action of the two systems is always antagonistic. Depending upon what that organ does in the body, the parasympathetic nerve either excites or inhibits its activity—but if the parasympathetic nerve excites the organ, the sympathetic inhibits it, and vice versa. Sympathetic and parasympathetic act like brake and accelerator, though which is which depends upon an organ's function.

This antagonism within the involuntary nerves is psychologically important. It means that the emotional responses that depend upon one set of nerves cannot coexist with the emotional responses that depend upon the other set. The sexual organs, which are swollen with blood by the parasympathetic nerves, are deprived of their supply of blood by the antagonistic sympathetic nerves, with the result that they become flabby. Neither affection nor desire can be aroused during fear or anger.

Conversely, the fear of a frightened child can be dispelled by caressing and stroking, as the pleasant sensations induce the brain to switch back to the parasympathetic from the sympathetic nerves. To quote the New Testament, 'Perfect love casteth out fear'.

THE JAMES–LANGE THEORY OF EMOTIONS

Having investigated the various aspects of emotional responses to stimuli, we are ready now to examine their interrelationships. The question was the subject of another of William James's influential theories.

James's second theory was concerned with the *order* of occurrence of the conditions related to the emotional state. The common-sense view is that in a state of emotion the conscious feelings are the first reactions one has to stimuli, that the visceral changes follow next, and that the overt responses are last. You see a lion, you 'feel' afraid, your blood pressure rises, and you begin to run.

In 1884, William James argued that the overt responses and bodily changes *preceded* the conscious feelings. The feelings of fear, rage, etc., were supposed to be merely the **awareness of the inner and outer changes,** which supposedly followed the stimuli directly. You saw a lion, you began to run, your blood pressure rose, and, because of the running and the rise in pressure, you felt afraid. This has come to be known as the **James–Lange theory of emotion,** because a Danish physiologist named KARL LANGE had the same idea at about the same time as William James.

Refuting the James–Lange Theory. Since the James–Lange theory holds that feelings are merely awarenesses of the bodily responses, it would be impossible, according to his theory, to have emotional feelings without awareness of the bodily actions.

To test this conclusion, Dr. C. S. Sherrington of Yale performed a clever experiment on a dog. He cut all the nerves carrying sensations from its nerve trunk back to the brain. Yet the dog showed anger, joy, and fear, when appropriately aroused.

Dr. Walter B. Cannon went one step beyond this, and cut the sympathetic nerves which *arouse* the bodily changes. Cannon's cats and dogs were not merely *unaware* of having bodily reactions, they actually *had* no bodily reactions. Still they showed the expressions and behaviour of emotions appropriate to the stimuli.

Unless the animals were pretending, which seems incredible, emotional feelings do not seem to depend upon sensations received from *within* the body.

THE BRAIN AND EMOTION

In studying emotion, it is convenient to distinguish two different parts of the brain. One part, the most complex, is called the **new brain,** because it is highly developed only in man, who evolved more recently than the lower forms of life. The most important part of the new brain is the **cerebrum,** particularly its surface, or **cortex.** The **new brain controls thinking and deliberate actions.**

The other part of the brain, the **old brain,** which is more animal-like than the human new brain, **controls automatic actions both inborn and acquired.** It is the primitive old brain that orders the sympathetic nerves into action in emergencies. The old brain, therefore, must be the location where sensations such as cold and pain are felt, since these sensations alert the sympathetic nerves. To put this fact into psychological language, **the old brain is the site of affectivity.**

Affectivity. Psychology gives the name affectivity to the dimension of feeling whose two poles are **pleasantness** and **unpleasantness.** These may be designated by the symbol **P–U.**

Affective tone depends upon our **organic state.** A hungry child will rate a mouthful of milk high on the P–U scale: a satiated child will rate it much lower; and a bloated child will rate it very low.

The affective tone of sensory impressions also varies according to the **repetition** and the **intensity** of the stimulation.

Considering **repetition** first, we know that the agreeableness of a piece of music can vary with its familiarity. You can even measure its artistic value by noticing whether its position on the scale moves towards P or U. A composition that 'improves upon acquaintance' is likely to have artistic merit while one for which 'familiarity breeds contempt' is artistically questionable.

The **intensity** of stimulation also determines its rating on the P–U scale. Water that is slightly salty is neutral, or mildly pleasant, and saltier water is decidedly pleasant, but very salty water is decidedly unpleasant. In general, there is a particular level of intensity for each sense, at which its stimulation will be most pleasant. Lesser intensities will be either neutral or unpleasant, while greater intensities will always be unpleasant.

The Affective Tone. While there is no doubt that emotional feelings can be pleasant and unpleasant, *no* emotional feeling has a *constant* affective tone. Anger, for instance, is sometimes pleasant and sometimes unpleasant. Also *no* sensory impression necessarily arouses a *particular* emotional feeling. Feelings depend not upon sensations, nor even upon perceptions, but upon conceptions. **An emotion is a reaction to a total situation as it is understood at the time.** Thus, the affective tone of an emotional feeling depends upon the entire meaning of the stimulus, and *not* only upon its affective tone.

Part of the meaning of a situation depends upon its immediate pleasantness as well as its future results. An emotional feeling, then, is in part a reaction to **anticipated pleasure or displeasure.** Such anticipations, like other forms of understanding, occur in the **new brain.**

Let us recapitulate the role of the brain in emotion. The **old brain** experiences **sensations** and controls the **automatic** bodily and behavioural responses. The **new brain** experiences **meanings** and controls **deliberate** behaviour.

Fig. 30 illustrates the role of the brain in emotional responses.

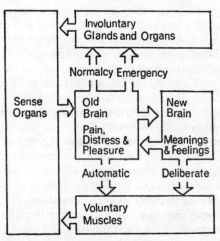

Fig. 30. The brain in emotion

In Fig. 30 the arrows represent the direction of nerve impulses. By following the course of an impulse from its beginning in a sense organ, it is now possible to answer in detail the question of order posed by the James–Lange theory. The order in which the aspects of an emotional response occur is probably as follows:

stimulus;
experience of pain, pleasure, or discomfort (affectivity);
feelings, reflexes, and the beginning of the inner changes;
deliberate behavioural response.

DEVELOPMENT OF THE EMOTIONAL PATTERN

You will notice in Fig. 30 that an arrow leads *back* from the new brain to the old. This arrow represents a set of nerves through which the **new brain can control the old brain.**

The nerves that lead back to the old brain from the new brain are of the utmost importance. Since the new brain can understand stimuli, it can reinterpret pain, cold, and other stimuli as being of little or no real danger, and can thus inhibit the degree of emotional reaction. The weaker the emotional response to a stimulus, the more free a person is to choose responses that are more adaptive than primitive conduct.

At birth, these nerves that connect the new brain to the old brain are not fully developed. Therefore the emotional responses of infants are uncontrolled. The infant reacts totally, without discriminating between different degrees and different kinds of stimulation.

Another important set of connexions are also not fully developed at birth. These are the connexions *within* the new brain, by which one item of experience is linked to another. As a result, the infant responds emotionally to fewer stimuli than does the adult. The infant also has fewer feelings, and far fewer behavioural responses.

With normal growth, nerve connexions develop *within* the new brain and *between* it and the old brain. As this maturation proceeds, the emotional responses of the individual develop along four varied paths. These correspond to the four aspects of emotion that we have been discussing: the **stimuli,** the **feelings,** the **internal responses,** and the **be-havioural** patterns. By comparing the emotional responses of an infant to those of an adult, we can see that these developments are in each case from simplicity to complexity.

Having before us a picture of the mechanisms governing the emotional processes, we can now consider how our daily life is related to these four aspects of emotion.

The Role of Stimuli in Producing Emotion. Through the process of **conditioning,** almost any stimulus can be made to provoke an emotional response. A sudden shriek emanates from a television set in the presence of an infant. The child is startled and starts to cry. Later, just the sight of a television set may act as a 'fear stimulus' to that child. By the same process, exploding balloons and screaming sirens become the source of a youngster's fear of a balloon vendor or a fire engine standing in the street.

Through similar conditioning, older children and adults will come to react with fear to many more stimuli than infants, who are aroused at birth only by pain and intensely unpleasant sensory shocks.

It is not surprising that no pattern emerged from the long lists of stimuli compiled by early psychologists like James. As we have seen, almost anything can arouse emotion, according to the **meaning of association** that it takes on for a person. Perfectly harmless stimuli can come to arouse the tensions and excitement of emergencies. By repetition or even by one association, if it is impressive enough, individuals may come to fear the dark, animals, water, or any other stimulus as a result of such negative conditioning.

In our chapter on Learning it was shown that conditioned fears could be extinguished by reconditioning. It usually takes much longer to eradicate a fear response than to establish it. However, it can be done. The previous fear-arousing situation must later be associated with an attractive, pleasant stimulus.

Emotional Habits in Everyday Life. The process of acquiring emotional habits is not restricted to fears. It is just as potent in the emotions of love and anger.

For instance, people often find themselves liking and disliking many things in life even though they have not previously experienced them. The reason for this *un*reasonable behaviour is that the new things are **associated** in their minds with objects that they already like or dislike. A refusal to try a new food may be based on its similarity in some respect to something unpleasant.

Often such a disturbing resemblance is the quality of colour. Thus, the colour yellow seems to be associated in many people's minds with things so distasteful that it often induces nausea in places where food is being served. Airline companies have had to exclude yellow from their interior decorations because it was found to aggravate the nausea of air-sickness.

Some people interpret as a sign of the mental illness that eventually drove the painter Vincent Van Gogh to commit suicide, his fondness for yellow paint. It not only predominated in his paintings, such as the famous 'Sunflowers', but he also painted his entire house the same vivid yellow. Of course, a liking or tolerance for the colour yellow is no reliable sign of mental illness. In Van Gogh's case, it seems to have reminded him of brilliant sunlight. In other words, for him it happened to have a pleasant association that was as strong as the unpleasant association it has for those who take *his* liking for it to be a symptom of derangement.

Red is widely regarded as an invigorating colour. Sometimes, as in ruby lips and rosy cheeks, red's power to arouse emotion is pleasant. In stop signs, and in blood, however, red can signify danger, provoking fear and anger. According to one theory these two reactions to red were originally conditioned from primitive reactions to blood, unshed in the case of pleasant responses, shed in the case of unpleasant responses.

Other colours may have equally powerful effects. The colour black tends to have negative connotations, ranging from mere conservatism in clothes to the utter negation of death. Blue may be associated with sadness, as in the expressions 'blue Monday' and 'singing the blues'. Green may have happier associations, based on flourishing plant life and natural abundance.

Such associations are not invariable or inevitable. We have seen that a known abnormal personality, Van Gogh, had an abnormal colour response. It would be interesting to determine the colour associations of colour-blind people. Even normal people, however, can and do have personal colour associations that run counter to the majority.

Conditioned Prejudices. Many other aspects of daily behaviour besides colour reactions are governed by the conditioning of emotional attitudes. Those racial and religious prejudices that are not caused by mere uncritical adoption of parental attitudes are frequently the result of single incidents. A single experience with one member of a race or creed can be vivid enough to accomplish the conditioning of an unpleasant association with the whole of that race or creed.

Prejudices can be positive as well as negative. Much advertising is designed to transfer a favourable emotional attitude towards pleasing figures in the entertainment world to the products associated with them. It is thus a recognized principle among advertisers and sales people that in 'pushing a product' an appeal to the prospective buyer's emotions is more effective than persuasion directed to the intellect.

Television stars and sportsmen were once shown smoking a certain brand of cigarette. An actress sleeps under a blanket made of the newest synthetic. An opera singer is shown eating her favourite cereal.

The method underlying such advertising is **psychological conditioning.** The idea is for the prospective buyer to associate lovely faces, athletic prowess, and all kinds of wondrous talent with the product for sale. The comparatively insignificant amount of space used to describe the product itself is conclusive testimony to the power of indirect emotional conditioning.

The Multiplication of Feelings. It was noted that at birth we can only distinguish two emotional feelings—the pain or discomfort involved in the stress and tension of 'excitement' and the calm pleasure of the emotion that Watson called 'love'.

At an early age, **general excitement becomes differentiated into distress and delight.** Each in turn develops a family of emotions. **Distress** becomes differentiated into anger, fear, disgust, and jealousy. **Delight** branches out into elation first and then joy.

The emotion of **love** lacks the violent nature of the emotions that derive from excitement until puberty activates the sex glands. The hormones they release have some of the internal 'emergency' effects of adrenalin, but operate through the parasympathetic nerves of 'normalcy'.

Thus sexual love partakes of the natures of both emergency and normalcy. This explains why sexual emotion can be more powerful than the other emotions, which are related only to one or the other state of the body.

In children, sexual love is not as strong as sensuous gratification. They are hungry for pleasure in general, not avid for erotic pleasure in particular. Any sensuous gratification will make them happy and calm, even if it is merely a piece of chocolate.

WUNDT'S THREE DIMENSIONS OF FEELING

One of the first experimental psychologists, WILHELM WUNDT of Germany, tried to classify the hundreds of emotional feelings by a system of **three dimensions.** Just as the location of an aeroplane can be fully described by giving its degrees of latitude, longitude, and altitude, the quality of a person's feeling was to be fully described by rating it on the three dimensions of **expectancy-release, excitement-calm,** and **pleasantness-unpleasantness,** or **affectivity.** Wundt's objective scheme, which is about as old as James's theoretical ideas, has stood the tests of time much better. The dimensions still seem valid today.

THE DIFFERENTIATION OF BEHAVIOUR

In our chapters on Child Development, we watched the growing child acquire a large number of physical habits that enabled him to adjust to his environment. In doing so his actions in general proceeded from **simple to complex, from random action to selective actions.** In the same way there needs to develop **selectivity and refinement of emotional responses.**

The usefulness of a strong emotional response for primitive man is easy to realize. The emergency values of the charge of adrenalin prepared him to fight his enemies, flee dangers, and give pursuit to obtain his needs. Such emotional response had an essential survival value in the evolution of man.

In civilized cultures almost the opposite circumstances obtain. It is a handicap for an individual to be governed by one's emotions too often or too easily. **Emotion interferes** with **thinking,** and thinking is the best tool known to man for solving the problems of life.

The emotionally excited person says and does things that not only fail to solve his problem but also create new problems. Even in the mildest state of emotion, the aroused person is somewhat confused mentally and is not capable of perfectly objective thinking.

More serious is the condition known as **diffusion.** In this state, the aroused or disturbed person makes many useless movements. He walks up and down, pulls his hair, drums with his fingers. He performs ordinary acts with excessive violence, slamming doors and shouting instead of speaking.

The diffusion of emotion is similar to the random responses of an animal faced with a trial-and-error learning problem. In the excited person's case, the making of numerous and violent responses helps to reduce his muscular tension. It uses up part of the energy that the body is providing for an emergency.

In a true emergency, the energy expressed in diffusion would be put to use. Strong emotions are valuable when spurts of violent effort are required. However, the need for true violence is small or non-existent in daily affairs while the need for reason is great. To 'lose one's head' places one at a disadvantage to one who 'keeps cool'.

There is a degree of emotion still more extreme than diffusion. Emotion can be so strong that the individual goes into the condition known as **shock.** In this state, the person's emotional reactions are incoherent and the behaviour is either delirious or stuporous.

EMOTIONS AND DISEASE

Besides having an inhibiting temporary effect on the ability to think, emotion can have a permanently harmful effect on the body. For a long time, doctors have known that illness and excess emotion go together, just as health and happiness do. Recent research in this area has led to the development of a branch of medical science and applied psychology known as **psychosomatics** or **psychosomatic medicine.**

The basic idea of psychosomatic medicine is that **many physical complaints are related to the patients' psychological reactions to life.** For instance, the physical disease of **peptic ulcer** may have its origin in emotional stresses. These emotional stresses are accompanied by excessive secretion of hydrochloric acid in the stomach, leading to ulcer formation and bleeding. **Colitis** is another disease of the digestive tract that may be psychosomatically caused.

Other parts of the body are susceptible to psychosomatic disease besides the organs of digestion. Strong emotions are sometimes found to be among the precipitating causes of such **skin diseases as hives,** such **circulatory troubles as high blood pressure,** and such **respiratory ailments as asthma. Migraine** headaches are precipitated by reactions to stress.

It can be seen that certain slang expressions, known to doctors and psychologists as **organ language,** are more accurate than one might suppose. Such expressions as 'It gripes me', 'I haven't the guts for it', and 'It breaks my heart' express the facts of psychosomatic medicine quite accurately.

Even when emotion does not *cause* a disease, it can interfere with the course of a disease. Emotion can very definitely work against successful treatment of tuberculosis, heart diseases, diabetes, and epilepsy. The effects of emotion are particularly bad in tuberculosis.

Eliminating Emotions. Aware of the many negative effects of uncontrolled emotion, some people argue that emotions should be eliminated. When such people are shown that emotions can be eliminated only by destroying a large part of the brain, they sometimes suggest a substitute. It would be sufficient, they say, to eliminate **awareness of emotions.** To accomplish this, they point out, would require very little damage to the brain. Just cut the nerves that convey feelings.

Such an operation has been performed not once but many times, on human beings as well as laboratory animals. It is called a **lobotomy,** in which the nerve connexions to the prefrontal lobes of the brain are severed. Lobotomies are only performed on mentally sick people whose emotional reactions are uncontrollably and unpredictably violent, and who have not been helped by other treatment. The partial subduing effect is definite but its therapeutic value remains in doubt. After lobotomy, the patients lose their terrible excitement. They may become relatively calm, less violent, or sometimes apathetic. For a while they may regress to childish habits. After a time they make progress and overcome their regressions, but the extent of the predictable correction of their psychoses is still a very moot question as judged by studies.

Controlling Emotions. It is obviously unnecessary to submit to a lobotomy in order to avoid the harmful effects of uncontrolled emotion. Emotions need not be eliminated if they can be **controlled.**

Psychologists would be the last to say that control should be pushed to the degree of eliminating all emotion. Still, one psychologist, Laurence F. Shaffer, has argued that at least one emotion, **fear,** would not be missed. In Shaffer's words, 'fear is a pure state of non-adjustment, and has no utility that can be discovered'. Happiness, however, and affection, meet with the approval of all psychologists.

Some Rules for Controlling Emotion. The first rule is to face the emotion. The person who boasts of being fearless in danger doubles his burden of fear. He not only fears the real danger but also fears being found out. Such additional sources of emotion can be avoided by facing the fact that you are afraid, or angry.

The second rule is to reinterpret the situation if possible. An emotion is the product of an interpretation. It is not stimulus-in-itself, but a stimulus-as-interpreted, that triggers an emotional reaction. Ordinarily, for example, a child will show fear if dropped, but if its father does the dropping with a clucking laugh it will respond with delight. An adult employee who is frightened by a request to appear at the head office can reduce his emotion by realizing that the request may be motivated not by displeasure but by a need for information. Reinterpretations are not easy to make. They require objective, imaginative thinking. Sometimes a person may need the help of an objective outsider in order to see his own difficult situation from a different point of view.

Sometimes a situation is too urgent to permit long-term reinterpretation. In such cases, the ability to see the situation with humour or detached realism can be of help. Laughter, even when unjustified, helps to relieve emotional tension. Realism keeps people from taking themselves too seriously. Part of the relaxing effect of humour is due to the fact that *any* activity helps to relieve the tension of emotion. The extra energy provided by the inner changes of emotion must be used up. Thus, a good rule for immediate relief is to engage in activity. The old ideas of running round the block or chopping wood to 'work off steam' are psychologically sound.

Of course, the best way to resolve an emotional condition is to perform an activity that is directly useful in correcting the provoking situation. It is easier to attack a problem than to control one's feelings about it. For example, instead of trying to control a general fear of losing a position, one should try to become so expert in the job that concern over job security will be groundless.

This advice leads us to a final rule for controlling emotion, namely, to practise dealing with problems. Feelings depend upon one's early estimate of one's relationship to any test situation. The well-prepared student welcomes an examination as an opportunity to prove himself; the unprepared student dreads a test. People who fear social situations can go a long way towards becoming confident by learning to master social amenities and skills. One's feelings depend very greatly upon such skills, and these can be developed and enlarged in scope by conscious thought and practice.

All of these rules for controlling emotion depend upon the fact that the new brain can overrule the old brain. In popular language, the 'head' *can* rule the 'heart' if it *wants* to, and therefore learns *how* to.

This statement holds true only for people in normal health. People whose internal organs are not working properly may be subject to moods beyond their control. We cannot always blame a bad temper on poor self-control, or baseless fears on negative conditioning. Many qualities of temperament are the result of glandular imbalances.

This *bodily* determination of temperament is most clearly seen in the female menstrual cycle. The chemical changes in the body which produce the menstrual cycle also cause changes in the individual's usual emotional reactions and tend to alter the personality. A fuller treatment of the physiological basis of psychological 'moods' is undertaken in the next chapter.

SUGGESTED FURTHER READING

Arnold, M. B. (Ed.), *The Nature of Emotion*. Penguin: London, 1968.

Cannon, W. B., *Bodily Changes in Pain, Hunger, Fear and Rage*. New edn. Harper and Row: London, 1963.

Cannon, W. B., *The Wisdom of the Body*. New edn. Oldbourne Press: London, 1963.

Lorenz, K., *On Aggression*. Methuen: London, 1966.

Strongman, K. T., *The Psychology of Emotion*. John Wiley: New York, 1973.

Young, P. T., *Emotion in Man and Animal*. 2nd revised edn. Robert E. Krieger Pub. Co.: New York, 1973.

13

PERSONALITY

Few people are entirely satisfied with themselves. Most individuals believe themselves to lack certain intangible qualities that make for 'social success'. Among these desired qualities is one that is popularly called 'personality'.

To psychologists, the word **'personality'** means more than just the quality of charm that makes us say of its possessor, 'There's someone with a lot of personality.' The personality of an individual is made up of *all* of his qualities. These qualities, or traits of personality, are abstracted from his behaviour.

Kinds of Traits. Some traits have to do with the manner of a person's acts. 'Persistence' and 'speed' are typical traits of manner. Other traits are more like attitudes—traits like 'sociability' and 'patriotism'. Even these attitudinal traits, however, tell us more about the style of a person's behaviour than they do about its actual nature. Differing political parties can all be patriotic, but they disagree about what deeds and policies will best serve the country's interests and needs. Still other traits describe interest—aesthetic, athletic, and so on. Among the most important traits are those of emotional temperament. These traits include such qualities as optimism and pessimism, irritability and moodiness, excitability and calmness.

The Choice of Traits to Measure. There are thousands of human qualities that society has found necessary to name in order to describe its members. The psychologist GORDON W. ALLPORT found 4,500 words that designate distinct personal forms of behaviour in the 1925 edition of the unabridged *Webster's New International Dictionary*. Which of a person's traits to measure is entirely a matter of interest. Recruiters of men for submarine duty are usually interested in traits of temperament such as 'placidness'. Employers are more interested in their employees' traits of 'general intelligence', 'persistence', and 'honesty'. The tests devised by industrial and military psychologists have reflected these interests. We can never actually observe a man's 'honesty', of course. We can only infer it from the results of tests and experiments—just as we infer 'intelligence' from I.Q. tests.

The Trait of Honesty. Two psychologists at the Yale Institute of Human Relations devised a series of experiments to detect and measure the trait of honesty. Professors Hugh Hartshorne and Mark A. May set up situations in which schoolchildren were sent to the shop and given extra change. They planned other situations in which the children could alter answers in marking their own test papers, copy from a schoolmate's paper, 'peep' in blindfold games, and 'solve' puzzles by illegal short-cuts.

Hartshorne and May made two major findings. First, almost every child tested was dishonest in at least one of the temptations. Some stole, others cheated, many lied, and a number were guilty of all the offences.

Perhaps more significant was their finding that a general trait of honesty—or its opposite, dishonesty—does not seem to exist. That is, children who were scrupulously honest in one situation would not hesitate to lie, steal, or cheat in another situation and vice versa. Similarly, adults who nonchalantly cheat the telephone company and transport system would consider it contemptible to pass a counterfeit coin at their local grocer's shop. Similarly, many individuals who wouldn't touch a penny of unattended cash would think nothing of taking hotel towels, ashtrays, Bibles, or other 'souvenirs'.

Situation Tests of Personality. If all we wanted to be sure of was a subject's knowledge of the rules of honesty, it would be an easy matter to construct an appropriate test. However, we wish to discover not what a person *can* do but what he *will* do in actual life situations. As noted in the example above, you must disguise the purpose of the test. You cannot expect natural and sincere behaviour from a man who knows that his honesty is being tested. Or, if the trait to be tested is perseverance, the person being tested may try to wear out the tester. A test of perseverance may be disguised with many kinds of verbal camouflage. The subject can be set to build as many words as possible from the letters of a given word under the impression that his vocabulary is being tested. He can be asked to stand on tiptoe as long as possible, thinking that his muscular fatigue is the trait being measured. Any single task like these brings in other traits, physical and psychological, but a battery of such tests measures persistence very well.

PROJECTIVE TESTS OF PERSONALITY

If we present a subject with a task that requires him to use his imagination, we can analyse the product of his **fantasy** to see his characteristic ways of feeling and thinking. A person tends to be himself most when occupied in free, unrestricted activity. He **projects his personality** through the ways he goes about the creative task.

There are many different projective tests of personality. One test requires the subject to complete a standard beginning of a story. Another, the **Thematic Apperception Test,** presents him with a series of illustrations and asks him to produce a narrative based on each. The details chosen for emphasis, and the attitudes revealed towards them, tell the trained psychologist much about the subject's interests and attitudes.

Another interesting projective test is one that instructs the subject to **'draw a person'.** In evaluating the results, the analyst ignores artistic ability. They are interested in the sex, age, posture, thoroughness, distortions, emphasis, and omissions of the drawn figure. The assumption is that the 'person' drawn is often based upon the subject's idea of himself. In the few cases where it is not a self-portrait, that fact is in itself informative.

Perhaps the most famous projective test of personality is the **Rorschach Test,** named after its inventor.

Rorschach came to use a collection of ten inkblots in which most people can 'see' shapes and figures, like the forms and faces that can

Fig. 31. Ink-blot test

be 'perceived' in clouds. Most of the blots are plain black on white. The others are coloured. Fig. 31 illustrates the general kind of ink-blot used, but is not one of the standard Rorschach series, since we wish to avoid invalidating the test.

When the standard series of blots is shown to the subject, he is asked to tell what he sees. He may see one thing after another in one blot. His responses are scored according to the answers to such questions as these:

How many responses does he make?
How quickly does he respond?
Does he respond to the blot as a whole or to its parts?
How original are his responses?
What proportion of them are human figures?
Are these human figures, if any, in motion or at rest?
How easily can the figures he sees be seen by objective observers?
Does he react differently to the coloured blots from the way he reacts to the black and white blots?

From the subject's scores on such questions the Rorschach tester draws surprising conclusions. For instance, seeing the blots as wholes indicates a preference for **abstract ideas,** while reacting to their details shows a preference for **concrete realities.** Seeing human forms in motion indicates a preference for **inner thought.** Responding differently to colour and to black reveals the role of **emotions.** Seeing new but verifiable forms suggests **creative originality.**

The best check on such projective tests as the Rorschach is to compare their findings with the results of other kinds of tests. When this is done, the analyses of personality made by *trained* users of the Rorschach method come out in favour of the method. However, it is not the last word in personality testing, because it measures mostly **stylistic** traits of personality. For **attitudes,** other kinds of tests are still necessary.

TESTS OF ATTITUDES

The questionnaire method is used to measure **attitudes** towards various ideas, institutions, and people. These are perhaps the least reliable of personality tests, since the subject's estimate of the tester's personal opinion of him will colour his responses. Sometimes, too, the subject is 'of two minds' on a certain question, or has not yet made up his mind. The incorrect prediction of the poll-takers in the 1948 American presidential campaign was due to overconfidence in the questionnaire method of measuring attitudes. With that famous example in mind, many people are still dubious about the results of another famous questionnaire—Dr. Kinsey's measurement of the kind and frequency of certain sexual acts.

Rating Scales. The most accurate way to express the *degree* of a person's possession of given traits is on a **rating scale.** A pair of opposing traits—like 'cheerfulness' and 'gloominess'—are made the end points on a line that represents a **dimension of personality.** Then the line is divided into sections, and the position of the subject along the scale is marked off on it.

Estimates of personality traits are liable to suffer from two errors, the 'halo effect', and the 'error of generosity'. The **halo effect** is the error of rating a person near the top (or bottom) in every trait if you have been favourably (or poorly) impressed by his excellence (or deficiency) in one trait. The good or bad impression is hard to shake off while making the other estimates. Estimators make the **generosity error** when they rate acquaintances more favourably than strangers. Sometimes, to compensate for these errors, estimators commit still another error, that of rating the subject more towards the centre of the scale than they first intended to rate him.

There are statistical methods for ruling out the effects of these errors. Merely pooling estimates often results in a cancellation of errors, as the biases of the estimators balance out.

Accurate ratings of personality traits are valuable to employers, superiors, and counsellors. Their particular interests have helped to decide the question of which traits to devise tests for. Tests constructed by some psychologists occasionally owe their existence to their inventors' beliefs about the prime importance of one or another single trait for personality as a whole. The psychologist Jung, for instance, thought the most important fact about a person was his standing on the dimension of personality whose extremes he called 'extraversion-introversion'.

Extraversion and Introversion. For many years, no dimension of personality attracted as much attention as the one expressed by this pair of words. As defined by Jung, the **extravert** was a person who was interested most in the external world of objects and people, while the **introvert** was most interested in his own thoughts and feelings.

Jung and his followers worked out many ways in which to tell extraverts from introverts. The extravert would live in the present and value his possessions and success, while the introvert would live in the future and value his own standards and sentiments. The extravert would be interested in the visible, tangible world of concrete reality, while the introvert would be interested in the underlying forces and laws of nature. The extravert would be practical, a man of 'common sense', while the introvert would be imaginative and intuitive. The extravert would incline towards action, and would easily make decisions, while the introvert would prefer analysis and planning, and would hesitate before reaching decisions.

These terms are still popular among laymen. Objective psychologists, however, have found that two important criticisms can be made about the traits of extraversion and introversion.

The first criticism is that the dimension of extraversion-introversion does not really describe one trait but three. It combines three separate dimensions in one:

> liking for thought *versus* liking for action;
> liking for solitude *versus* liking for society; and
> proneness to find trouble in life *versus* proneness to be content with things as they are.

This confusion would not matter if the three traits were always associated together in personalities. However, these traits are independent.

The Primary Dimensions of Personality. The way in which psychologists can prove whether or not two traits are independent of one another is called the **method of correlation.** A good sample of the population is first tested for one dimension of personality—say 'cheerful-gloomy'—and then for the other dimension of personality—say 'kind-cruel'. The people in the sample are then listed in order of their standing along each dimension. If the two lists coincide—that is, if the most cheerful person is also the kindest, and so on down the lists—then the two dimensions are equivalent. We say that there is a **correlation of one.** If, however, there is **zero correlation,** the two dimensions are separate and distinct.

Such correlation tests have been made of most of the traits that are reliably measured by existent tests. Table VII lists twelve dimensions—called **primary dimensions of personality**—that have very low correlations with each other, but whose defining traits have very high correlations with each other.

Table VII. Primary dimensions of personality

1 Easygoing, generous, genial, warm *versus* cold, inflexible.
2 Independent, intelligent, reliable *versus* foolish, frivolous, unreflective.
3 Emotionally stable, realistic, steadfast *versus* emotionally changeable, evasive, neurotic.
4 Ascendant, dominant, self-assertive *versus* self-effacing, submissive.
5 Cheerful, placid, sociable, talkative *versus* agitated, depressed, seclusive, sorrowful.
6 Sensitive, sympathetic, tender-hearted *versus* frank, hard-boiled, poised, unemotional.
7 Cultured, aesthetic *versus* boorish, uncultured.
8 Conscientious, painstaking, responsible *versus* emotionally dependent, impulsive, irresponsible.
9 Adventurous, carefree, kind *versus* cautious, inhibited, reserved, withdrawn.
10 Energetic, persistent, quick, vigorous *versus* daydreaming, languid, slack, tired.
11 Calm, tolerant *versus* excitable, high-strung, irritable.
12 Friendly, trustful *versus* suspicious, hostile.

Classifying Personalities. The second, even more important criticism of Jung's extraversion-introversion traits is a tendency among those who use them to think of the two terms as two **types or classes,** rather than as the **extreme points** on a scale running from 100 per cent extravert to 100 per cent introvert. Tests show that people are almost never complete extraverts or complete introverts. Most people are **ambiverts,** sometimes most involved in their environments, sometimes in themselves.

This desire to type personalities, place people into pigeonholes, is as old as it is unscientific. As far back as A.D. 180, a famous attempt was made to classify people according to their predominant trait of temperament. At that time, Galen, a famous Greek physician and writer, claimed that all men were predominantly **choleric** (irritable), **melancholy** (depressed), **sanguine** (cheerful), or **phlegmatic** (calm).

In modern times, an Austrian psychiatrist, Dr. Ernst Kretschmer, described two types of personality called **cyclothymes** and **schizothymes.**

The first type were supposedly cheerful, emotionally unstable, sociable, nasty, and good-natured. The second type were reserved, sensitive, fond of books, humourless, kindly, honest, and untalkative. The resemblance to Jung's types is obvious. A more recent classification of personality is that of Dr. William H. Sheldon. He defines three components of temperament: **viscerotonia** or internal calm; **somatotonia** or energy; and **cerebrotonia** or restraint. However, none of these over-simplified plans of fitting all people into one or another definite category has proven to be valid or workable.

THE PERSONALITY PROFILE

The most useful method for comparing individual personalities is known as a **personality profile.** It shows how a person rates in comparison to the general run of people in each of several traits. It is prepared from the results of standard personality tests. When the results are rated, the scales are combined into a diagram. Such a diagram is also called a **psychograph.** It cannot be held that a psychograph is a complete picture of one's personality. People are too complex, too rich in potentialities ever to be truly and totally portrayed by any psychograph, no matter how detailed.

One of the first psychologists to describe the richness of adult personality and point to the ineffectiveness of attempting a categorical characterization of personalities was William James, who has often been referred to as the 'father of American Psychology'. He wrote in 1892, 'A man has as many different social selves as there are distinct *groups* of persons about whose opinion he cares. He generally shows a different side of himself to each of these different groups.'

Personality and Physique. If a man's behaviour is not a totally reliable guide to his personality, what aspect of him *can* make his future personality predictable? Is there *any* objective expression of his personality?

The idea has long persisted that certain *bodily* attributes are linked with particular personality traits. In the year 1600, for instance, Shakespeare had Julius Caesar saying:

> *Let me have men about me that are fat;*
> *Sleek-headed men, and such as sleep o'nights;*
> *Yond Cassius has a lean and hungry look;*
> *He thinks too much; such men are dangerous.*

A study that received a great deal of notice was the work of Dr. Ernst Kretschmer. He classified 260 abnormal patients into four groups, on the basis of physique.

There were many systems of physical typing Kretschmer could have used. In 450 B.C. the Greek philosopher Hippocrates defined two basic types of body build—roughly speaking, 'thin' and 'stout', which he associated with tuberculosis and strokes respectively. In the 1700s, Dr. Haller described 'thin', 'thick', and 'athletic' types of people. In the late 1800s, the Italian D. Giovanni again divided all people into two types according to whether they were stout or lean.

Kretschmer, however, used four categories, to which he gave original names. The heavy-set, he called **pyknic.** The long slender were termed **leptosome.** Between the pyknic and leptosome were the **athletic.** All those who did not qualify as pyknic, leptosome, or athletic, went into a fourth catch-all group called **dysplastic,** or unsymmetrical.

After grouping his patients, Kretschmer compared their body build with diagnosed mental disorder. He claimed to have found a significant relationship between the kind of physique and the kind of disorder. In general, the stocky pyknics suffered the insanity of high-and-low moods called **manic-depressive.** The lean leptosomes suffered from withdrawn personality indicative of **schizophrenia.**

Extending the theory to normal people, Kretschmer created two personality types and associated them with the body types. According to Kretschmer, most pyknics are **cyclothymes,** having alternative high and low moods, and most leptosomes are **schizothymes** tending to be withdrawn and self-centred in their general outlook.

Kretschmer's Critics. Many criticisms have been made of Kretschmer's simple system of body types. When the figures are put to a statistical test, the results are not significant. The types overlap too much, just like psychological types. As Professor Laurence Shaffer points out, 'When exact body measurements are used instead of general impressions as Kretschmer employed, the differences become even smaller.' Professor Kimball Young calls Kretschmer's techniques 'rough-and-ready measurement'.

Sheldon's Three Extremes. Kretschmer's types were so 'rough-and-ready' that when Dr. William H. Sheldon of the University of Chicago attempted to classify 400 students, he could fit in only 112. He had 288 left over as so-called dysplastic mixtures. Sheldon concluded that trying to classify human physiques into three types 'was comparable to trying to build a language with three adjectives'.

Sheldon has since devised efficient, scientific methods of measuring body-builds. From his studies, he concludes that physiques do not fall into *classes*, but must be descended on a **scale,** as mixtures of three components. These three qualities are **endomorphy,** or softness, roundness, and fatness; **mesomorphy,** or muscularity; and **ectomorphy,** or thinness. He claims to have found relationships between the body rating and psychograph patterns. However, the question is still open.

Most psychologists believe that the relationship between body-build and personality is an individual and highly variable matter. Different people react differently to being tall or short, trim or fat. While an individual's personality is related to his particular physique, they can be related in many ways.

Other Physical Traits. Personality traits have also been 'related' to facial traits. The pseudo-science of **physiognomy** was based on certain false beliefs that still circulate. Among these are the unfounded notions that a high forehead represents intelligence; a square jaw, determination; spaced teeth, passion; bushy eyebrows, villainy; beauty, stupidity; and a fine nose, refinement.

Objective psychological investigations have shown that there is **absolutely no pattern of relationship between personality traits and such facial characteristics.** Nor are eye-colour, hair-colour, or skin-colour related to personality patterns.

The Four Humours. When Galen typed personalities into the four **temperaments,** he associated his types with four 'humours', or internal liquids, which Hippocrates had distinguished. Galen claimed that each type was the result of a particular pattern of imbalance of the four 'humours' of the body. Too much yellow bile made a man **choleric,** or irritable. Too much black bile, or **melanchole,** made him **melancholy,** or depressed. An excess of blood made him **sanguine,** or elated. A predominance of phlegm made him **phlegmatic,** or calm.

The Theory of H. J. Eysenck. One of the most influential psychologists in the field of personality at present is Professor H. J. Eysenck. Eysenck takes a scientific approach to the study of personality and argues that science is concerned with measuring and quantifying and that the psychology of personality must use the methods of science. He takes a **nomothetic approach—that is, he is looking for laws which influence the behaviour of whole groups** of people, rather than an idiographic approach.

Eysenck has identified **three dimensions of personality.** First, the dimension of **extraversion–introversion;** secondly, a **neuroticism** (unstable–stable) dimension; and finally a **psychoticism** dimension. Particular attention has been paid to the first of these dimensions. It has, for example, been found that introverts condition more rapidly than extraverts and that they need less stimulation from the external world. The extreme extravert tends to be more sociable and active.

Much research has been carried out to investigate relationships between the extravert and introvert and learning in school. The findings are rather complex and we need to take into account the age and sex of the pupil. In general it has been found that stable extraverted children tend to be more successful in the primary school but that at the secondary age a different picture begins to emerge. There is a tendency for a larger proportion of university entrants to show introvert qualities.

ENDOCRINOLOGY

This ancient idea of a correspondence between temperament and body fluids has been revived in the modern science of **endocrinology, the study of the hormones secreted by our glands.** This science has abandoned the list of specific 'humours' advanced by Hippocrates. It has kept the idea that certain **internal chemical substances affect the workings of the nervous system.**

The substances are called **hormones.** They are secreted into the blood by the **endocrine glands,** so called from the Greek words for 'internal' and 'secretion'. They are sometimes referred to as the **ductless glands,** because they do not have any tubes or ducts leading into specific parts of the body, as do such other glands as the salivary and tear glands.

Modern science has shown that the hormones are more numerous, more powerful, and more varied in their influence than Hippocrates supposed. We have already seen the effects that very small amounts of adrenalin will cause during emotional excitement. Dogs and other animals seem able to smell the adrenalin in the blood of a frightened man. The odour appears to stimulate their own adrenals to liberate extra adrenalin, making them angry and aggressive. This fact not only further confirms the physiological identity of fear and anger, it may help to explain the rapidity with which panic spreads in a crowd of people. Perhaps even human beings can detect the aroma of fear when there is enough of it in the air to stimulate the flow of their own adrenalin. However, this is merely conjecture; for an analysis of crowd panic we must still look to the social psychologist.

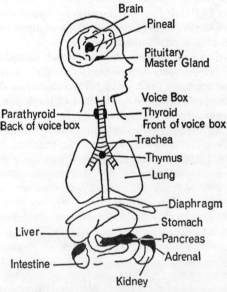

Fig. 32. The principal endocrine glands

Adrenalin is secreted by a part of the **adrenal glands,** which are two small caps on top of the kidneys. Each gland consists of an inner part called the **medulla** or pith and an outer part called the **cortex** or bark. The medulla produces adrenalin and the cortex cortin.

Animals deprived of their adrenal medullas survive in good health.

However, they die if they lose their adrenal cortexes. The fatal human disease that follows such destruction—which usually happens by tuberculosis—is called **Addison's disease,** after its discoverer. Its main symptom is extremely low blood pressure. Victims are fatigued, exhausted, and depressed. They show poor judgement, are unco-operative and irritable. These signs are removed by giving them **cortin.**

Other Endocrine Glands. Other glands known to produce hormones are the **thyroid,** the **parathyroids,** the **gonads** (sex glands), and the **pituitary.**

The approximate locations of these organs are shown in Fig. 32.

By removing a gland and noting the effects of the loss, and by supplying a gland's hormone by mouth or injection, physiologists have found that each has specific and general effects upon the temperament. Let us begin our survey of these important glands with the thyroid, which is the best understood of them all.

The Thyroid Gland. The thyroid gland lies at the base of the neck, in front of the windpipe. It normally weighs less than an ounce. When it enlarges, it is called a **goitre,** but this enlargement does not necessarily mean that it is not working properly.

The main job of the thyroid gland is to **speed up the chemical activity of the body**—especially oxidation. The thyroid hormone is called **thyroxin.** When thyroxin is deficient, chemical activity of the body—or **metabolism**—falls to a low level and the victim loses his former vigour and alertness. He sinks into a sluggish condition known as **myxoedema.** The skin becomes puffy. The muscles and brain become inert. The individual cannot concentrate. He cannot think and act effectively. He becomes slow and forgetful.

The cure of myxoedema was one of the triumphs of endocrinology. It was found that the normal state could be restored if the individual ate the thyroid glands of sheep, or an extract of such glands. The normal state is retained as long as the person continues to receive adequate doses of the thyroid extract. When there is an excess of thyroxin, the individual is restless, tense, unstable, and worried.

Embedded in the thyroid gland are the four tiny **parathyroid** glands. Removal or injury to the parathyroid results in convulsions and death. Extracts of the gland have helped some cases of epilepsy.

The Gonads. The gonads, or sex glands, have several functions. They develop eggs and sperm; and they secrete hormones that determine the secondary sexual characteristics. We have discussed some of these characteristics in our chapter on Adolescence. They include the growth of bodily hair, the deepening of the voice, and the changes in body form.

The male hormone is called **testosterone.** If injury, atrophy, or the effect of other glands keep the testes from secreting this hormone, the masculine traits do not appear. The shape of the body remains childish. It also tends towards a distinct type of obesity, fat accumulating on the hips and chest. The voice remains high in pitch. The beard is sparse or absent.

Males who have lost their testes are supposed to be weak, depressed, and sluggish. They are said to lack aggressiveness and determination. Whether these reports are all true, and if so, whether these traits are due directly to the hormone loss or to the psychological effect of the castration, still remains unknown. History shows that many of the most able individuals at oriental courts have been eunuchs.

Females have more than one sex hormone. One of them, called **theelin,** stimulates the reproductive organs and the breasts. It seems to correspond to the male testosterone, for it determines the female secondary sex characteristics. Theelin is secreted constantly through life until the onset of the menopause, or 'change of life'.

A different hormone, called **progestin,** regulates ovulation and menstruation.

Evidence is scanty as to the direct influence of these several sex hormones on the temperament. The supposed egotism, resentment, and self-pity of women whose ovaries have had to be removed looks very much like a defensive attitude formed as a reaction to the loss of an esteemed life function. Are all such traits, then, only **secondary** effects of glandular disturbance?

The Pituitary Gland. Before we answer the question raised above, let us conclude our discussion of the endocrine glands with the **pituitary.** This gland is often called the 'master gland' because it secretes several hormones that control the flow of the hormones produced by the other glands. One such, **thyrotropin,** controls the action of the thyroid gland. The kind of goitre in which the eyeballs protrude is due to this hormone.

Another pituitary secretion, the **master sex hormone,** is required if the gonads are to function properly. It goes beyond the effect of cortin in that it stimulates female sexuality as well as male. The pituitary sex hormone and the pituitary growth hormone are antagonistic. In normality, a correct balance is maintained between them, but excessive growth of the pituitary is usually accompanied by sexual immaturity, while sexual precocity is usually associated with stunted growth.

ENDOCRINES AND PERSONALITY

There is no doubt that endocrine glands have important effects on **temperament.** In addition to the temporary emotional states of irritability or depression that we have mentioned, social reactions to traits of temperament will also have an emotional effect upon the victim of the glandular deficiencies.

A person whose glandular balance makes him highly energetic will come to be different in attitude, manner, and even interests from a person whose metabolism is low. In so far as one's energy level will lead to particular experiences that might otherwise have been either avoided or sought, the endocrine glands can be said to be a contributing factor in the development of personality.

However, those endocrinologists go too far who say that 'glands *regulate* personality'.

Typing Personalities by Glandular Function. In 1925, when the science of endocrinology was still in its infancy, Dr. Louis Berman wrote a book called *The Glands Regulating Personality*. According to this treatise, your every act, emotion, or thought had an endocrine basis. Moreover, Dr. Berman typed individuals according to the endocrine secretion that seemed to be dominant in their make-up. His book referred to many famous figures. It had great public appeal, and was widely quoted by scientific writers desiring to attract popular fancy.

By 1930, men of science had voiced their disagreement with Dr. Berman's thesis. The viewpoint of Dr. Logan Clendenning, as expressed in his book *The Human Body*, is representative of the opinion held by scientists who are critical of Dr. Berman's position. Discussing the endocrines, Dr. Clendenning writes:

> The whole subject of their activities is so interesting, so many experiments have been performed, and so many of these are so bizarre, that the most unrestricted imaginative speculation has been indulged concerning them. Much of this, both that intended for laymen and that intended for physicians, is put forward with the solemn appearance of fact. Actually, it is pure armchair speculation. I refer to one notable example, a volume entitled *The Glands Regulating Personality*, by Louis Berman. Here we are told with the most solemn appearance of authority that Napoleon was a 'pituitary type', and other famous characters are similarly analysed. Now, of course, all such stuff is pure imaginative speculation.

Despite such criticism, the idea persisted for some time. In 1933, Dr. Louis Berg wrote a book called *The Human Personality* in which he gave quite detailed descriptions of the supposed types. Thus, according to Dr. Berg, a slight excess of thyroid secretion may ... 'produce a superior type who is above average intelligence, capable of reaching emotional and intellectual heights, alert, cheerful, and bright-eyed, with good colour in his cheeks, white teeth, and moist and flushed skin. He will be high-strung, lean, temperamental; he will have a rapid pulse and will tend to develop heart and nervous disorders.'

In contrast are the people with a slight thyroid deficiency, who, said Dr. Berg, are 'the stout, squat, dumpy, or blocky people who are phlegmatic and good-natured, disinclined to worry, and who make the best of life as they find it. They reach no heights and plumb no depth; they are kind and well-intentioned, are good to their families and constitute the "safe and sane" element of society. They take on weight easily and assume responsibility without grumbling, often being known as the "tired businessman" type.'

Criticism of Glandular Typing. Such characterizations, as Dr. Clendenning declared, are not scientific. Dr. Berg made claim to knowledge of correlations that psychologists, doctors, and other research scientists have yet to confirm. Science has no knowledge that thyroxin gives white teeth and cheerfulness. It has never been shown that normal intelligence can be raised by taking doses of thyroxin. Equally invalid is Dr. Berg's assertion of a connexion between a slight thyroid deficiency and the traits of kindness, goodness to one's family, and safe-and-sane attitude. There has been found no specific and proportional effect between the chemical and the psychological make-up of normal people. W. Freeman compared the various sizes of the endocrine glands obtained from 1,400 autopsies with the records of the patients' personalities. He concluded that the endocrines 'would seem to have little to say in the matter' of determining the total personality.

Endocrine enthusiasts commit their fallacy of exaggeration mostly because they fail to distinguish between **personality** and **temperament.** They ignore the great difference in kind between simple temperamental traits like excitability, irritability, apathy, and moodiness and intricate personality traits like egotism, pride, suspiciousness, altruism, and realism.

The fact is that the tensions produced by glandular activity are absorbed into the other tensions that dictate personal behaviour. Suppose, for example, that the adrenal glands secrete an excess of adrenalin. The flow will probably cause a vague emotional excitement. The way that this excitement is *handled* will depend upon the person's personality. Chemical changes induced by age or disease, by adolescence and the menopause, even by castration, are all handled by the individual in ways that fit in with his deep-seated habits and attitudes, even with his religion or other philosophy of life. The *meaning* of sexual activity to a person is far more important in controlling its nature and frequency than is the power of his sexual drive. The urgency of the drive, in other words, can be diminished by its conflict with other motives.

Personality, in short, is the complicated arrangement of internal forces that mould the way in which an individual goes about being the kind of person that he is. It is the system of desires and intentions that form his personal mode of adjustment to his environment. Motives are the keys that open the door to fuller understanding of the structure and workings of personality, and the development of emotional temperament.

For instance, motives explain apparent contradictions in personality, such as the fact that one and the same man may be dignified in church, rowdy in the locker room, courteous at the office, and rude at home.

Underlying such contradictory **traits of personality** are perfectly consistent motives—in this case, the desire to be accepted and to feel important. To understand a person, we must discover what desires and needs drive him to behave as he does.

SUGGESTED FURTHER READING

Cattell, R. B., *The Scientific Analysis of Personality*. Penguin: London, 1965.

Eysenck, H. J., *Fact and Fiction in Psychology*. Penguin: London, 1965.

Eysenck, H. J., *Readings in Extraversion/Introversion* (3 vols.). Staples Press: London, 1971.

Fransella, F. (Ed.), *Personality Theory: Method and Research*. Methuen: London, 1981.

Hall, C. S., and Lindsey, G., *Theories of Personality*. 3rd edn, John Wiley and Sons: New York, 1978.

Handley, G. D., *Personality, Learning and Teaching*. Routledge and Kegan Paul: London, 1973.

Hogan, R., *Personality Theory*. Prentice-Hall: New Jersey, 1976.

Lowe, G. R., *The Growth of Personality*. Penguin: London, 1972.

Lynn, R., *Dimensions of Personality*. Pergamon: Oxford, 1981.

Murray, H. A., *Explorations in Personality*. New edition, Wiley: London, 1962.

Pack, D., and Whitlow, D., *Approaches to Personality Theory*. Methuen: London, 1975.

Rabin, A. I. (Ed.), *Projective Techniques in Personality Assessment: A Modern Introduction*. Springer Publications: New York, 1968.

Rotter, J. B., and Hochreich, D. S., *Personality*. Scott, Foresman: New York, 1975.

Vernon, P. E., *Personality Assessment*. Methuen: London, 1969.

14

MOTIVATION AND PERSONALITY

Psychology is devoted to studying not only *what* people do, but *why* they do it. This 'why' of any human act is called the **'motive'**.

The psychologist's emphasis on motive as a means of understanding personality is not without basis. Experience has shown that it is not enough to observe an individual's behaviour in order to understand him. It is necessary to probe behind the actions themselves to find their origin or motive if we would understand the 'actor'.

There is a popular expression which states that 'things are not always what they appear to be'. Nowhere is this more true than in the realm of human motivation. In elaborating this principle, psychologist Richard Husband reminds us that 'motivation is the crucial issue in deciding upon a penalty for killing a human being'. It is pointed out that in premeditated murder, the guilty one may, until comparatively recently, have been given a death sentence. If murder is committed in the heat of a brawl, the sentence is apt to be ten years' imprisonment.

As we develop from infancy through childhood to adulthood, our behaviour becomes increasingly complex. Parallel with this development, that of our motivating forces also becomes vastly more complicated as we progress from infancy to adulthood.

The most fundamental motives are those that stem from our body physiology and chemistry. Observe a hungry baby and you see a squirming, squealing human yelling for food. Leave a safety pin stuck in the baby's buttock and you are greeted with the same disturbed behaviour. It is the same when the infant is thirsty, fatigued, or calling for maternal affection. These body forces which activate infants as well as adults (but each in their own way) are referred to as **'drives'**.

Analysis shows that the body forces to which we refer are persistent internal stimuli which demand attention. By definition then: **a 'drive' is a persistent stimulus, usually of physiological origin, which demands an adjustive response.**

In everyday discussion and often in technical psychological descriptions, the terms 'drive' and 'motive' are used interchangeably. We speak of the 'drive' to get ahead and the 'motive' to succeed. Having no desire to quibble over terms, we say it is primarily important to know how the two terms are defined. Whereas the 'drive' acts as the stimulus or pin-prick—**motive is defined as a tendency to activity, started by a drive and ended by an adjustment. The adjustment is said to satisfy the motive.**

From the above discussion, it is apparent that the particular adjustment any person makes to satisfy a motive depends upon several factors—the degree of maturity, one's physical condition and, especially, past learning.

The problem of 'adjustment' is to be the subject of the next chapter. At this point, it would be logical to start with a discussion of our basic wants or drives.

DRIVES OR BASIC NEEDS

The basic drives, including those for air, water, food, warmth, and the like, are caused by bodily wants. They are expressed by stimuli within the body.

Hunger is a typical example of a basic drive. The hunger stimulus results from a lack of food in the body. This lack makes the stomach contract rhythmically. By having a person swallow a balloon, these contractions can be measured and timed. Such observations always show that the pangs of hunger felt by a hungry person are sensory reports of stomach contractions.

These internal stimuli arouse general activity. When the individual lies on a bed that records motion, the graphs show that most restlessness occurs at the times when the stomach is contracting, whether or not the person is asleep. Other tests show that people can grip more strongly, and even score higher I.Q.s, during the stomach contractions of hunger. In this connexion, many confirming psychological experiments have shown that students do better in tests and that typists and other clerical employees work at greater rates of efficiency while they are reasonably hungry as compared with a feeling of being well fed just after a meal.

Outside the laboratory, in everyday life, a person normally puts to work this heightened capacity for response, satisfying the motive to eat. His initial restlessness soon gives way to a definite habit of adjustment.

In babies, as we know, the native responses to hunger are not specific. The hungry infant becomes active all over. He has not yet learned any definite forms of adjustive behaviour. All the infant knows how to do is to respond with his entire body. For that reason, as we saw in the chapter on Emotions, observers cannot tell from infants' overt responses just what stimuli are arousing them. The basic drives originally arouse mass activity. Only after **learning** does each different kind of stimulus arouse appropriate, particular habits of response.

Learning and Adjustment. Learning changes motivated behaviour in two ways. First, the individual learns particular **habits** of response that tend to satisfy the motives. The hungry cat, for instance, learns to beg in the kitchen, scratch at the door, or hunt in alleys. Human beings learn to ask for food, to wait until mealtime, to make a snack, or to buy food and prepare it.

A second effect that learning has upon a motive is the change in the **stimuli** that will arouse it. At first, only the *need* for food will make a person want to eat. Later, the sight or smell of food will make him hungry. Eventually, just talking about food will make his stomach contract and his mouth water.

Other Basic Drives. Hunger is not the only drive that expresses a bodily need. Other bodily needs, like those for air, water, warmth, and sex, make themselves felt through definite bodily stimuli. They too arouse random responses until the individual learns an appropriate habit of satisfying them.

Certain **external stimuli** arouse motivated behaviour in the same way as the internal stimuli. Body wounds which prick, cut, bruise, scrape, tear, or burn the skin are called tissue-injury stimulations. Adjusting to these stimuli is certainly as great a service to the body as satisfying its inner needs.

Like these inner needs, tissue-injury stimuli at first arouse the random responses of mass activity. The injured infant squirms and writhes exactly as the hungry infant does. Later, after maturing sufficiently, the infant learns how to *withdraw* from the source of pain. Still later, the child learns to avoid imminent injury, and then to withdraw from merely possible danger.

In every case there occurs **directly motivated behaviour as a result of the disturbing stimuli.** While in infancy and early childhood there may not be too much difference in the motivated behaviour occasioned by these same stimuli, it is interesting to observe the variations that take place with continued maturity into adolescence and adulthood. Thus, we find the stoic-minded individual will clench his fists, shut his mouth and calmly seek aid in removing or soothing a source of pain. Still another will give voice to the presence of a cut, bruise, burn, or other pain stimulus and grin and bear it while it is being treated. Reverting to the more childlike reaction we find the type who cries out, groans, and complains about any existing pain or injury. In general, their 'motivated behaviour' can be described as that of the emotionally immature. In the extreme these individuals are classed as hypersensitive or hypochondriac, exaggerating the magnitude of every existing pain and personal discomfort and also imagining the presence of many aches and pains that are non-existent.

POSITIVE MOTIVES

So far, we have been talking about annoying stimuli, which the individual wants to avoid. Each of these drives, whether the stimuli come from inside (as in hunger) or outside (as in pain), arouses responses that continue until the stimulus is stopped.

There is another group of drives which have attractive stimuli. These stimuli do not merely signal the absence of annoyance, but give pleasure in their own right. They include bright objects, sweet tastes, flowery aromas, and gentle stroking of the skin. Unlike their opposites—sour and bitter tastes, foul odours, and harsh itching—which arouse withdrawal responses, these pleasant stimuli arouse responses of approach. The behaviour tendencies activated by these stimuli are considered to be the result of **'positive motivation'**.

Through learning, the positive and negative motives become interrelated. To avoid one stimulus is almost always to approach some other stimulus. Hunger, for example, becomes not only a drive to reduce the pangs of an empty stomach but a motive to enjoy the flavour of food. After a while, the *absence* of a customary satisfaction can be annoying. Strongly motivated behaviour results. The best example of this is what takes place in cigarette smoking. It is usually begun through a variety of motivations including imitation, a desire for social approval, inner feeling of inferiority, and numerous other motives. Nevertheless, after smoking becomes a firmly fixed habit in the adult, abstinence comes to be more than annoying, to put it mildly.

The two steps in this learning process are:

Avoiding a bodily need becomes the same as seeking whatever will satisfy it.

Maintaining this satisfaction becomes the same as *avoiding* whatever will prevent it.

In this way, **positive and negative motives come to be inseparable.**

The Need for Sleep. In the same way that the hunger drive demands food, thirst requires fluids, passion seeks sexual gratification, so it is that fatigue calls for sleep. The body's demands for sleep cannot long be denied. The drive for sleep is one of the strongest. For all its partial success at explaining dreams, modern psychology is in the main ignorant of the causes and mechanism of sleep itself. This common state remains largely a tantalizing puzzle.

By experiments, psychology has been able to learn some facts about this universal human experience. We know, for example, that during sleep your blood pressure, pulse rate, metabolism, temperature, respirations, and muscle activities are greatly reduced. At the same time, the reflexes are more active. The secretions of the sweat glands are greatly increased. The rate of digestion continues normally and the contractions of the empty stomach may even increase.

People seem to vary widely in their individual needs for sleep. Some measurements indicate, however, that the range of variation is not as wide as is commonly believed. Many people famous for their ability to do well on only a few hours' sleep at night have been found to make up the difference with naps during the day. Thomas Edison was a devotee of this method of seeming to lengthen his work day. Other people seek to make up the difference on a week-end 'orgy' of sleep.

A more substantiated popular belief about sleep is the idea that the normal man needs eight hours of sleep a day. It might be more accurate, on the basis of the preceding paragraph, to say that the normal man needs an average of eight hours sleep a day. Two members of the Medical Research Council in London have reported findings that seem to confirm this way of putting the observation. Drs. H. E. Lewis and J. P. Masterton measured the sleeping periods of members of the British North Greenland Expedition. When the explorers were permitted to sleep at any time during the twenty-four-hour Arctic night, they went to bed and took naps at all times. It looked as if they were sleeping too much. But when sleep was totalled up for the *month*, it was found that the explorers averaged 7·9 hours a day, just as if they were at home in normal conditions.

What Causes Sleep? Despite such experimental findings, psychology does not yet understand the body mechanism by which sleep is produced. If this process were known, the knowledge might well help to overcome **insomnia,** the inability to sleep. Several theories have been put forth to explain the physiology of sleep. These theories fall into three groups:

> blood-circulation theories;
> chemistry-of-body-tissue theories; and
> sleep-centre-in-the-brain, or nervous-system theories.

Blood-circulation theories ascribe sleep to a reduction of blood in the head area as it shifts to the stomach area. The **chemical** theories hold that fatigue products such as lactic acid in the tissues depress the function of the brain. The **nervous-system** theories claim that a sleep centre exists somewhere in the brain that causes sleep when activated by nervous-system impulses.

One of the most interesting and revealing bits of evidence *against* the chemical and blood-circulation theories of sleep is presented by the unusual case of coalescent twins born in Moscow. Two boys, Galya and Ira, were born attached together. Unlike Siamese twins, who have individual bodies linked by a bridge of flesh, Galya and Ira had but one body. However, the common body had four arms, two necks, and two heads. Despite the fact that Nature usually aborts such unfortunates, these twins were born alive and survived for a year under constant care and observation at the All-Union Institute of Medicine.

Miss Helen Block, an American, reported on this rarity in the *Journal of Heredity*. She states, 'The conclusions arrived at from the study of the twins are very valuable to science, especially the discovery that the origin of sleep is *not* connected with the blood stream. This was proven by the fact that one twin would sleep, while the other lay awake.' Autopsy after death showed that the twins had one common circulatory or blood system but two separate spinal columns or nervous systems. Thus, if sleep was produced by some change of location or chemistry in the blood stream, these coalescent twins with a single blood stream would always have slept and awakened together. But such was not the case.

MOTIVES AND EMOTIONS

Since emotions involve the inner and outer workings of the body, they are closely related to motivation.

The positive motives, for instance, are involved in the emotions of delight and affection. Gently stroking or fondling an infant will arouse in him a desire for more of the same gratification. As soon as the child can, he will invite more of this sort of stimulation. Eventually, he will seek it actively, learning to want the company of people who will give it to him, and trying to evoke it by imitation.

The unpleasant stimuli of body needs and tissue injury are also connected with emotion. Here, the primitive emotion is **excitement,** which, with maturation, becomes differentiated into **rage** and **fear.** In these cases, the emotion connects the situation to the response.

The true importance of emotion in motivation can be seen *after* the outer stimulus disappears, for the inner changes of emotion persist for some time, reinforcing the original stimulus, and continuing to motivate the individual.

Emotional excitement **strengthens** and **prolongs** the effect of a stimulus. For this reason, most psychologists now feel that prompt gratification of a helpless infant's drives will help to keep him from learning to **over-react** to stimuli. Then, as soon as each stage of maturation permits, the child should be taught to satisfy his needs by himself. This will keep tempers controlled, tantrums to a minimum, and have a generally beneficial effect on the child's personality. The bodily drive of hunger will have been used to strengthen his social motive for independence—a motive which society approves.

The Social Motives. Motives derived from bodily needs are not the only motives that 'arouse, sustain, and direct activity', to quote Professor L. F. Shaffer's definition of a motive. Besides such **subsistence motives,** many **social motives** can be abstracted from human behaviour. As conduct is diverse, so too are the motives from which the conduct springs. Taken one at a time, we might have to name almost as many motives as there are acts of behaviour. It would be futile to try, as well as unnecessary. For convenience in study, it is perfectly possible to group motives according to the basic wants that they satisfy.

Professor Laurence Shaffer, for instance, lists the motives for **mas-**

tery, **social approval,** and **conformity,** as well as the **subsistence** and **sex** motives. People show strong tendencies to *master* their bodies, their environments, and even their fellows. People want to be *approved* in their own judgement and in the judgement of other people. They are also motivated strongly to conform to their parents' and peers' ideas of what is right, traditional, fair, and appropriate. Related to each of these motives is a desire for *security*, or the feeling of future safety and survival.

Social Motives *versus* Instinct. In the early days of psychology, the social motives were believed to be *inherent* in the human race. The desires to receive praise, to be spared blame, to mingle with friends, to be powerful, to be successful—these motives among many others were called 'instincts'. Subsequent research has shown that such motives are by no means nor in any way 'instinctive'. Ethnologists, the scientists who investigate different cultures, have found several primitive societies in which one or more of these social motives are exaggerated at the expense of the others. In one society you are considered to be out of step if you assert mastery and independence; in another society you are considered to be odd if you do not.

At various times, instincts have been confused with reflex acts, habits and acquired skills as well as learned attitudes. Popular writers tell of children shying away from dangerous animals 'instinctively'. Newspaper stories describe combatants as ducking 'instinctively' and 'rising to the kill instinctively'. There is nothing instinctive about shying away from animals, or killing an adversary. These are acquired traits.

A part of the blame for the confusion about the exact meaning of the term 'instinct' must be attributed to some early writings in the field of psychology. One of the first of such treatments was made by the famous William James. He claimed that man had more instincts than any other animal. His instincts included crying, curiosity, sociability, shyness, cleanliness, pugnacity, and sympathy. Following this there came the writing of Professor William McDougall who classified most behaviour as an expression of innate impulses. He added to the list, food seeking, sneezing, laughing, escape, and repulsion among others. Others included gregariousness, fighting, anger, mastery, and fear.

With the work of John B. Watson in the 1920s it was shown that these early writers were confusing acquired 'habits' with instincts. Professor Knight Dunlap supported Watson's findings by pointing out that all of these acts of behaviour which were being termed 'instinctive' were a result of, and affected by, 'learning'. They could not therefore be 'innate' which was a prerequisite of an instinctive act.

As a result of this early confusion about what is and what is not an instinct, it has been generally agreed by modern psychologists that the term instinct as applied to human behaviour is poorly chosen and best excluded from technical writing. In the words of Professor Robert S. Woodworth, in his publication *Psychology*, 'On the whole, we shall save trouble by minimizing the use of the terms instinct and habit, and leaving both to be terms of popular rather than scientific use.' Supporting this view Professor Gardner Murphy states in his textbook, *A Briefer Psychology*, 'Because of confused popular usage, the term instinct is disappearing from scientific use.'

In another work by this author the use and understanding of the term instinct were resolved in the following way:

In the field of animal behaviour, the term instinct is still applicable to such acts as building nests, migration, hibernation, copulation, suckling, etc. It is significant that although our biologists and zoologists have been successful in describing the physiological basis of many of these wondrous acts of animal behaviour, they properly continue to refer to them as instincts. These men are scientists. They know their ground. Thus, psychologically speaking, we should not make the mistake of removing from the class of instincts a truly instinctive animal act such as migration merely because the mystery of its accomplishment comes to be known.

We might suggest a path agreeable to both the psychologists and the biological scientists. The term instincts should be little used for human behaviour. Applied to animal behaviour it should be continued. Whenever used in its true sense, the scientific definition of the term instinct shall be implied. In its original, scientific, definition, 'instinct' applies to: innate, unlearned, relatively unchangeable behaviour in response to a normal environment, and is universal to a species. In other words an instinctive act must meet these four conditions—have a hereditary basis; should *not be* acquired; should be relatively unchangeable in a normal environment; should be universal to a species.

The Development of Social Motives. From the foregoing discussion it is apparent that social motives are not instinctive but are **acquired.** Psychological analysis has shown that they are largely acquired through modification of the subsistence motives and varied experiences from the environment.

We may then say that social motives are **derived** and expect that they will vary from one person to the next and from one social group to another. This is so because no two individuals are exposed to absolutely identical environments and the environmental cultures of different societies are also different. Thus, in Britain an individual may marry because he is motivated by a desire to enjoy the exclusive privilege of sexual cohabitation with his wife. This motive plays almost no part among Canadian Eskimos who consider it a privilege and a display of hospitality to share their wives as bed partners with friends and visitors.

Just as derived motives will be different for different cultures, they will also be similar when they stem from the same environments. To the degree that the learning experiences of individuals are similar, we can expect that their goals or motives will be similar. On this basis we can explain racial or national characteristics. Thus if fair play or sportsmanship is stressed in American schools it becomes associated with Americans as a national trait or character. Should perseverance against all odds be stressed in the training of English children, this becomes a generally recognized English national trait. We must bear in mind that although a trait may become a national characteristic, it is *never* innate.

It must further be recognized that the relationship between derived motives and the basic drives from which they stem is a *historical* rather than a continuing or functioning one. Let us stop and trace the development of such prime moving forces as the mastery motive, desire for social approval, the motives for conformity, security, and sexual expression. It will be interesting to note how a motive which is originally derived from a particular basic drive takes on an importance and momentum of its own, completely independent of the original drive.

The Mastery Motive. The motive for **mastery** is a strong human trait. People continually seek to be free, to be in control, to overcome obstacles. The great satisfaction that follows completion of a task, solution of a problem, or victory in competition shows the power of this motive.

Mastery seems to originate in the rage response of infancy. The child whose activity is restrained, struggles and grows excited. From this pattern of behaviour, the mastery motive develops by means of the two processes we have already mentioned in our discussion of hunger—namely, the acquiring of new stimuli and the modifying of the native response.

Rage responses are **conditioned** to many stimuli besides the physical hampering that provokes it originally. Other actions, then words, in addition to inert objects, come to have the same meaning of threatened or actual interference with voluntary motion.

Rage responses are also **modified** at the same time. A child eventually learns that mere kicking and screaming will not overcome obstructions. Through trial-and-error and instruction, the child learns more adaptive forms of problem-solving response. Into these new acts, the emergency energy of his rage emotion is directed until the reinforcement of the habit that is being formed leads the brain to reclassify the stimulus situation as no longer an emergency. When normal energies are sufficient to power the adjustment, the stimulus loses its ability to provide confusing excitement. Thus we see the scientist struggling with his problem *mentally*, though motivated by essentially the same desire for mastery that led him as a child to throw a temper tantrum.

The Social Approval Motive. The approval motive seems to be derived from the pleasure-giving positive motives previously described and from the satisfaction of the subsistence drives. Its history is similar to the development of the mastery motive, showing the effects of conditioning on its stimuli and of learning on its responses.

A newborn infant must receive all satisfactions at the hands of people other than himself, usually his mother at first. Soon the infant is conditioned to associate her mere *appearance* with pleasure. This is shown by his four-month-old smile of delight upon seeing his mother, *before* she gives him any food or attention. After a while, her loving language and loving smiles become desired stimuli. To evoke them, the child learns by trial-and-error to perform in certain ways. Value has become attached to love and praise because of their association with tender care. A motive for social approval has developed from bodily drives.

If this motive is weak, a person may behave antisocially. If it is too strong, a person may bury his originality and use up his adaptive energies in trying to discover and do the conventionally correct thing. If deprived of all such love and tender care throughout infancy so that the earliest form of the social approval motive has no chance to develop, the consequences can be child delinquency or other undesirable social developments.

Other Social Motives. There are many other motives. The motive to **conform** is probably based on early fears of possible loss of parental love. The desire for **security** is similar to the desire for **approval,** with the emphasis more on what is got than on those who give. The common motive for **acquiring possessions** is a blend of the motives for security, mastery, and social approval.

It would be repetitious to list and describe all of the social motives, since they are all complex habits that develop through learning from the bodily needs, the positive stimuli, and the emotional reactions to their deprivation and satisfaction. It is often difficult to disentangle the various social motives that determine a particular act. *All* of them frequently operate *at once*. Men work, as an example, not only to satisfy their **subsistence** motives with the food, drink, clothing, and shelter that money can buy, but also to express **mastery** of their fields, to enjoy the **approval** of society, and to maintain their marriages, in which they gratify their **sexual** motives.

The Sexual Motives. The **sexual** motives resemble the **subsistence** motives in being direct expressions of bodily needs, but they also resemble the **social** motives in becoming greatly modified. **Social con-**

ventions often thwart the direct satisfaction of the sexual drive when it first appears during infancy. Economic obstacles and social conventions again thwart its direct satisfaction when puberty reinforces the drive.

Because of all this thwarting, the drive becomes attached to many substitute stimuli and to many substitute responses. Pictures, descriptions, articles of clothing, and many other objects come to be sexual stimuli, while dancing, playing games, and other more remote responses come to be at least somewhat adjustive. These roundabout satisfactions, and the social conventions that cause them, make the sexual motives especially likely to cause serious maladjustments. These will be discussed more fully in the next chapters.

Habits as Motives. To our list of reasons why men work, we might have added another—that habits adopted to satisfy particular motives often develop motivating power of their own. As the American psychologist Woodworth put it, 'the mechanism furnishes its own drive'. For instance, what are the first responses that pop into your mind in the following little experiment? Give a companion word for: (1) up; (2) war; (3) bread.

It is almost certain that you thought of 'down', 'peace', and 'butter'. So well established are the associations in these pairs of words that the second word in each pair is almost invariably the response made to the stimulus of the first.

Professor Gordon Allport has called this development of motives out of force of habits **'functional autonomy'.** To critics who point out that some habits, such as walking, do not force people to walk when they don't feel like it, Allport replies that it is only **imperfect habits or uncompleted projects that act as motives.** The interruption is felt to be a restraint. It is reacted to with the stubbornness developed from the rage response.

It is certainly true that adults resist attempts to change their habits, even when it can be shown that different patterns of behaviour would be more efficient adjustments to their motives. A good example of this stubborn resistance to change is the refusal of many farmers to adopt better methods of agriculture merely because such methods are new.

In many such cases, of course, the apparent force of a habit is really a sensitivity to criticism. Vanity will often make a man retain a bad habit. In some cases, however, the 'functional autonomy' does indeed enable a mechanism to 'furnish its own drive', and habits act as motives. Thus we find the sailor, ashore on leave, rowing in the park, and the airline pilot spending his vacation flying a private plane. In this same category we find the retired farmer who was motivated to work all his life to save money to retire to a life of ease in the city only to find himself bored and restless until he returns to work on a farm once again.

Social Facilitation. The presence of other people influences the strength of one's motives. Having competitors will almost always increase the mastery motive. However, fear of failure may be so great that excitement makes us lose control. In this case, rivalry may harm performance, rather than improve it. We saw an example of this in our chapter on Child Development, where the most productive form of competition was found to be not between **individuals** but between **co-operative teams.** This enhancement of performance in the presence of companions is called **social facilitation.** It underlies group morale and what is known as *esprit de corps.*

Mob Psychology. An interesting example of social facilitation is the strong tendency towards agreement found among the members of an audience or mob. Let one laugh and all laugh; one cheer, all cheer. Should a great enough number seem willing, or at least not unwilling, the excited members of a mob may soon find themselves performing acts that none would do alone or by himself.

An early theory of such mob behaviour claimed that a mob had a 'group mind', an entity that made decisions for the members of the mob just as a single mind made decisions for the members of its body. This idea is false. The only minds in a crowd are those of its members. The idea is also unnecessary. Mob behaviour can be explained quite adequately without resorting to imaginary entities founded on analogies.

There are four reasons why the members of a mob will tend to agree, and often agree to immoral or criminal acts. In the first place, mobs do not usually assemble by chance. They almost always come together with a **common motivation.** Strikers gather to express a complaint, audiences assemble to be entertained, lynch mobs meet to 'get revenge'. Therefore the members of a **mob** tend to have more in common to begin with than do the people in a **crowd,** which is merely a group of people who happen to be near one another.

Secondly, all of the members of a mob are in a **common situation.** They are all subject to the same stimuli. It is not surprising that people with identical stimuli and similar motives will make similar responses.

Thirdly, the reactions are exaggerated by **social facilitation.** Each person's reactions are enhanced by those of the others. This effect of companionship is all the more powerful because the members of a mob are close together. It has been shown experimentally that social facilitation is increased by nearness. An audience will applaud more in an auditorium that it fills than it will when scattered in a larger one.

Finally, and most important, is the motive of **social approval.** Most people do not commit crimes or immoral acts because they have been taught that such behaviour will result in great social disapproval. The habits of morality endure until the individual finds himself in a group whose members seem to approve of usually forbidden acts. If the group is large enough to seem like all of society, its approval will temporarily satisfy his conscience, and he will agree to violence.

HIGHER MOTIVES AND CONSCIENCE

Mention of the conscience brings us to a group of motives sometimes called 'higher' because they are considered to be **ethically superior** to subsistence, sex, and social motives. They include the **altruistic** motives to sacrifice for family, friends, fellow citizens, and mankind, the selfless motives of **dedication** to ideals of truth, and the **honour** motive to behave morally even when no one would know otherwise.

These motives are obviously even more remote from basic drives than are the derived social motives, but they can still be shown to have developed from the stimuli of bodily needs. To illustrate this development, let us trace the history of a **conscience, that is, of the motive to perform socially approved acts in the absence of social pressure.**

We have already followed the development of the social approval motive—the desire to be thought well of, at first by parents, then by peers. After a person has formed the habit of desiring approval, he finds that immoral or unethical acts lead to disapproval. Since such acts are associated with unpleasant results, they become unpleasant in themselves through a process of conditioning. Functional autonomy— the force of habit—then makes it difficult for him to act unsocially even in private.

Conscience, therefore, is not a mysterious voice, but the anticipation of an unpleasant feeling associated with particular acts. Such anticipations are learned. Like other acts of learning, the acquiring of a conscience will be eased and speeded up by giving rewards and praise for success as well as punishment for failure. All of the rules for more efficient learning, which were given in our chapter on Remembering, apply to the formation of conscience. In this particular case, the punishment, or negative incentive to learn, can be the mere withholding of the positive incentives of reward and approval. Children are most willing to learn morality when their inevitable failures are not punished too harshly, and when their successes are rewarded with the approval for which they undertake the learning.

Choosing Between Alternative Acts. People often have to choose which of two conflicting motives to satisfy. Sometimes the conflict is between two pleasures. At other times, the conflict is between a pleasure and a duty. If a person in such a situation chooses the pleasure, he is commonly said to have a 'weak will'. If he chooses the duty, however, he is said to have 'will power'.

It is the duty of psychology to show what really happens when this so-called will-power is displayed.

In general, a strong-willed act is one that pays more attention to **future** satisfactions than to **present** satisfactions. To postpone trivial but immediate rewards for greater but more remote rewards is one of the best signs of a mature personality. In the eyes of less civilized personalities, a person who can bide his time seems to be doing something that he does not want to do. The man who turns down his friends' invitation to play cricket in order to stay home and mend things around the house for his wife is supposed to prefer cricket to pleasing his wife. Such an opinion is incorrect. The fact that the man stays home to tinker shows that he wants to do so more than he wants to play cricket. There is no other way to measure the comparative strength of two motives than to see which motive triumphs when the two conflict.

Measuring Motives. The relative strength of several motives has been measured by the **obstruction method** devised by F. A. Moss and modified by C. J. Warden. To reach the various incentives whose attractions are being tested, animals must cross an electric grid that gives a harmless but noticeable shock. The number of times an animal will cross the grid to reach a goal in a standard period of time measures the strength of the motive it satisfies. During the test for any given motive, the other motives are kept at a minimum.

In this way, the relative strengths of various motives of white rats was measured. In terms of the average number of grid crossings, the **maternal** drive was strongest. Next came **thirst, hunger, sex,** and the **exploratory** urge—this last having only one-fourth the strength of the maternal drive.

Unfortunately, human motives cannot be measured so easily. Man's imagination allows him to be satisfied with future, even with imaginary, gratifications. Individual persons differ in the weight they give to the various social motives. **The only way to see which motives are stronger in a person is to see which motives win in a conflict.** The chosen act shows the stronger motive.

The Rank of Motives. On the basis of his long experience with maladjusted people, Professor A. H. Maslow tried to rank the *kinds* of motives in the order of their usual urgency. First come the inner bodily drives, then the tissue-injury drives, followed by the sexual and other positive drives. Only after these subsistence and safety drives are satisfied does man seek to realize his higher aims, which Maslow gives as the need for love, then the need for self-respect and social-respect, and finally the need for achievement and the sense of belonging.

Studies of wartime conscientious objectors who volunteered to suffer semi-starvation confirm that *continuous* fasting and abstinence eventually coarsen rather than refine the personality. These subjects lost their humour, their sociability, and their emotional life. They become irritable, suspicious, and showed animosity to strangers. These are the very traits, of course, often seen all over the world in people who have been severely deprived of basic necessities. In the words of W. H. Mikesell and Gordon Hanson, 'We perhaps do not fully realize how much our psychological wants are dependent upon the fulfilment of our bodily wants. It is true that we don't live by bread alone except when we cannot get any bread.'

Other Factors in Choices. Assuming that a person's subsistence motives are adequately satisfied by his work adjustment to his environment, what factors besides bodily needs will determine his preferences?

The individual's **intelligence** is certainly important. Because an adolescent of very low intelligence cannot foresee the future, he will live only for present satisfactions. A student of superior intellect, however, can imagine the future continuous satisfaction that will eventually reward him for present study and effort.

Aptitudes also have motivating force. The particular talents of gifted people influence their decisions because their abilities give them a head start on the road to satisfying their more general social motives of mastery, approval, and security.

Fallacies About 'Will Power'. The ability to make intelligent choices is highly valued. Unfortunately, most of the popular beliefs about strengthening the ability to do so are not based on psychological facts.

We have already seen that too much hardship, for instance, *weakens* the will to invest present effort for future rewards. The hardship that pioneers, artists, and other dedicated people endure only *measures* the motivation of these people; it does not *cause* it. Too often, chronic infections and poor diet have extinguished both the willer and his will.

Just as useless as physical deprivation is enforced drudgery. Giving children very difficult assignments will not 'cultivate their wills' unless overcoming the difficulty satisfies some other motive. Real learning occurs only where the labour of study is seen at the time to promise some ultimate reward.

Actually, the inevitable failure met by the overburdened child is much more likely to 'break' than 'make' his will. He will tend to cut down the number and vigour of his responses, becoming discouraged, gloomy, and depressed.

Similar traits can be the result of faulty metabolism and glandular deficiencies. When psychological in origin, however, they are usually the result of the kind of failure feelings caused by demanding more of a child than he is able to give.

Another cause of weak effort is early pampering. If everything has been made too easy for a child, he will have to develop strong mastery motives. In adult life, he will continue to want others to take care of him. This is the other extreme of the pendulum. For practical purposes it is obviously best to employ moderate and immediate means of motivating children and growing adolescents when our aim is to develop mentally healthy, well-adjusted members of the social group.

The Will and Voluntary Efforts. Will-power, as we have seen, is not the ability to do what one does not like, but the ability to persist. To some extent, this ability depends upon a person's energy. We know from our analysis of the nature of emotions that in addition to its normal energy, the body has a certain reserve of 'nervous' energy, which can be drawn upon in emergencies. When this reserve is consumed, the individual becomes exhausted, and can make no further voluntary efforts.

Normally, few people actually drain themselves physically in their attempts to overcome the obstacles that thwart the satisfaction of their motives. Long before that point is reached, they have found some less exhausting adjustment to their problems.

Let us now see what kinds of adjustments people do make to the inevitable frustrations that their motives meet in their physical and social environments.

SUGGESTED FURTHER READING

Bolles, R. C., *Theory of Motivation*. 2nd Edn, Harper and Row: London, 1975.

Cofer, C. N., *Motivation and Emotion*. Scott, Foresman: New York, 1972.

Evans, P., *Motivations*. Methuen: London, 1975.

Maslow, A. H., *Motivation and Personality*. 2nd Edn, Harper and Row: London, 1970.

Vernon, M. D., *Human Motivation*. Cambridge University Press: London, 1969.

15

PERSONALITY ADJUSTMENT AND MALADJUSTMENT

Every day, our environment thwarts our motives. Disturbing stimuli
threaten us with all sorts of unpleasantness, ranging from hunger
through disapproval to boredom. Somehow we must adapt ourselves
to these various situations created by our motives. One way or another, we must solve our problems. We must **adjust.**

There are usually many possible ways to solve a problem. A person
faced with the emotional problems posed by business failure, for instance, can reduce his tension by making greater efforts, by changing
his line of work, by making excuses, by kicking his dog, or by blaming
his failure on illness or handicaps, to mention only a few of the many
possible responses.

People would generally agree that the first two of these adjustments
are better than the others. However, opinion might be more divided
on other questions. Is it better to fight for one's rights or to compromise for the sake of peace? Is it better 'to grin and bear it', 'suffer
in silence', or 'go down fighting'?

Questions like these make clear the fact that good and bad are
ethical, not scientific, ideas. The business of psychology is to describe
and understand behaviour. The psychologist is interested primarily in
explaining behaviour. Altering behaviour is the business of the therapist. We who write about the subject are interested in both.

MECHANISMS OF ADJUSTMENT

The various kinds of habits that people acquire in attempts to satisfy
their motives are called **adjustment mechanisms.**

Included among them is the mechanism of realistic scientific attack
on problems, as well as the more primitive mechanism of hostile aggression against obstacles.

Such mechanisms are not abnormalities, nor are they necessarily
symptoms of abnormality. They are certainly normal in the statistical
sense that every person is always resorting to one or another of them
at various times.

Which mechanisms a person uses in a given situation can be a matter
of habit. We say 'mechanisms' because a given situation has several
aspects. First, there are many possible reactions to the motive itself.
With what mechanism shall the individual react to it? Shall he call for
help, attack it on his own, flee from it, or try to ignore it?

After a pattern of response has been chosen, there are the particular *forms* these can take. If attack, will it be total war with no holds barred, or competition controlled by a sportsmanlike code of rules, or half-hearted attacks strangled at birth by lack of confidence in one's ability and righteousness?

Then, if the motive is successfully satisfied, there are the mechanisms by which the individual reacts to success. To cite a few examples, he may be grateful, he may gloat, he may feel guilty, or he may simply be content.

If, however, the individual fails to satisfy his motive, there are a variety of mechanisms of reaction to the fact of failure, to the implied personal deficiency, and to the still-unsatisfied motive. For instance, one may resent the fact of failure, shift the blame for it from oneself to others, and substitute a motive of revenge for the original and thwarted motive.

Mature and Immature Adjustment Mechanisms. The example just given of a typical sequence of adjustment mechanisms hints at a very important fact, that the adjustment mechanisms can be grouped according to the level of their maturity as well as by their part in the adjustment process. Everyday language expresses this fact that certain mechanisms are linked to stages of development. People commonly and accurately say, 'He's being *infantile*. She's being *childish*. I'm too *inhibited*. He has really *grown up*.'

The infant, of course, reacts to stimuli emotionally. Soon he learns that emotional excitement can be adjustive. It results in the satisfaction of his drives. A year later, his parents teach him that independence is *good*, praising him for eating, walking, and talking. Within another year, his parents teach him that he must *give up* a large part of his newly found independence, urging him to control his bowels and bladder and not to grab everything he sees.

Thus, certain mechanisms of adjustments are typical originally of *infants*, others primarily of little *children*, while others reflect the *development* of the conscience, and still others show the balanced development of the higher motives.

The following account of the most important adjustment mechanisms takes them in the order of their natural development, starting with the infantile mechanisms of adjustment.

INFANTILE ADJUSTMENT MECHANISMS

Heredity endows almost everyone with a rich array of equipment and abilities with which to adjust. At maturity, most people have energy and intelligence that is at least adequate to ensure their survival. Indeed, the growth of civilization argues that most people have always had more than enough intelligence and energy to solve the problems of day-to-day existence. The human race has had a surplus of these virtues.

In infancy, however, these gifts are nowhere near their adult state of development. The newborn child cannot talk, or even walk, let alone reason. Nevertheless, his drives are as strong as they will ever be, except for the sexual one. How does the infant adjust to their disturbing stimuli?

The infant reacts to the stimuli of his drives with the internal changes of emotional excitement, the reflex response of crying, and the random responses of mass activity. The overt responses win for him the care of his parents, upon whom he depends for his satisfactions. In short, he reacts **emotionally** to his motives, and gets them satisfied **dependently.** He reacts to his success first with calmness, then with delight, eventually with gratitude. To deprivation, he reacts with panic, which if severe, turns to depression.

Anxiety. For an adult to react with confusion and diffusion to an unsatisfied motive is thus seen to be an adjustment retained from days of infancy. Fortunately, most people whose initial reaction is one of emotional excitement, eventually arrive at the mature adjustment pattern of objective analysis. Many people *retain* the infantile pattern of *anxiety* as their prime response to their continuously demanding motives. Particular causes and effects of such adult anxiety are more fully elaborated in the chapter on Neurosis.

Forms of Dependence. As is well known, **dependence** is also resorted to often in adult life. Occasionally it is even the habitual method of attack.

In some, it takes the form of a desire for complete care. Such people make headline news when some government rule requiring registration, such as rationing or a census, drives neighbours or relatives to reveal the existence of a hermit who lies in bed in one room, never venturing out of it even to bathe, and demanding that meals be brought to him.

Somewhat less extreme than such utter womb-like dependence is the parasitic existence of people who are content to live off other people's labour. To 'earn' the favour of their patrons, such people will be submissive, humble, and agreeable, complying with every request. In return for their obliging behaviour, they receive the protection of the more powerful person on whom they depend.

Dependence takes other subtle forms. It may show itself in the continual asking for advice, which is then followed blindly. It also appears in those people who cannot bear to be alone. Sometimes it leads to imaginary illnesses that force a person to be taken care of by the members of his family. Although the illness may be imaginary, the physical symptoms which are experienced and displayed can be such as to make it appear real.

CHILDISH METHODS OF ADJUSTMENT

Maturation enables the developing child to modify his original diffuse activity into particular patterns of response. These were given in Chapter 12 as **attack, approach, flight,** and **surrender**—the acts appropriate to the emotions of rage, love, fear, and gloom.

The typical childish reaction to success is **boasting,** a mechanism quite commonly found among adults. To the failure of his effort to satisfy his desires, the child usually reacts with some form of **denial,** either of the fact itself, of the implied personal deficiency, or even of the motive itself.

Let us study the particular forms of these all-too-common mechanisms of childish adjustment.

Approach. The child goes to the desired goal and tries to take what he wants. If indulged in this sort of behaviour, the child may grow up convinced that the world is his for the taking. People whose first or only mechanism of adjusting to a desire is to take what they want are known as **psychopathic personalities.** (A further description of them will be given in the chapter on Abnormality.)

When the desired goal is *not* an object but an intangible quality, like praise, or its conditioned symbol, **attention,** it may give rise to **attention-getting mechanisms.** Any behaviour that gets the child the attention he desires will become habitual, whether it be asking questions, complaining, interrupting, or even disobeying. Adults may become notorious for disagreeing, dressing oddly, or other practices whose purpose is only to satisfy their motive for attention.

Aggression. If an obstacle blocks direct approach to the goal, the child will attack it in a fit of rage. A child's attack is total war, the object being to overwhelm the obstacle or adversary, to destroy or kill it. Once learned, this habit of aggression is no easier to unlearn than any other acquired habit. Actually, in a version modified by the intelligence, aggression is the mechanism basic to the scientific method. Attack, therefore, is not *inherently* bad. It is only bad when, as in children who have not yet been adequately socialized, it is total, unthinking, and inconsiderately directed against the agent and not the source of frustration.

Unfortunately, primitive aggression is often found in the arsenal of adult adjustment mechanisms. In some people, this mechanism shows up as a proneness to blind rage. Such people are irritable, temperamental, unthinking. In others, it is generalized into a habit of hostility. Such a person always acts as if the only *possible*—let alone the 'best'—defence is offence. He finds fault with everyone, picking cruelly on their deficiencies. He is suspicious, and trusts nobody.

Much delinquency is due to aggression. The delinquent, *unlike* the psychopath, acknowledges the existence of **moral** obstacles to the direct satisfaction of his motives, but refuses to submit to them.

In another form of the aggressive mechanism of attack, the individual tries always to dominate the situation. Such a person always attempts to 'take over', to gain control. This attitude may be subtly expressed in sexual seduction or other forms of salesmanship. It may also lead a person to avoid all social and professional situations in which he cannot be superior.

Withdrawal. Should a child's approaches to his goals be blocked by indestructible obstacles, he may acquire the habit of **flight.** He may go so far as to hide, or he may be content merely to avoid chances of further pain, shame, and frustration. This form of withdrawal is very common among adults. Some individuals will avoid associating with people who are superior to them in any way. Sexually inhibited women may avoid the society of men, and any situations that would lead them to become close to men.

Another form of withdrawal is called **retrogression,** or **regression,** as it is often called. It is a retreat to an adjustive mechanism more appropriate to a lower age level. For a child, it is retrogression to act like an infant; for an adolescent, to act like a child; and for an adult, to act like an adolescent.

Jealous children of two or three often retrogress from independence to dependence in attempts to win for themselves the more tangible kind of love once given them and now given their infant siblings. Bedwetting is a typical instance.

'Homesickness' is a retrogressive sign in adolescents and adults. So is the common adult idea that childhood is a period of pure pleasure. This incorrect notion has been called **'The Old Oaken Bucket delusion',** after the nostalgic song that includes the lines,

> *How dear to my heart are the scenes of my childhood,*
> *When fond recollection presents them to view!*

Actually, childhood is a much more fearful time than maturity, full of more unforeseen and unassailable frustrations. It is not surprising, therefore, that the childish adjustments include many mechanisms for dealing with the aspects of failure.

Childish Reactions to the Fact of Failure. The infantile reaction to the failure to achieve satisfactions is panic. In children, the reaction is at first one of anger, until they understand that their anger is a source of satisfaction to their enemies. Then they begin the habit of **denial** that can be so dangerous to mental health. At first, the child will claim merely that 'I don't care'. Adults who habitually adjust to failure with this mechanism maintain neutrality, isolated from disturbing situations. Such a person never really gets close to anyone, though he may betray intense emotion in his work or hobbies.

Going beyond detachment is the denial device of pretending to like the condition of frustration. This is the attitude of the Pollyanna who always sees the bright side of things, won't acknowledge that he feels helpless and hopeless and tells himself that he's happy. In fact, he forces himself to be happy. His optimism must keep jumping from one subject to another, however, as his natural pessimism returns.

Related to this is the mechanism of **comedy.** This type of behaviour is used by people who feel very awkward in social situations. Finding it difficult to be with people, they cover up their discomfort by clowning and displaying wit.

An extreme form of the denial of frustration is the unjustified **elation** of certain emotionally sick people. This device of mania will be discussed in its proper place in the chapter on Abnormality.

A far more normal way of reacting to the fact of failure is simply to forget it. This is a form of denial, too, but accomplishes its purpose by inhibiting the unpleasant recollection, without the erection of false emotional attitudes. It is mentally safer merely to forget than to pretend. However, the device of forgetting can be pushed to a rather severe extreme known as **amnesia.** In this condition, the individual inhibits the recall not only of one but of many events and even periods of his life. Like other extreme forms of the various adjustment mechanisms, this one too will be treated at greater length in a subsequent chapter, in this case the one on Neurosis.

Childish Reactions to Personal Inadequacy. To a child, a failure to win is an indictment of his ability, and ability is childishly thought to be the only sign of worth. Therefore, a child is just as liable to deny responsibility for failure as to deny the fact of it.

The most common adult form of this mechanism for denying one's responsibility is to blame others. Thus we see the poor workman blaming his tools, the impotent man blaming his mate, and the failure blaming 'the system'. This mechanism is popularly known as 'passing the buck'. One form of it is to blame the incidental cause of failure. The child who stumbles over a toy turns and kicks it.

Another device children use to deny their feelings of inadequacy is to act as if they were superior to everyone else. They express the opinion, 'I am unique. I am remarkable. I have exceptional qualities. I am *not* worthless and helpless. I am valuable and I am able.'

This device is seen in an extreme form in the psychosis known as **paranoia.** In that illness, the patient has delusions of grandeur—false beliefs that he is God or Napoleon or some other powerful being.

Compensation. 'Inferior' people sometimes over-emphasize a trait to compensate for their supposed or actual lack. The poor student glories in athletic success while the poor athlete glories in academic success. Another reaction to inferiority is to believe in the false 'Doctrine of Balances'. The pretty girl is 'beautiful but dumb', the bright child is sickly, and quick learners do not *retain* as much as slow learners, supposedly because 'easy come, easy go'. Actually, measurements show that such ideas are often false.

Childish Reactions to Thwarted Motives. When direct attacks upon obstacles fail, the child will often turn his aggression against some innocent object or person, exhausting his emergency excitement.

The Nazis made scapegoats of the Jews so that the German people could keep their resentments focused on targets other than their true tormentors. Through this mechanism, anything can come to represent the hated obstacle. Some crime is said to result from attitudes of hatred developed against people and institutions symbolic of thwarting and frustration.

Not only the obstacle but the goal can be symbolized. Instead of trying again to do what is really desired, but dangerous to self-esteem, the child may do something similar which is safe. Masturbating instead of having mature sexual relations, playing cards with people instead of arguing with them—such are familiar adult instances of this adaptive mechanism.

Related to both of these mechanisms is the device of bullying, in which the unsuccessful attack is turned against a weaker person or animal and a substitute satisfaction is gained from seeing the victim's signs of suffering. In extreme forms, bullying is a symptom of the emotional illness known as **sadism,** in which the individual must inflict pain in order to experience sexual pleasure.

A more normal kind of satisfaction is obtained by means of substitute gratification. The person solaces himself for the frustration of one motive by gratifying body drives. Eating is the most common form of such behaviour. Many cases of excessive weight are due to the subject's habit of eating food or sweets whenever he feels disappointed, lonely, or depressed. Other people take a bath, or have sexual relations, to compensate themselves.

In order to justify substitute gratifications, the child will usually adopt the familiar 'sour grapes' attitude. In the old fable, a fox who could not reach the grapes he wanted finally said that they were sour. Similarly, a jilted man finds fault with his ex-fiancée, or declares that he never wanted the job from which he has been fired.

Perhaps the most common way to withdraw from the real goal is to attain it in fantasy. 'Make-believe' is a normal phase of a child's imaginative life. The child finds it very easy to imagine that satisfactions have been attained when, in reality, they have not. The resulting habit of daydreaming is dangerous when carried to extremes, or when not turned back into the real world through the media of the arts. It wastes time, and keeps the daydreamer from undertaking real accomplishments.

Not all daydreaming is maladjustive. Some fantasy is involved in planning. Creative thinking, as was shown in the chapter on Thinking, requires imagination.

Another adjustive form of fantasy is dreaming. Many of our dreams represent the fulfilment of our desires. In the 'wet' dreams of male adolescents, the fantasy leads to real gratification, without any external stimulation.

DREAMING

According to modern psychology, dreams have aspects of three compensation mechanisms—**symbolization, gratification,** and **fantasy.** The Freudian school of psychology has always placed great emphasis on the **latent** meaning supposedly symbolized by the **manifest** content of dreams. At first, the Freudians thought that the symbols were almost invariably constant—that is, an object or relationship had only a few or even one particular symbol by which it was most always represented in dreams. To illustrate this early theory, we quote at length from Dr. Louis Berg's book *The Human Personality*. Dr. Berg writes:

Symbols have both a racial and an individual basis; many are based upon myths, legends, folklore, and the common archaic material of the race. But above all, we must recognize that, most often, we deal not as much with individual symbols—which are few in number—as with racial symbols. The thigh, the staff, and the snake are well-recognized universal symbols for the phallus and for the associated qualities such as power, domination, and procreation. The male organ is not infrequently referred to in conversation as a staff, the physical similarity making it a convenient symbol for those ignorant of or ashamed to use the scientific term. King and queen stand for father and mother; parting is the symbol for death.

A house is a fairly well-known dream symbol for the body—the 'house' of the soul: thus, a tall building in a dream refers to a tall person; a low building to a short one. The foot is a phallic symbol as seen in dreams. Although it may mean speed and power also, it has, in the myths of the race, come to stand for fertility. The gods are frequently pictured making corn, wheat, and flowers grow where their feet have trod upon the earth. Civilized man, with his fitting of the feet with sandals or shoes, has increased the archaic value of this sexual symbol.

Fire is frequently a symbol of love. In our minds, the implication of passion is heat: we speak of people aflame with love, compare love to a fire that burns fiercely and then dies down; and the constant colloquial and literary use of this metaphor helps to carry over the symbol into our dreams. The lion is a universal symbol of courage; the tiger for ferocity of attack; the oak for sturdiness. There are also linguistic connexions between symbols and the idea they call forth in a dream: thus, a man who thinks of himself as fast on his feet, dreams of a race between two deer in which the smaller one wins. The explanation is that he is a small man who symbolizes himself as quick as a deer, and that he conquers his opponent in real life, *through* a dream.

The emphasis upon the **racial** basis of symbols has since come to be a feature of the school of Carl Jung. Freudian psychoanalysts now place much more stress upon the **individual basis of dream symbols.** Thus a house may stand for a body, as in the above, but it may be merely what it seems to be, a house; or it may mean something else. Modern psychoanalysts scorn, as too literal and crude, the kind of simple one-to-one symbol relationships described above. They feel that it is the relationships *within* a dream that give the most valid clues to its meaning. It is obviously extremely difficult to prove that a particular interpretation is correct. This impossibility of objective validation keeps a large part of the psychological world from accepting this aspect of psychoanalysis. Psychoanalysts retort that their interpretations are consistent, and meaningful to their patients. What part suggestion plays in the determination of their dreams has not yet been learned.

Some Facts About Dreams. Studies have shown that dreams can be studied objectively as well as subjectively. In a series of experiments at the University of Chicago, two scientists recorded brain waves, body movements, and eye movements made during sleep. Drs. Nathaniel Kleitman and William Dement found that eye movements during sleep are connected with periods of dreaming. In 130 of 160 cases studied, dreams were recalled by subjects awakened after eye movements. Some subjects were awakened five minutes, and some fifteen minutes, after the dream—as shown by the stopping of eye movements—ended. Those awakened after the five minutes could recall far more of the dream than those awakened after fifteen minutes.

Drs. Dement and Kleitman report that the *direction* of the eye movements is related to the content of the dreams. Up-and-down eye movements are connected with dreams of climbing. Side-to-side eye movements correlate with dreams of horizontal activities.

The University of Chicago studies also indicate that dreams vary in length. Contrary to older ideas that dreams are always brief, the researchers found that individual dreams can last as long as an hour. They also found that the average person spends about two hours a night in dreams. Before dreaming, there is much turning and twisting in bed, or moving of the arms and legs. Once the dream starts, body movements stop, except for such minor ones as finger twitching. At the end of the dream, the large body movements are resumed.

These movements resemble those of a theatre audience that twist and turn in their seats before the performance starts. Once the curtain goes up, the audience remain relatively still, until the curtain falls, when they again start moving.

Fiction and Fantasy. The reference to dramatic performances illustrates the close relationship in spirit between novels, stories, plays, ballets, films, etc., and dreams. From the psychological point of view, fiction is a ready-made fantasy, useful to the adjustments of both artist and audience, though in different ways. The acceptance by the audience of the artist's fantasy relieves him of guilt feelings, just as the public nature of the fantasy relieves the audience from guilt feelings about enjoying it.

Related to this use of fantasy is the 'Peeping Tom' method (*voyeurism*) of seeking to satisfy sexual drives. In this condition, the individual must see the object of his desires, but will not try to establish normal contact, thus he derives vicarious satisfaction.

Identification. Here the individual derives satisfaction from other people's success. For instance, parents, by identifying with their children, may encourage them in fields in which they themselves have failed. Or a child may identify with a parent, pretending to have that parent's power and rights. Later, the child identifies with other heroic figures, then with groups, and finally with abstract ideas.

Through this process, **ideals** are absorbed that would otherwise be foreign to the self-centred personality of the child. The child becomes **socialized,** submitting his urges to the modification of conscience.

Unfortunately, this process of identification can go too far. The child may become *over*-socialized, developing too strict a conscience. This happens in a perfectly understandable way. From experiences with strict parents, the child learns that the best way to gain approval of the parents is to exercise severe control over body drives. The result is an **inhibited personality.**

Let us scan the mechanisms by which the inhibited personality will adjust to its drives and desires.

INHIBITED REACTIONS TO MOTIVES

The mechanism of inhibition is sometimes called **repression.** The layman's word for inhibition or repression is 'burying'. It is as if the subject said to himself, 'If I don't know about my dangerous impulses, I won't have them at all. I will forget them, and then they won't exist.' Inhibition is very common, and socially necessary, up to a point. In serious maladjustment, people may totally inhibit as powerful a drive as sexual desire. So vital a force cannot always be 'buried alive'. It must eventually erupt, creating symptoms that will be examined in Chapters 16 and 17.

In addition to repressing a feared desire, the inhibited person may try to ensure that it will not be acted upon by crippling the organ needed to satisfy it. The most important organ that would be used in the threatening situation fails him. The reasoning at work is, 'Since I cannot avoid the threatening situation, I must protect my integrity.' Examples of this mechanism of voluntary **organ failure** are impotence in men, frigidity in women, headache, loss of appetite, paralysis of certain muscles, hysterical blindness, and so forth. When the decision to be ill remains in consciousness, the mechanism is called **malingering.** If all memory of the decision is itself repressed, the individual is said to be suffering a **hysterical neurosis.**

Another way of handling 'undesired desires' is to desire the exact opposite. This form of over-compensation is sometimes called **reaction-formation.** This is the mechanism by which insecure people yearning for loving care convince themselves that they really desire self-reliant independence. People who resent disapproval use this device to turn their aggressive urges into motives for conformity and law-abidingness. When such excessively moral people break down, they may have thoughts of excessive violence and sexuality.

Still another way of denying one's true desire is to renounce responsibility for them. In schizophrenia, the patient will dissociate himself from his own motives, saying, 'I am not responsible for what I think and feel. These terrible thoughts and urges come to me from outside.' This mechanism will be shown at work in the next two chapters. At this time, it is interesting to notice how this device resembles the artistic doctrine of inspiration. Some artists say, 'I am merely the secretary of the Muse. I note down what She dictates.'

A related mechanism is called **projection.** The individual perceives in others the motive he denies having himself. Thus the cheat is sure that everyone else is dishonest. The would-be adulterer accuses his wife of infidelity.

'Turning against the self' is another mechanism. Here the subject directs towards himself an impulse that was first directed against someone else. 'Instead of hurting him, I will hurt myself. Then I will not be punished.' Usually, the impulse is a hostile one. In its extreme form, this mechanism leads to suicide. In less extreme forms, the subject is depressed, discouraged, and angry with himself.

The inhibited personality is afraid to satisfy motives directly. Such a person may attempt to justify his behaviour by giving false but acceptable reasons for it. This is the mechanism of **rationalization.** The more aware he is of what he is doing the more his rationalizations verge on *lying*. True rationalization is automatic—that is, habitual. The subject acts as if he wanted to be able to say, 'I am not afraid. I am not guilty. I have no conflict. What I have done is perfectly sensible and reasonable.' The less serious rationalizations try to vindicate acts of cowardice; the more serious rationalizations, acts of cruelty. The first type of rationalizer includes the man who says, 'I am just doing my duty'; the second type includes the boss who, in the name of efficiency, hounds his subordinates.

A very common device for relieving the anxiety aroused by desires is to follow rigid rules of behaviour. The inhibited personality will seek ritual ways of going about the business of living, insisting upon certain routines in work, or particular systems of introduction.

A similar approach could be called limitation. A girl who is strongly attracted to men may see them only infrequently. The formula is that a dangerous act will be permissible if limited. For another example, a woman who feels guilty about sexual relations may leave on some article of clothing or require that the lights be out while engaged in them. She then feels that she has not given herself fully and is therefore not guilty.

Another method of limiting a motive's satisfaction is to compromise. Compromising personalities will not dare do what they want to do unless they spoil, qualify, or partly deny it. One way to do this is to manoeuvre another person to persuade them to do what they really wanted to do all the time. The emotional responsibility then seems to fall on the other person. More commonly, they spoil their enjoyment with worry, which, oddly enough, may relieve them of their guilt feeling.

Sometimes the inhibited personality compromises the satisfaction of a dangerous urge by counteracting it. For instance, a man who does not want to depend upon his wife but who does not want to lose her may be kind in her presence but unfaithful in her absence. To his way of thinking—or rather feeling—the acts of infidelity free him from the bondage implied by his kindness. Meanwhile, the kindness 'atones' for his adultery.

The inhibited personality is one who has learned, rightly or wrongly, that certain motives are evil, ugly, or disgusting. Therefore such a personality will feel anxious about many normal desires and guilty about many of the normal satisfactions of life. Often, to feel 'forgiven' for having 'forbidden' urges, the inhibited person will indulge in **self-debasement.** The subject accuses himself of all sorts of failings, including sins not only of commission but of omission as well.

After any widely publicized crime, police are swamped with people who volunteer confessions to the crime. Some of these people are so convinced of their wickedness that they believe themselves capable of anything. In extreme cases, the person is not just a sinner but the greatest sinner in the history of the world—Satan himself, in human form.

Since the inhibited person fears success, it is not surprising that failure is often *enjoyed*. The lack of gratification is rewarded with the approval of the person's conscience. Carried to extremes, this puritanical mechanism is seen at work in **masochism.** In this 'perversion', the individual cannot obtain sexual relief without suffering pain. Masochism is thus seen to be a kind of compromise between conflicting body drives and high ideals.

THE GOOD ADJUSTMENT

The reader is now in a better position to judge adjustments on a psychological as well as an ethical basis. However, even with an understanding of motives and adjustments, one cannot answer too glibly the important question, 'What is a good adjustment?' At first thought, it might seem that adjustments are good when they fully and directly satisfy a person's drives. This is certainly true of the adjustments to bodily needs. When one is hungry, thirsty, and suffocating, there are no satisfactory substitutes for eating, drinking, and breathing.

Adjustments to the more subtle psychological motives cannot be judged so easily. The fullest, most direct satisfaction of the approval motives would be the kind of constant flattery and petting that Roman Caesars got from their courtiers and concubines. Likewise, the mastery motives would be best satisfied by the kind of complete power over one's enemies and rivals enjoyed by those same Caesars. History shows that such utter gratification bored the Caesars, and degraded their personalities.

Another point can be made against the pleasure-theory of adjustment. A man cannot play golf while basking in a bath. He cannot earn a living while swimming in a pool. The unlimited satisfaction of one drive may thwart the fulfilment of other ends.

In fact, the man who one-sidedly devotes himself to reducing one drive at the expense of the rest is just the man who needs help. **Good adjustments tend to satisfy all of a person's motives, regarded as an integrated system.**

In addition, one cannot ignore the person's social environment. He must do his adjusting in a society of other people who have their own personalities, motives, and mechanisms of adjustment. When the interrelated motives of a person are satisfied without exaggerating or slighting of any one motive, and without exaggerating or slighting the rights of other people, good adjustment exists. To put it another way, **a good adjustment is one that manages to satisfy subsistence, social, and higher motives simultaneously, through effective behaviour in the real world.**

The Mechanisms of Mature Adjustment. Truly mature adults solve their personal problems with the same objectivity which they apply to impersonal problems. They consider the situation objectively, reviewing all of the evidence. Then they evaluate the importance of each item of data, and the interrelationships between them. To ensure a realistic point of view, they check their understanding against the opinion of an outsider. Then they imagine various courses of action. They weigh the immediate and long-range results of each plan. Finally, they decide which plan to follow, and in what order to switch to other plans if some unforeseen event eliminates their first choice. They act on their decision at once, vigorously and wholeheartedly. If, in spite of all their pains, they fail, they do not reproach themselves, since they can honestly say they did their best.

Analysing this process in the same terms applied earlier to the infantile, childish, and inhibited mechanisms, one can say that the **mature reaction to a motive situation is objective analysis.** The response chosen may be a realistic attack upon the problem, postponement of immediate gratification, or even mature renunciation of the motive. To success, the true adult reacts with a feeling of satisfaction, or 'a job well done'.

The well-adjusted person fails at least as often, and perhaps more often, than the maladjusted, since he attempts more. He is far more interested in correcting the failure and learning from it, than he is in attributing blame for it. Therefore he accepts the fact of failure, reappraises his goals and his methods, and then either renounces, postpones, or substitutes satisfaction, or reviews his attack on the source of his problem. Through all of this he remains perfectly aware of 'what's going on'. He does not try to fool himself.

Security and Confidence. Why should anybody feel it necessary to fool himself or others? Why do some people feel dreadfully ashamed of failure, when other people, while regretting it, chalk it up to experience and forget about it? Why do some people go to great lengths to conceal their fear, when other people, even in crises, may not feel it at all, but do their best and take what comes 'like men'.

The answer lies in the difference between the emotional attitudes of well-adjusted and maladjusted people towards their environments and towards themselves. The well-adjusted person feels secure and confident. He trusts his environment, and he esteems himself. To the maladjusted person, however, the environment seems hostile, and his self seems inadequate. No matter how comfortable and talented he really is, he feels insecure and inferior.

Improving One's Own Adjustments. How can a person who is not too sure of himself improve the quality of his adjustment? Regardless of the particular schools of psychology upon which psychiatrists base their personal method of therapy, they agree on the following general rules of effective living:

Maintain good physical health. Since adjustment involves the entire person, a person who seeks to improve his own adjustments should visit his physician. As was seen in a previous chapter, some personality defects are due to organic disturbances, like endocrine gland upsets. Worry over pain and discomfort can spoil the quality of all adjustments, while poor *physical* health will lower one's zest for living.

Do satisfying work. One of the greatest forces for balanced personality is the sense of satisfaction and completeness that comes from the successful conclusion of important work. Try to plan, undertake, and complete tasks that are socially useful and personally interesting.

Rest and recreation. Rest and recreation are valuable for several reasons. They increase physical well-being. They give undesirable emotions and ideas time to die out. If the work is temporarily difficult, recreation supplies satisfactions to balance the frustrations met in the work.

Participate in society. Social activity is as necessary as individual activity. People in a group forget their immediate difficulties, finding satisfaction in mutual achievements. Anxiety is hard to maintain among people one likes and is liked by.

Have a confidential relationship with another person. One of the best ways to reduce tensions is to talk about one's difficulties to an equal. When a person communicates the nature of a problem to another mind, he is forced to consider it more objectively. The role of confidential listener is not limited to physicians, psychiatrists, and psychologists. Parents, wives and husbands, clergymen, teachers, and friends can prove themselves to be discreet and sympathetic confidantes.

Plan and do something about every problem. As we saw in our chapter on Learning, vigorous and varied responses increase the odds of finding solutions to problems. Of course, mere random activity is not enough. One must use one's objectivity and insight.

Be objective. The objective person opens his eyes to the facts, instead of being blinded to them by his desires. He is therefore able to manipulate the forces of his environment to gain a balanced satisfaction of his motives. By paying attention to other people's motives and feelings, he can compromise more easily on trivial issues to earn co-operation of important matters.

Seek insight. Well-adjusted people try to be objective towards their own personalities as well as towards their environment.

Normal people are able to evaluate their personal share of gifts rather accurately. Of the wide range of possible careers and purposes presented by the world, they choose those goals that seem achievable by their particular talents. They do not set their standards so high that failure is likely, nor so low that life presents no challenge. Such people are realistic. They do not try to cover up their shortcomings and failures.

Don't take yourself too seriously. The well-adjusted person can laugh at himself. He sees the ridiculous in his own conduct. In fact, the more mature a person is, the less he laughs at others—not only to spare their feelings, but because he knows he is no wiser.

Live in the present. It is essential for good adjustment to live with each situation as it arises, and to attack it at once with all of one's resources. Anxiety about the future and regret about the past do nothing to help one solve current problems. In fact, they hinder adjustment, as we know from our chapter on Emotion. The past is to be learned from, and the future is to be planned for, but only in relation to one's present difficulties.

Sometimes, of course, one's present difficulties are so great, or are caused by illnesses so hampering, that one must have professional help in overcoming them. The next chapter will discuss illnesses that are emotional—the *neuroses*.

SUGGESTED FURTHER READING

Dicks, H. V., *Marital tensions. Clinical Studies Towards a Psychological Theory of Interaction*. Routledge and Kegan Paul: London, 1967.

Freud, S., *The Interpretation of Dreams* (*1900*). Hogarth Press: London, 1953.

Gathercole, C. E., *Assessment in Clinical Psychology*. Penguin: London, 1968.

Gorer, G., *Grief and Mourning*. Cresset Press: London, 1965.

Jahoda, Marie, *Current Concepts of Positive Mental Health*. Basic Books: New York, 1958.

Kluckhohn, C., and Murray, H. A. (Eds.), *Personality in Nature, Society and Culture*. Jonathan Cape: London, 1953.

Maier, N. R. F., *Frustration*. Crescent Press: London, 1961

Pope, B., and Scott, W. H., *Psychological Diagnosis in Clinical Practice: With Applications in Medicine, Law, Education, Nursing and Social Work*. Oxford University Press: New York, 1967.

Quay, H. C., *Research in Psychopathology*. Van Nostrand: London, 1963.

Sanford, N., *Self and Society: Social Change and Individual Development*. Atherton Press: New York, 1966.

Shaffer, L. F., *The Psychology of Adjustment*. 2nd Edn. Constable: London, 1956.

16

THE NEUROTIC PERSONALITY

Despite the universal human desire to be happy and healthy, many people become the victims of psychological illnesses. These take the form of a personality impairment which fall into two categories, broadly referred to as the **neuroses** and the **psychoses.** The less severe of the two are the neuroses in which a function of the personality escapes conscious control. In some cases it is the emotion of fear. In other cases, control of ideas is lost. In some situations there may be uncontrolled disturbing behaviour patterns, loss of control of body parts, or debility of involuntary organs with no 'physical' cause.

In the conditions known as the psychoses, the normal ability to perceive and interpret stimuli correctly is affected. The psychotic person inhabits an imaginary world, which is a more-or-less distorted version of the real world. As a rule, individuals suffering the effects of a true psychosis have to be hospitalized. In the next chapter we will explore the causes, kinds, and effects of such severe abnormalities. At this time we shall discuss in greater detail the various aspects of neurosis or the neurotic personality.

ANXIETY

One of the commonest neurotic symptoms is a state of continuous fear. Unlike *normal* fear, which is a response to threatening stimuli in the immediate *present*, neurotic fear is a response to anticipated future trouble. To distinguish one kind of fear from the other, neurotic fear is called **anxiety.**

Anxiety can be mild or intense, and occasional or continuous. When it is mild but continuous, it is called worry. When occasional but intense, it is called panic.

The average individual feels that worry is justified. Psychiatrists cannot deny that the world contains dangers and discomforts, both seen and unforeseen. It is undoubtedly wise to take precautions against inevitable or probable events. However, to fear such events in advance is useless and even harmful. Even when such events occur, if they do occur, fear is useful only if physical flight is the best adjustment. This is hardly ever so, and certainly not in the case of one's own death. Yet death and possible injury to oneself or one's kin are common subjects of worry. This indicates that worry, for all that it seems to be a reasonable reaction to future woe, is really a fear of something else.

Attacks of panic give stronger evidence that neurotic fear is not really caused by its apparent stimuli. For one thing, they often occur for no apparent reason at all. All at once, without any warning, the individual will suffer an attack of intense fear. It lasts only a few minutes, or even less, and then subsides. Such an attack may occur once a month, once a week, or even several times a day.

During attacks of panic, the individual may be afraid of particular events, like dying or going 'crazy'; or of the fact that he is an insignificant part of a tremendous universe; or of nothing in particular. Sometimes the individual has no conscious feeling of fear, but is troubled by all of the internal states typical of fear. You may recall from an earlier chapter that the bodily signs of fear include palpitation of the heart, rapid pulse, difficulty in breathing and swallowing, perspiration, need to urinate or defecate, and dizziness. Occasionally only a few, or only one, of these signs of fear will be felt during an attack of acute anxiety.

The Causes of Anxiety. Worry that continues after precautions have been taken, and panic that occurs 'spontaneously', are signs of a fear whose stimuli have been inhibited. Anxiety is a symptom of repressed emotional excitement.

Emotional excitement, as was shown in an earlier chapter, is a reaction to frustration. Anxiety, therefore, is a sign of repressed frustration. At one time or another, the victim of such anxiety must have repressed the memory of a motive, an obstacle, or a resulting impulse to fight or flee. One or more of these elements of frustration frightened the individual, and the entire situation was repressed.

The psychiatrist confronted with an anxious patient may have a good idea of just which of the victim's motives were or are being frustrated.

Nevertheless, a psychiatrist will want to try certain techniques that have been found useful for uncovering repressed material.

Detecting Repressed Stimuli. One way to find out what stimuli are really causing the inappropriate emotional responses of anxiety is called the method of word-association. In this technique, the tester instructs the subject to utter at once the first word that springs into his mind in response to words read one at a time from a standard list. As the subject does so, the tester records his response to each stimulus word. He also records the exact time interval between the two. He then examines his records, looking for the following signs of emotionally disturbed word associations:

An overlong reaction time in giving the word.
An extremely short reaction time.
Strange, apparently senseless responses.

No response at all.

Repetition of a response made previously.

On a later retrial with the same stimulus, a defective reproduction of the response given the first time.

Apparent misunderstanding of the stimulus word.

Repetition of the stimulus word itself.

From the clues given by these disturbed responses, the tester can prepare new lists of stimulus words with which to further test his subject.

The results of these subsequent tests will tell him which senses of the original stimulus words upset the subject. In the hands of an experienced clinician, the results of an extensive word-association test can be very useful in getting at the crucial points in the subject's emotional history—the points at which his habits of repression were formed.

Typical Repressed Material. When the causes of an anxiety neurosis are brought to light, they are usually found to be such wishes, needs, and memories as have met with strong parental or other societal disapproval. The need for approval has led the individual to form the habit of inhibiting those desires whose direct expression would have cost him the desired approval. Just what those motives are depends upon the particular life experiences of the person. Almost any drive or motive can become associated with disapproval.

Chief among the drives that people learn to inhibit is the sexual drive. No other biological drive is so thoroughly regulated. Indeed, it is the *only* body drive whose continued frustration will *not* lead to the individual's death—although the human race would, of course, die out if the sexual drive were completely frustrated.

THE SCHOOL OF FREUD

This fact led the famous Viennese psychoanalyst SIGMUND FREUD to build a school of psychological thought based almost entirely on observations relating to sexual frustration. As continued research showed that the social motives are just as effective causes of anxiety as sex, Freud extended his own definition of the sexual drive until it came to include almost all of the other body drives and social motives. He called this general urge 'libido'. An early associate of Freud, ALFRED ADLER, later decided that all of the motives were really aspects not of a sexual drive, but of a **mastery** drive. Still another one-time Freudian, C. G. JUNG, concluded that the one motive that embraced all of the others was **the desire to belong.**

Freud's great contribution was certainly not the dubious redefining of sex to include all vital drives and motives; nor was it even the needed emphasis on the importance of sex in neurosis; but rather the demonstration that **repression was the mechanism of neurotic anxiety.**

The Failure of Repression. The mechanism of repression leads to maladjustment because it fails to do its job. If repression worked by *extinguishing* a memory, the traces of painful events could be wiped from our minds. Actually, **repression works by inhibiting a memory.** An earlier chapter showed that inhibition is the process whereby a substitute response is related to a stimulus. In the case of repression, the substitute response is the response of not recalling. Freudians would say that the memory is repressed into the **'unconscious'** part of the mind. Objective psychologists prefer to say that the act of recall is simply *not* completed in its original form. However, the term is convenient as a label for material that has been repressed. If taken as a synonym for 'repressed', and not as the name of an entity, it is perfectly scientific.

Like any acquired act, the repression of a particular painful stimulus may not be learned perfectly. In 1914, Freud published a book called *The Psychopathology of Everyday Life* in which he showed that such apparently 'normal' acts as slips of the tongue revealed unconscious memories and motives. The repressed material continues to provoke responses.

If secondary conditioning has associated the emotional responses made to the original stimulus to substitute stimuli, the latter may provoke the original emotion whenever encountered. Chance words, snatches of a song, tones of voice, smells, colours—almost any substitute stimulus can arouse the emotion that has been transferred to it from the inhibited stimulus. This is the explanation of panic attacks.

In worry, too, the emotion proper to one stimulus is aroused by likely or possible events in the future. Fear is transferred from past anticipations to present anticipations. Since the future never ends, worry is continuous. It is not reduced by favourable outcomes. It is merely transferred to a new future possibility.

PHOBIAS

When repressed fear is transferred to a *particular* object or situation, the resulting fear is called a **phobia.**

Most people have one or more mild phobias, usually of mice, snakes, insects, or other vermin. In some individuals, however, such fears are so intense as to be overwhelming. Closed or open places, heights, animals, the dark, and a multitude of other special situations and objects will reduce these unfortunate people to terror. Their fear reaction to any one or more of these particular circumstances is so intense as to be termed a phobia or a form of neurosis. When it reaches the proportions of a neurosis, their personality distortion or impairment is so grave as to interfere with their normal living, restricting their freedom or requiring the constant presence of another person.

All phobias are unreasonable fears. The victims suffer from a variety of converted or disguised emotional apprehensions. Some original fear, associated with guilt or shame, is repressed. It becomes converted into fear of something else. It thus conceals some conflict or frustration. Phobias are more serious than anxieties because an additional maladjustive learning step has taken place. In an attempt to rationalize his anxiety, the phobic individual has associated it with previously innocent objects. These objects thus become **symbols** of the true cause of the anxiety. In treatment, therefore, the individual must unlearn the symbol as well as the original inhibition. Therapists do not allow the patient to be satisfied with mere unlearning of the symbol. Unless the true cause is unearthed, the fear will merely become attached to a different object, creating a new phobia.

OBSESSIONS

An obsession is a persistent, conscious idea or desire that is recognized by the individual as being more or less irrational.

The obsessive neurotic does not accept the obsession, but cannot avoid it. Many otherwise rational individuals confess their inability to give up prejudices in the same breath with their acknowledgement that the bias is unreasonable. The suspicion that one is really an orphan and that one's supposed parents are really unrelated could be an obsession with emotionally insecure children. The tormenting idea that one did not turn off the gas and lock the front door is another common obsessive idea. More serious than these obsessions are sudden desires to commit indecent or criminal acts.

The obsessive neurotic intellectually rejects his obsession. He usually fears or dislikes it. Still, he cannot help dwelling on it, returning to it again and again, much as the tongue keeps exploring a cavity in a tooth. No matter how much he despises the obsessive thought, he cannot abandon it or keep it out of his consciousness. When one remembers how annoying it is to be unable to forget a certain tune, the extreme discomfort of a frightening *idea* can be easily imagined.

COMPULSIONS

The obsessed neurotic will often try to counteract his terrifying thought by a specific action. This action is termed a **compulsion.** If, for instance, an individual is obsessed with the horrifying idea of killing his father, he may feel compelled to utter a protective wish, or to fold his hands in prayer. In another vein, he may feel compelled to wash his hands if his obsession tells him that every object he touches is covered with deadly germs. In fact, hand-washing is one of the most common compulsive acts. Sometimes hand-washing is carried to such an extreme that the hands become painfully irritated.

A related compulsion drives some housewives to keep their homes so spotless that their families find it impossible to live in the place comfortably.

It is obvious that only a person who is desperately afraid of 'dirtiness' would elevate cleanliness into a passion. Compulsive acts and obsessive thoughts are always found to be about such socially touchy subjects as excretion, sexuality, and aggression.

THE COMPULSIVE PERSONALITY

When the personalities of compulsive and obsessive neurotics are examined, they are found to have certain common traits. They are usually very orderly, very stingy, and very courteous. At the same time, they will occasionally show the opposite traits of extreme sloppiness, generosity, and cruelty. The traits reveal a basic concern about cleanliness, sharing, and sympathy. Apparently, the compulsive–obsessive type of personality is still uncertain of its self-control. To make sure that no forbidden impulses are acted upon, the compulsive–obsessive neurotic does as much as possible in a ritualistic, patterned way. Little is left to 'chance'—that is, to impulse. The calendar and clock reign supreme, new experiences are avoided, and life is lived according to rules and regulations rather than by spontaneity and whim.

As in the other neuroses, the repression ultimately fails. The forbidden impulses, denied expression in deeds, denied even voluntary consideration, appear in the consciousness as obsessive ideas. Under pain of anxiety, the obsessed neurotic must then perform a compulsive act to 'cancel' the obsession.

KLEPTOMANIA AND OTHER MANIAS

Grouped under the heading of **manias** are conditions much like the compulsive neuroses, in that the individual commits certain acts 'against his will'. Unlike compulsive neurosis, the manias compel a person to **commit unlawful acts,** such as stealing, setting fire, committing assault, rape, and murder. It is as if an **obsessive thought were carried out instead of countermanded.**

When not engaged in these illegal acts, mania neurotics behave normally. They are perfectly aware of the illegal nature of their maniacal acts, and of the risks they run by committing them. Usually, these neurotics get no material benefit from their crimes. Kleptomaniacs can usually buy what they steal, or else have no particular use for it. During the crime, these neurotics experience great emotional relief, but guilt and self-punishment follow later.

Underlying the manias is repressed fear and resentment of rejection, real or imaginary, present or past. The acts are committed partly in revenge, partly to gain attention, partly to feel important, and partly to be punished—punishment being better than no attention at all.

A mechanism that 'satisfies' so many motives is not easily given up. It takes a long time for a therapist to help the victim of a mania uncover the repressed causes of his compulsion. Such neurotics often have the time to spare. Because of their desire for punishment, many of them are easily caught, convicted, and imprisoned. Unfortunately, most prisons still lack adequate psychiatric staffs. The chance given by imprisonment to help these sick people is largely wasted.

DISSOCIATED PERSONALITIES

A group of neuroses called **'dissociations'** represent still other attempts to avoid the anxiety associated with forbidden impulses. In these conditions, the **unity** of the individual is disturbed. Several different processes go on simultaneously, or are kept separate in consciousness.

Somnambulism, or Sleep-walking. In the dissociation of **somnambulism,** the individual tries to carry out in his **sleep** acts which he unconsciously desires but which inhibition keeps him from doing while awake. In this respect, sleep-walking resembles those dreams in which wishes are fulfilled. Like most dreams, episodes of sleep-walking are forgotten in the morning.

Except for the physical danger of walking about at night while not totally alert, sleep-walking would be harmless, if it were not for the fact that somnambulism does not really solve the problem that causes it. Until the repressed desires are acknowledged, understood, and accepted, either sleep-walking or some other mechanism of avoidance will continue.

Fugue, or Flight. When a certain stimulus threatens a neurotic personality with the likelihood of entering a situation in which he fears he will misbehave, he may soon find himself, after a time, in a strange place, without knowing how he got there. The condition he was in during his transportation from his normal habitat to the new locale is called **fugue.**

During a fugue, the dissociated neurotic may simply wander off, or buy a railway ticket, or simply spend all his money and time on shows and drinks. The fugue may last only a few hours or as long as several days.

Fugue is a reaction to a situation of stress. It is partly an escape, and partly a compensation. In addition to literally running away from trouble, the neurotic in fugue satisfies certain needs or consoles himself in his plight by having a good time. Fugue is a caricature of going on holiday.

Amnesia, or Loss of Identity. Every neurotic reaction involves repression—usually the memory of certain events in the neurotic's life. In the dissociation of **amnesia,** this disturbance of memory becomes the predominant problem.

People disturbed in this way suddenly forget who they are. They cannot recall their name and addresses, and often cannot recognize these signs of identity even when supplied by police or relatives.

Amnesias usually last from a few hours to a month. They rarely persist for years. The neurotic may recover memory spontaneously, or may require hypnotic or other treatment.

Amnesias represent a way of avoiding the anxiety of conflict. By forgetting their identities, these neurotics shut their problems out of awareness. The dramatic quality of an amnesia usually overshadows less startling symptoms of general maladjustment.

Double Personality. Sometimes a dissociated neurotic who develops an amnesia for his true identity **replaces it with another identity.** This replacement is not consciously performed. Rather, the individual becomes suddenly convinced that he is a different person, with a different name and interests. While in this condition of double personality, the individual has no conscious knowledge of his previous name and life.

After many weeks, months, or even years, double personalities suddenly remember who they really are. In the same instant, they forget their alternate identity, and as in a fugue, cannot recall how they reached their present situations.

Like somnambulism, fugue, and amnesia, the dissociation of double personality is an attempt to solve a conflict of motives, by giving in to the forbidden motives only when not 'truly' conscious of the dereliction.

HYSTERIA

This group of neuroses are most noteworthy for their expression in **bodily conditions.**

To describe a condition in which a **psychological conflict is converted into a physical symptom,** Freud coined the term **'conversion hysteria'.** The word 'hysteria' goes back to ancient Greek medicine. It is derived from the Greek word for uterus. Its use reflected an old belief that hysteria was exclusively a feminine disease, due to disturbances of the womb. In popular use, the word means a condition of extreme emotional excitement: 'She was hysterical.' In psychiatric use, hysteria refers to the condition of an individual who converts anxiety into symptoms which then become more or less independent of the rest of the hysteric's personality.

For example, a soldier whose anxiety in battle becomes unbearable may suddenly lose his sight. Examinations will find nothing organically wrong with his eyes. Still, the hysterical soldier will insist that he is blind. Not until he is removed from the front lines will his vision return and even then his non-organic but psychologically induced (i.e. hysterical) blindness may persist. **Hysterical paralysis** is another common mechanism used by people who passionately desire to avoid situations that will distress them. An arm will begin to hang limp. Muscle tone, as measured by reflexes, diminishes. The limb becomes cold and bluish. If the hysterical paralysis continues for many years, the muscle may *actually* waste away.

Unlike malingerers, or people who consciously pretend to be ill, hysterics are **unaware of the psychic origin of their illnesses.** An hysteric will often show inconsistencies which a malingerer would take pains to avoid. Told to say 'yes' if he fells a pinprick, and 'no' if he does not feel it, an hysteric claiming a loss of feeling in a limb will often respond with a series of yesses and noes, even when blindfolded—failing to see the absurdity of reporting an absent sensation.

Another indication of the conscious sincerity of the hysteric's symptoms is the fact that they usually conform to popular ideas of anatomy rather than to the actual facts of body structure. An intelligent malingerer, before claiming to have lost feeling in his hand and arm, would do some research. Discovering that true anaesthesias occur in patches, he would not claim to have lost feeling in all of the skin below the elbow. However, this is the anaesthesia most commonly claimed by hysterics. It is called 'glove' anaesthesia, because the area that has supposedly gone dead covers the arm like a glove.

Behind a glove-anaesthesia, blindness, paralysis, convulsions, and the other symptoms of hysteria, stand several repressed emotions and motives, which these symptoms express and satisfy. There is, first of all, a great desire to avoid doing or experiencing some act or situation. Second, there is a great desire to be taken care of. It is this dependent streak that makes the hysterical personality particularly liable to suggestion. Many paralyses have been removed by giving sugar pills, called **placebos,** with the assurance that the medicine always works. Authorities other than the medical can also perform 'cures'. Almost certainly, the 'cured' individuals return to their old symptoms or develop new ones. The power of suggestion is limited to hysterical symptoms. It cannot eradicate their cause.

NEURASTHENIA

The term 'neurasthenia' was once applied to almost every neurosis. It is now limited to a condition whose predominant symptom is **continuous fatigue.** It is most common in the so-called 'nervous housewife' who is neglected by her family. It represents a repressed desire to stop functioning. This desire is a response to a feeling, also repressed, of inferiority and insecurity. By naturally leading to periods of rest, relaxation, and sleep, the symptom also satisfies a repressed desire to be dependent. It also wins attention and sympathy.

PSYCHOSOMATIC MEDICINE

In discussing hysterical paralysis of the arm, it was pointed out that the arm might actually shrink from disuse if the hysteria continued for a long time. This shrinkage, with its resultant true paralysis, would be a **secondary** effect of the repressed emotion causing the hysteria.

In some cases, it has been found that repressed emotion has direct, **primary** effects upon the body. These conditions have been termed '**psychosomatic**'. They express the fact that it is a '**somatic**' or bodily condition having a '**psychological**' origin. The evidence does not warrant the broad generalization that *all* illnesses are 'psychosomatic' as some psychiatric zealots would have us believe. However, there is no longer any doubt that **the distinction between mental and physical illnesses is not nearly as sharp as was previously thought.**

Of course, the **temporary** effects of emotion upon the body have always been acknowledged. This century, however, has seen the discovery that emotion, if repressed, can cause durable physical effects.

Among the physical complaints that have often been found to be related to their victims' traits of temperament and emotionality are ulcers, colitis, asthma, hives, high blood pressure, migraine headaches, impotence, and frigidity. The reader who recalls the internal changes of emotion described in a previous chapter will see that the complaints listed above are extreme and more durable forms of those changes.

THE MEANING OF NEUROSIS

By now it is clear that the symptoms of a neurosis are the results of unsuccessful attempt to adjust. A neurosis is an extreme form of an attempted adjustment mechanism. The neuroses are maladjustive because they do not get at the underlying cause of painful feelings. The person who adjusts by compensating, or withdrawing, or repressing, is like a person who keeps on taking aspirin for an aching tooth instead of going to the dentist to have it filled or extracted.

Like any other responses, these devices can become habitual. Such habits limit and distort the personality of the person who forms them. They keep one from various broadening and even reassuring experiences. They spoil human relationships.

If neurotic adjustments do not really adjust, why do people retain them? Doesn't the Law of Effect say that people learn through the reinforcing effect of success? If the neurotic mechanisms are maladjustive, how do they come to persist?

The persistence of maladjustive mechanisms can be accounted for by the fact that habits of adjustment are begun many years before the intelligence is fully matured. Neither the true meaning nor importance of parental taboos and other obstacles are apparent to the infant and child. The immature child responds to an immediate and narrow view of a situation. Children cannot distinguish the enormously important difference between self-control and self-frustration. Instead of understanding that parents and society want drives and motives channelled and directed, children think that drives and motives are to be thwarted and frustrated. In this way, the repressed personality is created. At puberty, force of habit makes the adolescent apply childish methods of 'control' to the sexual drive, with some form of neurosis as a possible result.

Traumatic Neuroses. Not all neuroses are the results of long-repressed conflicts. Any severe, sudden shock that can be interpreted as a real threat to existence may cause drastic changes even in a normal personality. Such disruptions are called **traumatic neuroses,** from the Greek word for shock, 'trauma'.

The symptoms vary. In mild cases, the patient is irritable and sensitive to noise. He perspires too much, his hands tremble, he suffers dizzy spells, and he feels nauseous. He tires easily and his efficiency drops. In severe cases, he may become paralysed and confused. He suffers terrifying nightmares, when he lives through the original accident or catastrophe again and again, or else he is destroyed, injured, or humiliated repeatedly.

These symptoms occur as often in people who are not harmed physically as in those who are wounded. The close approach to death makes them feel that they are helpless, and the world is hostile. Until pleasant life experiences or therapy reconditions them to confidence, the neurosis may persist. It has been called 'shell shock', 'battle fatigue', or 'war neurosis', and its soldier victims called 'psychos'.

METHODS OF PSYCHOTHERAPY

The goals of psychotherapy are to relieve neurotics of their symptoms, to increase their ability to be happy, to increase their efficiency, to aid them in social adaptations, to increase their spontaneity, and to adjust their bodily functions.

These effects can be achieved by any method that will increase the neurotic's feelings of esteem and security, release their repressed impulses, and increase their insight, self-acceptance, and striving towards positive goals.

Several methods of therapy have been developed that can help accomplish these ends. Some methods concentrate on only one of them. **Release therapy,** as indicated by its name, attempts to relieve the anxiety of inhibited children by getting them to express through play with dolls and toy furniture, the emotional responses they are learning to suppress. A similar technique for adults, called **psychodrama,** aims beyond mere release. By actually acting out improvised dramas, the participating adults gain insight into their true motives and concerns. In **group therapy,** a half-dozen neurotic patients freely discuss their difficulties and problems. The therapist contributes his interpretation of their problems. After a while, the members of the group come to see the fundamental identity of their problems and maladjustive solutions. They come out of their neurotic isolation, grow to like each other, and learn to accept the truth about themselves.

By far the most common therapeutic technique, however, is **individual therapy,** which centres on a conversation between therapist and patient. The therapist aims to have the patient, sooner or later, touch on *all* significant aspects of his life. He may guide the conversation or merely listen. In either case, the patient derives great relief just from talking about his troubles to an objective adult. Because the therapist listens without condemning, censoring, or being shocked, the patient loses his fear of motives and feelings. The patient is also influenced by the therapist's prestige, and he believes that he has strong help in facing the world and mastering his problems. If, in addition, the course of therapy succeeds, the patient will have learned that it is possible for him to form a healthy, affectionate, and self-respecting relationship with at least one individual—the therapist. This new ability is carried over to daily life, so that the patient is able to relate himself well to other people in his life.

What, besides listening permissively, does a therapist do? According to the nature of the neurosis and the personality of the patient, the therapist may:

> **interpret** the meaning of the patient's reactions;
> **reassure** him of his essential normalcy;
> **advise** the patient of possible alternate responses;
> **guide** towards rewarding experiences;
> **train** in social behaviour;
> **teach** how what he has learned in therapy can be integrated with the personality;
> **suggest** ways in which life can be stabilized and enriched;
> **re-condition** fears away;
> **change** his environment, either by getting the co-operation of the patient's family, or by putting him into an institution.

This last alternative is *always* chosen in cases of maladjustment so severe that the patients are liable to injure themselves or others, or to be injured economically or psychologically by continued freedom. Such maladjustments are much more likely to be among the psychoses

than the neuroses. The difference between these two groups of disorders, and the differences between the various kinds of psychoses,
will be the subject-matter of the next chapter.

The preceding section has discussed means of treating behavioural
'problems' using an analytical approach. A different method of treatment—and one whose value is gaining much recognition and acceptance—is based on the principles of learning theory and is broadly
referred to as **behaviour therapy**. The supporters of this approach argue
that neurotic behaviour is **a learned response** and should therefore be
treated by procedures based on mechanisms of learning. Broadly
speaking there are three main kinds of behaviour therapy:

Systematic Desensitization. This is a method of treatment used to
help eliminate phobias (such as extreme fear of open spaces, particular
animals, and so on) of normal (that is, not psychiatrically disturbed)
people.

There are at least three stages in carrying out treatment by systematic desensitization. First, it is necessary to draw up a hierarchy of the
situations which give rise to anxiety in the sufferer. Supposing, for
example, the patient was afraid of the sight and barking of dogs to
the point where a phobia had developed. Treatment would be likely
to take the following course. At the bottom of the hierarchy might be
imagining looking at a small, friendly dog. The second stage would be
to train the sufferer of the phobia to relax. In the third stage the
situations in the hierarchy would be proceeded through, starting with
the lowest and least anxiety-arousing, until the patient felt happy to
be standing beside and indeed pat a dog.

Aversion Therapy. This form of treatment has tended to be used to
eliminate behaviours which are regarded as socially unacceptable, such
as alcoholism or drug addiction. It usually takes the form of giving a
noxious stimulus—such as an electric shock or a drug which will produce a state of nausea—when the undesirable behaviour occurs. Thus
undesirable behaviour will become associated with an anxiety reaction
with the result that on future occasions the gratification which would
usually be provided by, say, taking drugs is **replaced** by a feeling of
anxiety and discomfort. Treatment using this form of therapy tends to
be quite brief and initial success is often followed by a high rate of
relapse.

**Operant Conditioning. This method of therapy is based on the princi-
ples of learning established by B. F. Skinner** and discussed in Chapter
4. Essentially operant training involves giving reinforcement to
those behaviours to be encouraged whilst ignoring those behaviours it
is hoped to eliminate. Thus **the desired behaviour is shaped by the use
of reinforcements.**

It is not always possible, however, to arrange a programme such
that reinforcement can be given immediately for appropriate be-

haviour. One way of dealing with such a problem has been to use the **token economy** system. This method is used in some psychiatric hospitals and involves giving patients tokens for behaviour deemed appropriate. These tokens act as **secondary reinforcers** and can later be exchanged for tangible rewards such as sweets, viewing a television programme, or going on an outing.

SUGGESTED FURTHER READING

Brown, D., and Padder, J., *Introduction to Psychotherapy*. Tavistock Publications: London, 1979.

Caplan, G., *Principles of Preventive Psychiatry*. Tavistock Publications: London, 1964.

Fordham, F., *Introduction to Jung's Psychology*. Penguin: London, 1953.

Foulkes, S. H., and Anthony, E. G., *Group Psychotherapy*. Reprinted with revisions, Penguin: London, 1973.

Freud, Anna, *The Ego and the Mechanisms of Defence*. Hogarth Press: London, 1961.

Freud, S., *Two Short Accounts of Psychoanalysis*. Penguin: London, 1962.

Haslam, M. T., *Psychiatry Made Simple*. Heinemann: London, 1982.

Orford, J., *The Social Psychology of Mental Disorder*. Penguin: London, 1976.

Ransom, J. A., *An Introduction to Social Psychiatry*. Penguin: London, 1971.

Rycroft, C. (Ed.), *Psychoanalysis Observed*. Penguin: London, 1968.

Sulloway, F. J., *Freud: Biologist of the Mind*. Fontana: London, 1980.

Wolf, S., *Children Under Stress*. Penguin: London, 1973.

17

THE ABNORMAL PERSONALITY

People whose behaviour differs widely and steadily from normal social requirements are called **abnormal.** Since societies differ in their requirements, an act that is normal in one place may be abnormal in another. There is no society, however, that does not have *some* moral, ethical, or criminal laws. In every society, consistent, serious, and inappropriate disobedience of the written and unwritten laws is considered a sign of abnormality.

Some abnormal personalities are harmless. Inventors of perpetual motion machines, food faddists, and some tramps and hoboes are usually quite harmless. Other abnormal personalities may harm themselves or others, either by acts of violence or by failure to act responsibly. As a rule, such dangerously abnormal people need to be put into institutions, for their own good, and for the good of society. Psychotics whose particular derangement is a passionate belief that everyone is about to kill them must be cared for in mental hospitals, since they feel obliged to attack everyone near them. As more and more criminals are found to be mentally retarded, severely neurotic, psychopathic, or psychotic, prisons take on aspects of the therapeutic institutions.

DELINQUENT PERSONALITIES

The problem of crime has fascinated the popular and professional mind throughout history. Criminal traits, like desirable traits, have been variously attributed to heredity, to environment, and to the interplay of both. Those theorists who blame juvenile and adult delinquency on environmental factors differ among themselves, disputing whether the family or the society is more influential.

Psychologists now believe that no one theory has a monopoly of the truth. Some delinquency may in part be due to mental retardation. Today, however, it is recognised that in attempting to explain delinquency we must look for multicausal agencies.

Many crimes against people and property are committed by individuals suffering from the neuroses known as the **manias.** Theft, arson, rape, assault, and manslaughter are some of the terrible acts that kleptomaniacs, pyromaniacs, and other maniacal neurotics feel compelled to commit.

Some criminal acts are committed by otherwise normal people in situations of great emotional stress. The outraged husband who kills his wife's seducer, the unemployed father who steals to buy food for his hungry family, are not uncommon figures. Such 'criminals' are usually dealt with lightly, on the grounds that crime is not their habital adjustment.

What about people who are not mentally retarded, not neurotically maniacal, and not emotionally excited when they plan their crimes—the so-called professional criminals? Just what is wrong, besides their behaviour, with burglars, robbers, confidence men, racketeers, gangsters, and killers?

Some psychologists would probably preface an answer to this question with a question of their own: 'Does the given criminal feel guilty about his crimes?' If the answer is yes, the psychologist would be apt to say that the criminal's maladjustment is the result of imperfect socialization. Such a criminal never *fully* incorporated into his own personality the ideals of society. That he *partially* adopted social ideals is shown by his guilt. Guilt feelings on the part of the professional criminals are by no means uncommon. Some criminals actually seem to invite capture, by stupid oversights not befitting their general intelligence. Apparently, these criminals unconsciously desire punishment, to relieve repressed guilt feelings. The element of childish rebellion and revenge is often present, too.

Not all professional criminals feel guilty, however. Some are convinced that their acts are justified. Others do not truly understand the immoral nature of their acts. These last are the psychopathic personalities often referred to as 'psychopaths'.

PSYCHOPATHIC PERSONALITY

The psychopathic personality has no moral scruples—no conscience. He does, is, and takes what he wants, as the whim moves him. He has no guilt feelings, and lies glibly. To express this attitude, we might turn to a pair of once popular songs whose refrains have passed into the language:

> *'Oh, the world owes me a living!'*
> *'Oh, there ain't no strings on me!'*

The psychopath is to be distinguished from other kinds of delinquents. Unlike them, he is not acting in rebellion. He acts as he does because his personality lacks an ideal self. The psychopath is totally unsocialized. He is incapable of self-criticism because there is no part of his personality in opposition to his drives.

When their life histories are investigated, some psychopaths are found to have been over-indulged in childhood. Their every whim was gratified, their every deed condoned. They were favoured and forgiven in everything. Other psychopaths seem to have suffered severe deprivation and rejection in childhood.

Not every maladjustment with this cause is severe enough to be labelled psychopathic. Still, people who have been consistently over-indulged or severely deprived show the following characteristics:

> Selfish, demanding behaviour.
> Very low tolerance for frustration.
> Difficulty in adjusting to authority.
> Difficulty in tolerating monotony and routine.
> Lack of discipline.
> Impoliteness.

Such people, whose lives are one continuous search for gratification, are miserable when not indulged, and—as the lives of certain Caesars show—bored when they are indulged.

PSYCHOSIS AND INSANITY

It was pointed out before that some criminal acts are committed by psychotics—that is, by people whose personalities are so severely disturbed that they are totally out of touch with reality. The psychological word for such a disordered condition is **psychosis.** Not all psychotics commit *criminal* acts, but all of them behave in ways that most people would agree are inappropriate to their situations. (Psychotics are the unfortunate people often referred to by some as 'crazy', 'mad', 'nuts', and 'insane'.)

Actually, the words 'insane' and 'psychotic' are not exactly equivalent. Insane is a **legal** word. It means being ignorant of the difference between right and wrong, or being unable to control one's actions in the normal way. Psychotic is a **medical** word. It means being maladjusted at all levels of personality.

PSYCHOSIS AND NEUROSIS

If a psychotic is totally maladjusted, lacking in normal self-control, and unrealistic, how does he differ from a neurotic?

A neurosis certainly interferes with the enjoyment and control of reality. However, there is nothing seriously wrong with the neurotic's perceptions and conceptions of reality. Outside the area of his symptoms, he is in normal touch with his environment.

Turning to the more serious maladjustments, we find a different situation. The psychotic person is quite out of touch with his environment. He is either unable or unwilling to check the truth of his conceptions against the facts of his perceptions. Therefore, he gives up distinguishing between fantasy and reality. To fit his ideas of himself and the world, he distorts reality, sometimes up to the point of denying its true nature completely.

To be sure, some degree of distortion and denial is to be found even in normal people. According to their mood, they see the world as more or less pleasant, and guide their behaviour to fit the estimate. In times of trouble, they may find themselves wanting to shift the blame away from themselves. When lonely or bored, they may catch themselves drifting into daydreams.

However, normal people do not fool themselves for long. They are *amused* by their distortions. The neurotics acknowledge that there is something vitally wrong with themselves. Not so the psychotics. They are unaware of reality in the throes of their distortions.

There are three ways of being so unrealistic that behaviour becomes profoundly maladjusted. A psychotic personality can have:

imaginary perceptions called **'hallucinations'**;
unjustified conceptions, called **'delusions'**;
inappropriate emotional states which take the form of deep **melancholia** or an uncontrolled euphoria.

Hallucinations. Hallucinations are sensory experiences for which no adequate sensory stimulus can be discovered. If a person claims to hear a voice at a time when no sound is audible, this experience is called hallucinatory. Shapes and objects reportedly seen when no such stimuli are visible are likewise hallucinatory. Strictly speaking, such normal experiences as dreams, fantasies, visual memories, and anticipations are all hallucinations.

What distinguishes psychotic hallucinations from such normal hallucinations? In general, the psychotic is not as likely as the neurotic or normal person to realize that his hallucinations are caused by internal stimuli. However, some psychotics do realize that their hallucinations are not real. Likewise, some perfectly normal people have mistaken daydreams for reality. Under hypnosis, hallucinations can be suggested with ease to people who are definitely not psychotic.

Actually, the only difference between psychotic and non-psychotic hallucinations is the fact that psychotics are so much more wrapped up in their problems that they make less effort to tell imagination from reality. Therefore they are more liable to include hallucinations among their reported experiences.

The material of hallucinations, including dreams, is formed from the individual's memories, both conscious and repressed, both recent and long past. Hallucinations reflect the motives, the interests, the preoccupations, and the experiences of the individual. Since a psychosis, like a neurosis, is a way of responding to great stresses, it is not surprising that most psychotic hallucinations are unpleasant.

Typically, a psychotic sees enemies threatening him, hears voices cursing him, smells foul odours, tastes putrid flavours, and feels disgusting touch sensations, such as being bitten or crawled upon by vermin.

This last hallucination, depending as it does upon an interpretation of a tactile sensation of prickling, verges on being a delusion.

Delusions. Delusions are beliefs or convictions that are firmly held despite objective evidence to the contrary. Delusions go beyond neurotic obsessions, as the obsessions go beyond prejudices. A normal person can, if he wishes, usually eradicate a prejudice; a neurotic cannot eradicate an obsession, but is critical of it; however, a psychotic accepts his delusion wholeheartedly. There are three general classes of delusions; the expansive, the derogatory, and the persecutory.

Expansive delusions are direct compensations for feelings of inadequacy. These are beliefs in the possession of immense abilities or property. They include **delusions of grandeur,** in which the psychotic may believe himself to be a president, Napoleon, Satan, Jesus, or God.

Derogatory delusions include convictions of worthlessness, evil, depravity, or sickness. In this type, psychotics may believe themselves to be suffering loathsome diseases, guilty of the unspeakable sin, or literally rotting away internally.

Persecutory delusions are unjustified beliefs in the existence of enemies dedicated to the injury of the individual or his loved ones. Sometimes these imagined enemies are believed to have taken control of the psychotic's body, either to inflict pain or to lead him into danger.

Because delusions satisfy emotional needs, rational arguments do not affect them. The psychotic's intellect is utterly at the mercy of his emotions.

Disordered Emotions. Another difference between psychotic and neurotic or normal behaviour is the exaggerated and inappropriate nature of psychotic emotions. The psychotic is either too happy or too sad, too optimistic or too pessimistic, too irritable or too calm.

Which emotions will predominate in any given case depends upon the kind of psychosis suffered by the individual psychotic or the transitory stage of the psychosis. Psychosis, like neurosis, takes more forms than one and many of the forms blend into one another even though we may describe them as separate entities for ease of comprehension.

THE KINDS OF PSYCHOSES

Some psychoses, like all of the neuroses, seem to be caused by purely psychological factors. No detectable deteriorations in the victim's nervous systems account for their symptoms. All that can be said is that the personality does not function properly. These are called **functional** psychoses.

Other mental hospital patients suffer from psychoses that have been shown to follow physical changes and deteriorations. These are called **organic** psychoses.

THE ORGANIC PSYCHOSES

Organic psychoses are attributed to many different kinds of causes; inborn brain defects; brain infections; intoxication; head injuries; circulation disorders; seizures; bodily changes of growth and ageing; tumours or cancers; and unknown physical causes.

Each of these conditions can alter behaviour so severely that it appears irrational and prevents effective adjustment. For purposes of study, let us select the three most important of these organic psychoses: **general paresis, alcoholic reactions,** and **senile dementia.**

General Paresis. This condition is caused by syphilitic damage to the brain. Because of modern control and treatment of venereal disease, only a small percentage of people who contract syphilis develop **general paresis.** The condition appears from two to thirty years after the original infection. It comes on gradually. There is an increasing indifference to neatness, punctuality, and previous interests. The paretic becomes irritable or over-sentimental. Efficiency, memory, and energy decline. Soon the intellect is affected. Speech defects appear; the paretic cannot easily pronounce such phrases as 'Methodist Episcopal', 'General Electric', 'rough-riding artillery brigade', or 'truly rural'.

If not treated, general paresis rapidly leads to a vegetative state, followed by death within a year or two. Luckily, modern fever therapy can improve the majority of cases of general paresis.

Alcoholic Reactions. The use of alcohol and other drugs to relieve anxiety and guilt feelings is literally as old as history. Here we shall discuss alcoholic reactions as one example of the broad area concerning the inappropriate use of drugs.

Brewing, like baking, is based on fermentation of grain; grain requires farming; and farming leads to markets, roads, and civilization, and thus to history. Civilization, like alcohol, was a by-product of agriculture. Since their common origin, they have remained inseparable.

Alcohol relieves the tensions of civilized life by depressing the nervous system, starting with the highest and most complex structure, the cerebral cortex, which is the site of discrimination. The behavioural effects of alcohol are therefore **regressive.** The drinker grows more and more immature as he drinks. First to go is the conscience, which has accurately been called the 'alcohol-soluble part of the personality'. Second to go is emotional control; next, speech patterns are affected; then motor control is lost, including control of the bladder and bowel.

Since this technique of dealing with problems is temporary, it does nothing to solve them, and indeed creates new problems; excessive drinking is obviously a maladjustive mechanism.

At any of these levels, but particularly at an acute stage, the drinker is actually (though temporarily) psychotic. The individual's personality will determine the form and content of the psychosis; but in *every* case, the alcoholic release of learned inhibitions will coarsen the personality, since the motives normally repressed are aggressive, sexual, and excretory.

In **pathological intoxication,** the individual reacts violently to even small amounts of alcohol, with an amnesia for the extreme behaviour when recovered. In *Arrowsmith*, Sinclair Lewis gives a good description of pathological intoxication—a drunken student named Duer, whom the hero keeps from killing a man, fails to remember the incident the next day.

In **acute alcoholic hallucinosis,** the individual hears accusing voices, which frighten him extremely, the more so because he is otherwise well oriented and alert. The hallucinosis rarely lasts more than two weeks.

Another psychotic reaction to alcohol is **delirium tremens.** This condition is quite serious, contrary to the joking attitude of cartoonists and comedians, who laughingly refer to it as the D.T.s. The symptoms of delirium tremens usually appear in chronic alcoholics with years of heavy drinking behind them. Following a drinking bout, the individual suddenly has vivid and terrifying hallucinations, becomes confused, fatigued, tremulous, and unable to sleep. The delirium lasts from three to six days. During such exhausting episodes, at least 3 per cent of the patients die of heart failure.

Since heavy drinkers prefer drinking to eating, forget to eat, or cannot afford to spend whisky money on food, they usually suffer vitamin deficiencies, particularly of vitamin B. This deficiency has permanent effects on the brain, nerves, liver, and kidneys, and with the alcohol, causes a psychotic reaction called **Korsakoff's syndrome.** This psychosis is marked by the forgetting of recent events, the telling of lies to cover up the amnesia, disorientation in time and space, and emotional instability. It lasts as long as two months, and may be permanent.

The Problem Drinker. A problem drinker is defined as a person whose excessive drinking repeatedly interferes with his health or personal relations, and whose work is thereby reduced in efficiency and dependability. As in any other disease, the symptoms of problem drinking must be recognized before help can be given. (The following is a description of the usual steps in the development of a problem drinker.)

The Pre-Alcoholic Stage. The first steps towards alcoholism begin when drinking is no longer social but psychological—a release from tension and inhibition. Though still in reasonable control of his drinking, the problem drinker begins to show a definite behaviour pattern. These pre-alcoholic symptoms include:

Gross drinking behaviour. The individual begins to drink more heavily and more often with his friends. 'Getting tight' becomes a habit. When drunk, he may develop a 'big-shot' complex, throw his money around, make pointless long-distance telephone calls, and so on.

Blackouts. The individual starts to forget what happened 'the night before'. These blackouts are not the result of passing out, but a sort of amnesia. They sometimes happen to ordinary drinkers, but in people moving towards alcoholism they tend to develop into a pattern.

Gulping and sneaking drinks. More and more dependent on the pampering effects of alcohol, he tends to 'toss off' his drinks, rather than sip them. He sneaks extra drinks, or has a couple before the party. He feels guilty, and avoids talking about drinking.

Chronic hangover. As he becomes more and more reliant on alcohol to cushion the shocks of daily living, the 'morning after' becomes increasingly uncomfortable and more frequent. This is the final danger signal; next step—alcoholism.

Early-Stage Alcoholism. Until now, the problem drinker has been drinking *heavily*, but not always *conspicuously*. More important, he has been able to stop drinking when he chooses. But beyond *this* point, he will develop the symptoms of early-stage alcoholism with increasing rapidity:

Loss of control. This is the mark of the alcoholic. In this phase, he can refuse to start drinking, but can't stop drinking once he starts. A single drink is likely to trigger a chain reaction and he will drink himself to complete intoxication.

Alibi system. He feels guilty and defensive about his lack of control. He therefore erects an elaborate system of 'reasons' for drinking, partly to answer family and associates, but mostly to reassure himself.

Eye openers. Now the individual needs a drink in the morning to 'start the day right'. This 'medicinal' drink helps kill the effects of increasingly painful hangovers: feelings of guilt, remorse, and depression. He cannot face the day without it.

Changing the pattern. Under pressure from family or employer, he tries to break the hold alcohol has upon him. He sets up rules on when or what he will drink. He may 'go on the wagon' for a while. But one drop of alcohol can start the chain reaction again.

Anti-social behaviour. The problem drinker comes to prefer drinking alone, or with other alcoholics no matter what their social level. He broods over imagined wrongs. He thinks people are staring at or talking about him. He is highly critical of others. He may become destructive or violent.

Loss of jobs and friends. His continuing anti-social behaviour causes him to be dropped from jobs, and leads his friends to turn away from him. As a defensive measure, he may quit before he can be fired, and drop his friends first.

Seeking medical aid. Physical and mental erosion caused by his uncontrolled drinking leads him to make the rounds of hospitals, doctors, and psychiatrists. But he seldom receives lasting benefit because he refuses to co-operate or admit the extent of his drinking.

Late-Stage Alcoholism. Until he reached this point, the alcoholic had a choice: to drink, or not to drink; though *once he began*, he had no control of his drinking. In the later stages of alcoholism, there is no choice: the problem drinker must drink however and whenever he can. The symptoms of this stage are:

Benders. The individual now drinks for days at a time, getting blindly and helplessly drunk. He utterly disregards everything—family, job, even food and shelter. These periodic escapes into oblivion mark the beginning of the final, chronic phase of alcoholism: drinking to escape problems caused by drinking.

Tremors. The alcoholic develops 'the shakes', a serious nervous condition. The alcoholic diseases already discussed often begin at this time. After these attacks he swears off, but cannot stay away from alcohol for very long.

Protecting the supply. Having a supply of alcohol available is the most important thing in his life. He will do or sell anything to get it, and will hide his bottles to protect them for future needs.

Unreasonable resentments. In the late stages of alcoholism, the problem drinker shows hostility towards others, both as possible threats to his precious liquor supply and as a turning outward of the unconscious desire to punish himself.

Nameless fears and anxieties. Now the problem drinker is constantly afraid of something which he cannot pin down or even put into words. He feels a sense of impending doom and destruction. Nervous, shaky, he is utterly unable to face life without the support of alcohol.

Collapse of the alibi system. No longer able to make excuses for himself, or put the blame on others, he admits to himself that he is licked, that his drinking is beyond his ability to control. (This admission may be made in earlier stages, too, and be repeated many times.)

Surrender process. If the problem drinker is to recover at this stage, he must give up the idea of *ever* drinking again, and must be willing to seek and accept help. This must take place with the collapse of the alibi system. Only when they occur *together* is there any hope of recovery.

Helping the Problem Drinker. Alcoholism can be caught and successfully treated long before it reaches these final phases. For specific information, one can consult the local Health Department or the local branch of Alcoholics Anonymous. In general, the first step in treatment is to stop the patient's drinking. Next, his personality must be rebuilt, to exclude the maladjustive mechanism of drinking, and to include the adjustive mechanism of direct problem-solving. Voluntary associations like Alcoholics Anonymous often can help with the first and second step, and psychotherapists or behaviour therapists with the third step. Thus far, however, no method has been successful in every case.

Senile Dementia. As alcoholism is less hopeful of cure than general paresis, still less hopeful than alcoholism is **senile dementia.** This condition is the result of the degeneration and disappearance of nerve cells in the brain, due to normal ageing.

In the early stages of senile dementia, there is a gradual loss of inhibition and social learning. Slowly the range of interests shrink, thinking slows, memory fails, orientation in time and space is lost, delusions occur, and emotions become disturbed. At last the patient dies.

Some of these symptoms are due to the brain damage itself. Others are the individual's reactions to the impaired functioning. This is true of *all* of the organic psychoses. The psychological changes result not only from a direct disturbance of the brain but also from the individual's reaction to the disturbance. Thus, when brain cells wither away, a person's emotional control and memory suffers. Since the person becomes ashamed of his behaviour, additional irritability results.

Symptoms of Organic Psychoses. In general, all victims of organic psychoses show three kinds of symptoms: **release; interference; compensation symptoms.**

Release symptoms are those that result from weakening inhibition. The alcoholic shows very clearly the behavioural effects of progressive loss of cerebral control over primitive drives and urges.

Interference symptoms result from the loss of awareness and learning ability. In extreme form this loss of awareness is unconsciousness. In lesser degree, it shows itself in amnesia, dementia, and aphasia. In **amnesia** there is a loss of memory for events, places, persons, and in the extreme an unawareness of the victim's own identity. In **dementia** there occurs a loss of contact with reality. **Aphasia** is shown as a psychological loss of the ability to communicate with symbols. Some aphasias impede speech. Other aphasias interfere with the expression of ideas through symbols. The individual cannot speak or write.

Compensation symptoms reveal the individual's attempts to deal with the interference symptoms. These attempts use the adjustive mechanisms discussed in an earlier chapter. The impaired individual avoids situations where defects would be noticeable; or replaces the abilities with others, real or imaginary; or repeats what few forms of response remain. This perseveration, if verbal, takes the form of 'automatic phrases'. The victim meets every situation with the same response, such as 'Well, what do you know!', 'I'll try to do my best,' 'Yes, yes,' 'I see,' or some other phrase, once appropriate but now useless.

FUNCTIONAL PSYCHOSES

If a person behaves peculiarly enough to be adjudged psychotic, but has no physical symptoms of organic impairment, the psychosis is called **functional.** These psychoses are assumed to be reactions to a lifetime of psychological discord. Psychologists believe that the primary problems of functional psychotics, like those of neurotics, are transformed into an attempt to escape anxiety. However, the psychotic has either not used the usual neurotic mechanisms for dealing with anxiety, or has been forced to abandon them by the continuing severity of his problems. **Psychotic behaviour may thus be thought of as last-ditch efforts to deal with the anxiety aroused by psychic shocks.**

The personal significance of symptoms is not easily discovered. Once a psychosis is well under way, the patient does not co-operate well with attempts to understand him. In fact, his symptoms often serve as a defence against possible insight. Probing and persistent study show, however, that the psychotic symptoms about to be described express the same kind of fear expressed by neurotic symptoms. They are anxious fears of catastrophe. At the same time, they *are* catastrophes. That is, they express complete discouragement and giving up in the face of the problem.

Psychotic Depression. Psychotic depression is expressed in three ways—**emotionally, physically, and intellectually.** The depressed patient feels discouraged, worthless, and hopeless. His sadness continues even in funny situations. He finds it hard to become interested in his surroundings. He must exert great effort to do anything. He works slowly and he thinks slowly. He has to force himself to answer questions. In extreme depression, called **stupor,** the patient says and does nothing. He must be fed and otherwise taken care of.

Psychotic depression goes beyond the neurotic depression of neurasthenia. It lasts longer, goes deeper, and is more likely to result in suicide. It is the main symptom in two functional psychoses, **involutional melancholia** and **manic-depressive psychosis.** These are called affective disorders, because their major symptoms are **derangements of emotion.**

Involutional Melancholia. To certain people who have had no previous mental illness, late middle age brings a period of depression so deep as to be considered psychotic. This condition is called involutional melancholia. For a long time, it was considered to be an *organic* psychosis, caused by endocrine disturbances or other first signs of beginning old age. However, no hormones yet known improve cases of involutional melancholia. It is now felt that the approach of old age may represent enough of a psychological shock to cause psychotic depression in people who have not prepared themselves to deal with it. For the first time in their lives, they fully realize that human life is mortal, that they will have increasingly less energy and time to fulfil their purposes, and that they have wasted their lives on trivia.

As one watches an involutional melancholic, the overwhelming impression is of great regret of the past, and fear of the future. The depression coexists with anxiety, preoccupation with thoughts of death, and delusions of bodily decay. The danger of suicide is very great.

Some people in the deep despair of melancholia will imagine they are already dead. They will tell you the date, hour, and means of their death.

Most victims of melancholia have feelings of guilt and uselessness, based on the sexual changes they are undergoing as they live through the **climacteric,** or 'change of life'. In women, the climacteric is called **menopause.** Strictly speaking, this term refers to the stopping of the periodic menstrual flow in women. Menopause usually takes place sometime between the age of forty and fifty, and stretches over a period of one to two years. It is usually attended by mild personality disturbances. Only in extreme cases does a woman develop involutional melancholia. Even normal women, however, sometimes fear that sexual impotence has occurred. This is a groundless fear. For many women, as Walter Pitkin says, 'Life begins at forty'. For the first time in their marital life, they are able after menopause to have sexual relations without the fear of pregnancy. Continued development in contraceptive techniques, particularly in widespread use of the 'pill', is, of course, now having a radical effect on this fear.

The Male Climacteric. In the popular mind, 'change of life' is associated only with women. However, the masculine sex also experiences a comparable climacteric period. Few men, and even fewer women, are aware of this fact. Fore-knowledge of the physical and sexual changes that occur in a man at this time of life can save husbands and wives much heartache.

During their climacteric, some men will become irritable, anxious, and restless. Others will experience headaches, heart palpitations, dizziness, sleeplessness, slight forgetfulness, and depression. These symptoms usually pass off with a return to normalcy in a few months. Meanwhile, people will be saying of such a man, usually in his fifties, 'I don't know what's come over him; he's so different.' As in the case of the female, there will be a small percentage who succumb to the irrationality of involutional melancholia.

In his fifties, even the most vigorous male may experience a period of sexual inability that can last from a few months to possibly a year or more. Uninformed wives wrongly accuse their impotent mates of infidelity. This male lapse is usually temporary. It is generally followed by return to sexual virility *and* fertility, unlike the case of the female, who retains her desire but loses the ability to become pregnant (fertility).

No man should feel humiliated or despondent over his lack of virility, or inability to complete the sex act, during his climacteric period. Such inability is a normal occurrence. No artificial forms of restoring or prolonging virility have ever been adopted by the medical profession as a whole. Aphrodisiacs, love potions, and gland grafts are worthless. However, while science has not yet discovered the secret of prolonged sexual power, it does know how to treat the physical and psychological changes that accompany these 'changes in life'. Male and female sex hormones can prevent or alleviate the hot and cold flushes, mental depression, sleeplessness, and irritability of both men and women during their climacterics. Unfortunately, one in two thousand people will become mentally unbalanced despite such treatments.

Manic-Depressive Psychosis. When psychotic depression occurs earlier in life, particularly before or after an episode of **wild elation,** it is considered to be a symptom of the other affective disorder, **manic-depressive psychosis.** This disorder usually occurs in alternating episodes of depression and elation. Some patients suffer only periods of depression. Others have only elated periods. Still others alternate between the two extremes. It was these cyclical patients who gave the psychosis its name.

Psychotic Mania. In contrast to the depressed patient, the manic patient is extremely outgoing. He keeps moving about. He talks almost without stopping to breathe. He laughs, he shouts, he sings. He seems to be overjoyed. His mind is so active that it flits from one idea to another.

In mild cases, or in the early stages of mania, the individual behaves more rashly than usual. He talks a lot and laughs freely. He spends his money freely. His sexual behaviour is looser. This state is called **'hypomanic'.** It may clear up by itself, or after treatment, or it may lead to a fully manic state.

The manic patient obviously expresses a sense of freedom from restraint. He is having a 'fling'. Flouting his usual moral code, his symptoms express the attitudes that are normally repressed. He is sexually promiscuous, arrogant, bold, and exhibitionistic. The manic patient overcomes the moral obstacles of the world by ignoring them.

Attacks of depression and elation may develop slowly or suddenly. They last from six months to a year. They often, but not always, recur. Between attacks, patients are essentially normal for as long as several years. There are no permanent intellectual or emotional after-effects of an attack of depression or elation. The general history of manic-depressive psychosis may reveal anywhere from two to five or more periods of hospitalization and remission in a lifetime.

SCHIZOPHRENIA

Manic-depressive psychosis was named towards the end of the last century by the German psychiatrist Emil Kraepelin. In describing that disorder, Kraepelin contrasted it with a different illness which he termed **'dementia praecox',** or precocious dementia. He so named it for two reasons. From his limited observations, he believed that the condition always led to deterioration of the intellect, and always showed itself early in life. Subsequent observations and studies have indicated that this disease does not always dement its victims nor occur necessarily early in life. Therefore, present-day psychology has adopted another name for it, **schizophrenia,** which means 'split mind'. This name was given to it by Eugen Bleuler, another German psychiatrist. Bleuler emphasized the splitting from reality commonly observed in this ailment. When he coined the word 'schizophrenia' he was describing the inconsistency between the behaviour and emotion of the schizophrenic patient. For example, the victim may claim to be Napoleon, but he does not mind waiting on tables in the hospital cafeteria. He may be emotionally indifferent to the 'fact' that he is being tortured. He may stand before you with full serenity and say, 'How can I go to work when I haven't any feet?' He is no longer motivated by real goals and facts, but by the whims of shifting fantasies.

One of the main differences between schizophrenia and manic-depressive psychosis is this lack of consistency. In the latter disorder, all of the personality functions—thought, emotion, behaviour—express the patient's mood of elation or depression. The excited manic patient will respond fleetingly or exaggeratedly to changes in surroundings that the excited schizophrenic patient may ignore. The schizophrenic reacts largely to the hallucinations that are exciting to him. Thus, the schizophrenic is often apathetic. The feelings he does show have nothing to do with his surroundings. They express reactions to his imaginary experiences.

Individual schizophrenic patients have different kinds of symptoms. However, they all deny objective reality, disregarding the evidence of their senses. They replace reality with hallucinations, or false perceptions. These hallucinations express delusions, or false beliefs.

Primarily the symptoms of schizophrenia express the condition of withdrawal from reality into fantasy. The schizophrenic is emotionally detached from his environment. He does not care whether or not he communicates with the people around him. If he does talk, it is not to converse but to express his fantasies. The patient's language often cannot be understood. There are five forms of schizophrenia: **simple; acute; catatonic; hebephrenic;** and **paranoid.**

Simple Schizophrenia. Simple schizophrenics have few delusions or hallucinations. The major sign of their psychosis is a mild withdrawal from social and personal relationships. They lack interest in other people and they are indifferent to social standards. Simple schizophrenics may become vagabonds or minor delinquents, wandering around the country doing odd jobs, stealing, seemingly indifferent to pain, discomfort, filth, hunger, danger, and disgrace.

Acute Schizophrenic Panic. Patients who suffer acute schizophrenic panic have a sudden, severe psychosis that runs a short but stormy course. An extremely agitated panic is accompanied by delusions and hallucinations. This psychosis accounts for many so-called **'nervous breakdowns'.**

Catatonic Schizophrenia. In contrast to the simple schizophrenic's indifference to society, the catatonic schizophrenics are hostile to society. Their hostility is shown in either or both of two ways: through a general inhibition of all movement, or through excessive and excited aggression. They may sit motionless for hours or bounce around excitedly bubbling over with the pressure of talk and activity.

The inhibition of movement resembles the negativism of childhood. The rigid, apparently stuporous catatonic is actually alert, keenly observing the environment. His complete, statue-like inactivity is also comparable to the frozen immobility of hunted animals.

If the catatonic shifts to the excited state, the underlying hostility is clearly evident. Aggressive catatonics have no equals for sheer aggressive energy. They may run amok, killing and destroying with superhuman strength. This general aggressiveness resembles childhood, temper tantrums, exaggerated by mature power and deranged purpose.

This regressive form of schizophrenia has the best chance for complete recovery. From the many first-hand reports of cured catatonics, psychologists learned that even the motionless catatonics were watchfully alert against members of society they hated.

Hebephrenic Schizophrenia. The word hebephrenic comes from two Greek words meaning 'youthful mind'. It is this form of schizophrenia that most people have in mind when they call someone 'a crazy fool'. Its chief symptoms are silliness, dissociation of emotion from intellect, and peculiar delusions and hallucinations. In addition, the hebephrenic makes apparently meaningless grimaces and gestures. If not treated, the intellect appears to deteriorate rapidly and permanently, although this may be the effect of an inability to communicate. All of this behaviour reflects the hebephrenic's complete break with the usual human concepts of reality. The hebephrenic lives almost entirely in a fantasy world of his own. He takes figures of speech literally. The words in his sentences are connected by sound rather than sense, or by purely private meanings. His actions are symbolic, though the symbolism is usually too private to be understood. In short, the hebephrenic has not only withdrawn from reality but has substituted a synthetic reality for it. This makes it doubly hard to cure him.

Paranoid Schizophrenics. Appearing somewhat later in life than the other forms is paranoid schizophrenia. The paranoid schizophrenic also has much of the disordered emotion and thinking of the other schizophrenics. The major symptom, however, is **systematized delusions of persecution and grandeur.** These delusional systems are very resistant to therapy. Like the hysterical neurotic's physical symptom, the paranoid schizophrenic's delusion enables him to dissociate his anxiety from its true source. In paranoid schizophrenia, this source of anxiety may be a result of repressed homosexuality. The social taboos against homosexual activity create conflicts, fear, and feelings of insecurity and guilt. By projecting these feelings, and by compensating for them, the paranoid schizophrenic reduces his anxiety, at the cost of rationality.

Paranoid States. From about the age of thirty-five on, or at the time when the individual first starts to experience sexual and business competition from younger people, a person may develop a brief delusion of persecution, following a situation of failure or frustration. These episodes are called paranoid states. Except for the delusion, the individual's hold on reality is normal, and the outlook is very good for a return to complete normality. For these reasons, the paranoid states are distinguished from paranoid schizophrenia.

Paranoia. An infrequent but important psychosis is the disorder called paranoia. It is important because quite often the condition goes unrecognized for years. It is a perfect, permanent paranoid state. Except for his complex, consistent, and dangerously persuasive delusional system, the paranoiac may appear normal, without hallucinations, and without intellectual impairment.

The paranoiac applies all of his adult intelligence and energy to creating and perfecting a hypothesis that is factually false but emotionally 'true'. He will not test its objectivity, focusing his critical ability only on its internal logical consistency, so that he may overcome objections with subtle reasoning. It is quite possible for paranoiacs to achieve political leadership, in which case they can be very dangerous. Psychiatrists have speculated that Ivan the Terrible and Adolf Hitler became paranoic personalities.

THE TREATMENT OF PSYCHOTICS

The main difficulty in treating psychotic patients is their failure to acknowledge reality. This makes it hard to communicate with them.

There is no way to be sure that one's words have their normal dictionary meanings to the psychotic mind.

It can be unnerving to have one's words ignored, misinterpreted, or reacted to with violence. Down through history, psychotic symptoms have aroused fear in the majority of the population. Until fairly recent times, and to some extent still today, society has preferred torturing or avoiding abnormal personalities to understanding them. Called fools and madmen, and thought to be possessed by devils, psychotic people have been allowed to roam at will or have been brutally imprisoned. The word 'bedlam' is a mispronunciation of 'Bethlehem', the name of an institution in London in which psychotics were once cruelly confined, but are now, of course, treated permissively and with the latest techniques.

Three Trends in Treatment. During the last century, however, three trends of thought arose that have combined to form the positive attitude of modern psychiatry. One was the **humanitarian** attitude towards helpless and unfortunate people. It emphasized the right of psychotic patients to be treated as human beings. Another was the **medical** approach to psychiatric problems. In the belief that all psychoses have organic causes, careful and systematic observations were made of their symptoms. Though only the organic psychoses have been shown to be the result of physical changes, the observations brought order out of the chaos of symptoms.

The most recent trend in psychiatry might be called the **psychological** approach. It is based on the idea that personalities do not become abnormal by accident or only because the brain is damaged. The emotional meaning of the symptoms is sought. The interest is not merely on the patient's present state but on the psychological origin of this state. The emphasis is on personal history.

Put into practice, these three attitudes have led to the establishment of humane mental hospitals, in which a variety of physical and psychological methods of treatment are used to make contact with the patient and help him achieve a certain degree of insight. **Sedatives** are used to calm him, giving his body a chance to rebuild its exhausted energy reserves. **Narcosis,** or prolonged sleep, permits a frightened mind to put time between itself and its remembered hurts. **Diets** improve general health and energy. **Fever therapy** cures a large percentage of paretics. **Shock therapies, electrical or chemical,** temporarily break through delusions and dissociations, enabling therapists to help the individual learn how to accept physical facts and psychological feelings.

THE TRANQUILLIZING DRUGS

The tranquillizing drugs as a class are known to doctors as **ataraxics.** The root word means calmness, untroubled by mental or emotional excitation. The drugs relax patients, and give them a feeling of peace and contentment, freeing them from anxiety. The first two tranquillizers were an extract of the ancient Indian snake-root *Rauwolfia serpentina* and a synthetic compound called Chlorpromazine. Many drugs with similar effects have since been introduced.

The drugs affect animal as well as human experience and behaviour. Siamese fighting fish under the influence of reserpine and meprobamate, two tranquillizers, will not only refuse to fight but will retreat, usually backward. Given another tranquillizer, chlorpromazine, the fighting fish are quiet, not even swimming about, until attacked by an untreated fish, whereupon they too refuse to fight and swim away. In contrast, barbiturate sleeping drugs depress the fish but do not alter their readiness to fight when goaded.

In humans, too, the action of the drugs is believed to be quite different from the action of long-used sedatives. The sedatives depress mental functions. The new tranquillizers apparently bring peace without loss of alertness. The drugs have been used widely and successfully in treatment of high blood pressure, hypertension, and psychiatric conditions. However, used to excess, the drugs might have an *adverse* effect on the mental state of patients.

However, research is continuing on the use of drugs and it is quite possible that future developments in this area will make a valuable contribution to the treatment of the mentally ill or even to open new fields of discovery in psychological methods and ways of thinking.

SUGGESTED FURTHER READING

Allen, F. H., *Positive Aspects of Child Psychiatry*. Norton: New York, 1963.

Boyers, R. (Ed.), *Laing and Anti-Psychiatry*. Penguin: London, 1972.

English, O. S., and Finch, S. M., *Introduction to Psychiatry*. Norton: New York, 1964.

Freeman, T., *Psychopathology of the Psychoses*. Tavistock Publications: London, 1969.

Gathercole, C. E., *Assessment in Clinical Psychology*. Penguin: London, 1968.

Hargreaves, D. H., Hester, S. K., and Mellor, F. J., *Deviance in Classrooms*. Routledge and Kegan Paul: London, 1975.

Haslam, M. T., *Psychiatry Made Simple*. Heinemann: London, 1982.

Huxley, A., *The Doors of Perception*. Chatto and Windus: London, 1959.

Laing, R. D., *The Divided Self: A Study of Sanity and Madness*. Tavistock Publications: London, 1960.

Martin, B., *Abnormal Psychology*. Scott, Foresman & Co: New York, 1973.

Resnik, H. L. P. (Ed.), *Suicidal Behaviours: Diagnosis and Management*. Little Brown: Boston, 1968.

Rycroft, C., *Anxiety and Neurosis*. Penguin: London, 1970.

Sullivan, H. S., *Schizophrenia as a Human Process*. Norton: New York, 1962.

Wells, B., *Psychedelic Drugs*. Penguin: London, 1973.

18

ISSUES IN SOCIAL PSYCHOLOGY

Many of the previous chapters in this book have been concerned with the behaviour of the individual—how he perceives, learns, remembers, thinks, and so on. The areas of interest of the **social psychologist** tend to differ somewhat from these. It is difficult to define the subject matter of social psychology in exact terms but broadly speaking the social psychologist is concerned with studying the behaviour of individuals **in social contexts.** He is thus concerned with issues such as attitudes, prejudice, group behaviour, social interaction, etc.

The scope of social psychology is, however, wide and many books have been written on this area of study. Clearly, therefore, in a single chapter it is possible to give only a brief introduction to some of the key issues. Suggestions for further reading which will help to give further insight into this field are given at the end of the chapter.

We begin with a discussion of **attitudes** as these have been briefly mentioned in an earlier chapter and are central issues of study for social psychologists. At the outset we must recognize that attitude is essentially a **construct.** Many definitions have been proposed and it is indeed difficult to give an exact definition. A useful approach, however, has been put forward by Secord and Backman, who suggest that attitudes can be seen as:

Certain regularities of an individual's feelings, thoughts, and predispositions to act towards some aspect of his environment.

Thus, they are suggesting that an attitude has three components: the first, **feelings,** they refer to as the **affective component,** the **thoughts** as the **cognitive** component and, finally, the **predispositions to act** as the **behavioural component.**

WHERE DO OUR ATTITUDES COME FROM?

Clearly we are not **born** with attitudes as such but develop many attitudes as we go through life. In our early years a number of different attitudes are developed through relationships with parents and other members of the immediate family. If the child begins to develop and display attitudes which are favoured by the parents they are likely to **reinforce** by approval and praise his expression of such attitudes. **Learning** of the attitude therefore takes place. As the child grows older, and particularly when he begins school, other social groups influence the attitudes he adopts. We often conform because we wish to be accepted by a particular group and take on the attitudes held by members of the group in order to feel accepted.

Finally, attitudes are often formed as a result of **direct experience with an object.** For example, if a person purchases a new car and finds that a number of irritating faults rapidly develop he may soon come to hold a negative attitude to all cars made by the particular company in question.

WHAT FUNCTIONS DO ATTITUDES SERVE?

If we accept that all of us do have attitudes we should go on to ask what functions such attitudes serve in our everyday lives. Various **functional categories** have been proposed by psychologists; one widely used categorization is that proposed by **Daniel Katz.** Katz suggests that there are four functions which attitudes perform for the individual. These he calls (1) **the adjustive function,** (2) **the ego-defensive function,** (3) **the value-expressive function,** and (4) **the knowledge function.**

The Adjustive Function. We tend to adopt positive or favourable attitudes towards things which 'reward' us and negative or unfavourable attitudes to those which 'punish' us.

The Ego-defensive Function. This refers to the ways in which our attitudes defend the image that we have of ourselves; that is to say, our **self-image.** An example of this function given by Katz is 'when we cannot admit to ourselves that we have deep feelings of inferiority we may project those feelings on to some convenient minority group and bolster our egos by attitudes of superiority towards this under-privileged group'.

The Value-expressive Function. Some attitudes have the function of giving positive expression to the central values held by the individual and to the concept which he has of himself. Thus, a person may see himself as having a liberal outlook and would express this in the particular causes and reforms which he supports.

The Knowledge Function. Here Katz is proposing that the individual has a 'need to give adequate structure to his universe' and that such a need can be served by the attitudes which he holds.

The categories outlined above should not, however, be applied rigidly to all our attitudes. It is not uncommon for many of the attitudes which we hold to involve combinations of more than one function.

MEASURING ATTITUDES

Reference to the assessment of attitudes has been made in Chapter 13 and it has been stated that questionnaires are frequently used as a means of assessing attitudes. Two of the most frequently used attitude scales are the **Thurstone scale** and the **Likert scale.** The Thurstone method consists of presenting the **respondent** with a large number of statements relating to the attitude in question, and he is asked to indicate agreement, disagreement, or neutrality towards each statement. His overall score is the average scale score on all the items for which he has indicated agreement.

The Likert method is in some ways similar to the Thurstone scale. The respondent is presented with a number of statements and is asked to indicate agreement or disagreement on a scale ranging from 'strongly agree' to 'strongly disagree'. Often, five possible responses are presented and these would be strongly agree, moderately agree, neutral or undecided, moderately disagree, and strongly disagree.

There are problems in assessing attitudes by means of such scales as those discussed above. The scale tends to assume that the respondent has an attitude towards the issue in question and this may not necessarily be the case. **He is nevertheless required to respond as if he did have an attitude towards the issue and his score is thus likely to be misleading.** Furthermore, we must also allow for the **social desirability** of responses. The respondent may respond not in a way which reflects his true attitudes to the issue but in a way which he feels either to be socially desirable or which he believes those issuing the questionnaire would prefer or expect.

CAN ATTITUDES BE CHANGED?

It can often prove difficult to change or modify attitudes. This is not really surprising when we consider the various functions which attitudes serve for the holder. Nevertheless, we know from our own experience that people do change their attitudes and psychologists are interested in both why this occurs and in establishing those factors which are likely to influence attitude change. It has, for example, been found that the credibility of the communicator attempting to change the attitude of another is important. His **prestige** is likely to influence whether or not we accept his communication. **Hovland, Janis,** and **Kelley** have identified two important components of the credibility of the communicator. These, they term **expertness**—does his education, position or age increase our belief in him and the validity of what he says, and **trustworthiness**—what, if anything, does he stand to gain if we alter our attitudes as a result of what he says? The encyclopedia salesman will aim to persuade a prospective customer that a positive attitude towards the acquisition of wide general knowledge will be of immense value both to his family and himself. Realisation that he stands to gain through commission if we accept his communication is likely to lessen the effect of his persuasive arguments. On the other hand, the medical practitioner who attempts to change the attitudes of a patient who smokes heavily is more likely—but by no means certain—to meet with some degree of success. He is viewed as a credible source and has little to gain personally if he brings about a change of attitude in his patient.

A further factor influencing attitude change is that of the **communication itself.** Advertising compaigns aimed at changing attitudes towards such issues as smoking, the use of safety belts in cars, dental hygiene, insurance, and so on often make an emotional appeal to the audience. It was once believed that a strongly presented appeal which would increase the concern and awareness of the audience would have the greatest and most long-lasting effect. This, however, has not always been found to be the case.

In the 1950s **Janis and Feshbach** carried out a series of experiments to study the effects of three different intensities of **fear appeal** in a communication on dental hygiene. **These were strong, moderate and weak appeals.** It was found that a **strongly worded** emotional appeal in which stress was placed on the resultant pain and disease when dental hygiene practices were not followed had the greatest **initial** impact. The most effective and **longer lasting** appeal, however, was the one which suggested the least threat and was referred to as the **minimum appeal.** Here, far fewer references than in the strong or moderate appeals were made to the consequences of poor oral hygiene practices.

EXPLANATIONS OF ATTITUDE CHANGE

The theory of attitude change which has probably received the most attention is that proposed by **Leon Festinger** and termed the **Theory of Cognitive Dissonance.** He argued that an individual's attitudes are usually consistent with each other and he behaves in accordance with his attitudes. Inconsistencies do, however, occur from time to time and when there are inconsistencies this gives rise to a state of **cognitive dissonance.** Experiencing such dissonance is unpleasant for the individual concerned and he is therefore motivated to reduce or avoid the dissonance. Festinger speaks of **reduction dissonance and achieving consonance.** Thus if a person believes that smoking is harmful and yet continues to smoke heavily he is likely to experience dissonance. He may reduce the dissonance by deciding to give up this habit. On the other hand, he may seek information which would cast doubts on his previous acceptance of the harmful effects of tobacco and thus in this way achieve consonance.

There have been various criticisms and revisions of Festinger's original theory. It has been argued that the original theory was too simple. **Brehm and Cohen** have proposed that a person must be **committed** to an attitude or behaviour before any clear statement can be made about its dissonant relationships to other cognitive elements. If there is not this commitment the individual can usually dismiss the attitude or behaviour before dissonance can be aroused. A further modification has been suggested by Aronson, who has argued that Festinger's original definition of dissonance was **too broad** and resulted in many poorly supported hypotheses. Aronson has proposed that **a dissonant relationship is one that involves inconsistency between the individual's self concept and a cognition about his behaviour.**

ATTITUDES AND BEHAVIOUR

We sometimes hear it said that **if we know a person's attitudes we will be able to predict how he will behave in a particular situation.** This is, in fact, frequently, although by no means always, the case. An early empirical study on the relationship between attitude and behaviour was carried out in America by **LaPiere,** and the results of his research published in 1934. A white sociologist travelled across America in the company of a smartly dressed Chinese couple. During their journey they stayed and ate at a large number of hotels and restaurants **and were refused service only once.** Later, letters were sent to all of these establishments asking if the proprietors would serve Chinese people. In about 90 per cent of the replies received the answer was **no**—i.e. that Chinese people would not be welcomed. **This expressed attitude is in marked contrast to the behaviour** towards the Chinese couple in their travels with the sociologist.

There are, however, a number of possible explanations of this discrepancy between attitudes and behaviour. Refusal by letter to accept particular guests is far less embarrassing than would be the case in a face-to-face situation. The various proprietors at that particular time may well have feared that they would receive large numbers of minority group visitors if a positive reply was given to the written request. Furthermore, in dealing with a written request the proprietors would have in mind a **stereotype** of Chinese people; in the face-to-face situation different and additional cues are usually available.

THE ROLES WE PLAY ALSO INFLUENCE OUR ATTITUDES AND BEHAVIOUR

The concept of **role** is not clearly defined in psychology but broadly speaking refers to **behavioural expectations** which are associated with holding particular positions in society. Thus we speak of sex roles, kinship roles, occupational roles, and so on. **During the course of any one day we are each likely to occupy many different roles.** It has been argued by **Stanley Milgram** that roles can influence the behaviour we engage in not only by providing patterns of behaviour and attitudes we adopt as part of playing that role but further, in the case of some roles such as the subject in a psychology experiment, requiring us to accept the influence of others to a significant degree. Milgram demonstrated this in a series of experiments involving role play situations. Volunteers were required to play the role of 'teacher' in a learning experiment. Each time the student **(who was a confederate of the experimenters)** made an error he was given—or so the teacher believed—an **electric shock.** The strengths of the shocks increased in intensity as the experiment proceeded. Although a number of 'teachers' protested to the experimenter and argued that the situation was becoming dangerous many nevertheless passed what they believed to be high intensity electric shocks through the 'student' **when urged on to do so by the experimenter.**

A further study illustrating the influence of roles on attitudes and behaviour was carried out by **P. Zimbardo.** Subjects in the experiment were randomly assigned to play the roles of prisoners and warders. A makeshift prison was constructed and it was planned that this experimental study of role play should last for up to two weeks. The experiment, however, had to be terminated after a few days as the situation was getting very much out of hand. Those playing the role of warder had become so aggressive and developed such negative attitudes towards those playing the role of prisoners that the situation had become so tense that the experiment had to be abandoned. Zimbardo interpreted his findings as indicating the degree to which a person occupying a particular role may be influenced not only in behaviour but also in his feelings and attitudes towards others.

PREJUDICE—A PARTICULAR KIND OF ATTITUDE

It might well be said that the 'warders' in the study outlined above had shown a particular **prejudice** to those playing the role of prisoner. Prejudice, like so many terms used in social psychology, is difficult to define unequivocally but is generally regarded as an extreme and usually negative attitude which is generalised towards a particular class or group of people. Whether or not a prejudiced individual will behave in accordance with his attitude depends upon a variety of factors, such as the situation at the time.

SEVERAL TERMS RELATE TO THE CONCEPT OF PREJUDICE

Discrimination is viewed as the differential treatment of individuals considered to belong to a particular social group. Usually, discrimination is the behavioural expression of prejudice. Generally the individual who is discriminated against is denied some privilege or right that is given to other members of the society who do not belong to the minority group.

Stereotyping. The issue of stereotyping has been mentioned previously in relation to the LaPiere study. In general the term refers to the action of assigning particular attributes to a person purely on the basis of the class or group to which he belongs. Many groups in our society assume some stereotyped characteristics which are attributed to all members of the group. **Prejudice frequently involves stereotyped views of a particular group.** Such views are often the outcome of hearsay rather than experience and frequently are used to justify discrimination.

EXPLANATIONS OF PREJUDICE

A number of theories have been put forward in an attempt to explain why some individuals tend to show more prejudice than others. Such explanations can broadly be grouped as follows:

Syndrome Theories. The first of such theories is often referred to as the **scapegoat or hostility displacement theory.** This theory assumes that the blocking of a goal directed activity results in frustration which in its turn leads to aggression. It may well be the case that whatever or whoever is the cause of the frustration is too powerful to be attacked by the individual concerned. As a result his aggression is displaced and redirected towards a less powerful or minority group.

Such a theory is derived from **psychoanalytic principles,** as is the theory of the **authoritarian personality.**

Authoritarian Personality Explanations of Prejudice. This theory proposed that particular child-rearing practices result in a pattern of traits which show an important relation to prejudice. Parents have exercised rigid discipline and given affection to the child only as a means of approval of his behaviour. Thus submission on the part of the child and dominance of the parents are emphasized. The child is unable to express his hostility towards the parents and as a result develops **repressive mechanisms** for disguising his hostility and controlling his impulses. This leads to a rigid and authoritarian attitude towards others **and is often expressed in the form of prejudice.**

There are, however, criticisms of this theory since much of the evidence on which it was based was **correlational.** It may well be true that many adults who are authoritarian and prejudiced had, as children, parents who followed a strict code of discipline but **it does not follow that this method of child rearing caused the development of prejudice.** It could well be argued that the child learns prejudice from his parents through the **social learning processes** of **imitation and identification.**

Group Level Explanations. Group rather than individual levels of explanation of prejudice argue in terms of **in-group over-evaluation** and **out-group rejection.** This is referred to as ethnocentrism.

CAN PREJUDICE BE CHANGED?

Like attitudes, prejudices can be changed but effecting the process of change may often prove difficult. As is the case in some countries, the social structure itself may support prejudiced attitudes and group pressure may result in difficulties for those wishing to bring about change. Fear on the part of some possible outcomes if prejudices are changed can also give problems to those advocating change.

GENERAL EFFECTS OF GROUP PRESSURE—THE CONFORMITY ISSUE

Conformity has been mentioned above in relation to the maintenance of prejudice. The presence of other people often alters the behaviour of the individual. In some circumstances his behaviour may be **facilitated** whilst in others the presence of others may **inhibit** the individual's behaviour. In many cases the presence of others leads to behaviour which is referred to as **conformity. The essence of conformity is that yielding to group pressure** (or what the individual perceives to be group pressure) **is involved.**

Several experiments have investigated this phenomenon. In one study subjects are presented with sets of lines of varying length and asked to identify which of these matches exactly a 'standard' line. One subject finds that all other members of the group select a line which he has little doubt is longer than the standard. These members are, of course, 'in league' with the experimenter and have previously arranged to give a common response. The individual subject, unaware of these previous arrangements, finds himself in a **conflict situation;** the evidence of his perceptions would clearly seem at variance with that of other members of the group. In such circumstances it has been found that the individual frequently **conforms** to the views expressed by other group members.

In other experiment the subjects were placed in a fully darkened room in which a single point of light was just visible. Normally the light appears to move—this is referred to as the **autokinetic effect**— and the subjects required to estimate the amount of apparent movement. In a group situation where individuals could hear the judgements of others there was a tendency for such judgements to converge upon a common norm. Thus the members of the group were influenced by the judgements made by others **and conformed to these when giving their own estimation of the apparent movement they had witnessed.**

CONCLUDING COMMENTS

At the beginning of this chapter it was indicated that the areas of interest of the social psychologist are wide and that it is possible here to touch on a small number of these. Investigation of attitudes, prejudice, and aspects of group behaviour are central issues that the reader will have appreciated are studied by the social psychologist using a variety of techniques and methods ranging from observation in the field to controlled laboratory experiments. At times deception is employed and the reader may perhaps question the ethics of using such practices in psychological investigations. For those who wish to pursue their interest in social psychology further a selection of reading is given below. These suggestions include both 'general' texts covering a range of topics and texts dealing with specific areas within social psychology.

SUGGESTED FURTHER READING

Adorno, T. W., Frenkel-Brunswick, E., Levinson, D. J., and Sanford, R. W., *The Authoritarian Personality*. Harper and Row: New York, 1950.

Ajzen, I., and Fishbein, M., *Understanding Attitudes and Predicting Social Behaviour*. Prentice-Hall: New Jersey, 1980.

Brown, R., *Social Psychology*. The Free Press: New York, 1965.

Eiser, J. R., *Cognitive Social Psychology*. McGraw-Hill: London, 1980.

Gahagan, J., *Interpersonal and Group Behaviour*. Methuen: London, 1975.

Krech, D., Crutchfield, R., and Ballachey, E., *Individual in Society: A Textbook of Social Psychology*. McGraw-Hill: London, 1962.

Reich, B., and Adcock, C., *Values, Attitudes and Behaviour Change*. Methuen: London, 1976.

Secord, P. F., and Backman, C. W., *Social Psychology*. McGraw-Hill: London, 1964.

Warren, N., and Jahoda, M., *Attitudes*. 2nd Ed, Penguin: Harmondsworth, 1973.

Wheldall, K., *Social Behaviour*. Methuen: London, 1975.

GLOSSARY

Abstraction. A characteristic held in common by several different individual objects.

Adaptation. A change in the sensitivity of a sense organ resulting from continued stimulation. More broadly any change that enables an organism to respond more effectively to its environment.

Adjustment. The way in which a person becomes efficiently related to his environment.

Adolescence. The period of transition from childhood to adulthood.

Adrenalin. A hormone, secreted by the pith of each adrenal gland, that duplicates the effects of the sympathetic nerves.

Affectivity. The dimension of feeling whose two poles are pleasantness and unpleasantness. Sometimes called the 'P–U scale' from the initials of those two words.

After-image. A visual sensory experience that persists after the external stimulus has been removed. For example, the coloured spots seen after staring at the sun.

Ambivert. A person whose personality is a balanced mixture of extravert and introvert traits.

Amentia. The condition of subnormal mental development.

Amnesia. A dissociation in which a part or the whole of an individual's past experiences becomes completely repressed.

Anatomy. The science of the structure of animals and plants.

Animism. The tendency, characteristic of pre-school children, to attribute life to all lifeless things.

Antagonism. The opposite effect, upon a given organ of the body, of impulses sent along the sympathetic nerves, to the effect of impulses sent along the parasympathetic nerves.

Anthropology. The science of the cultures, arts, and morals of the races of mankind.

Anthropomorphism. The primitive, self-centred tendency to see human motives at work in natural objects and events.

Anxiety. Neurotic fear of anticipated trouble. Called 'worry' when mild but continuous, and 'panic' when occasional but intense.

Aptitude. An ability to form a certain kind of habit efficiently.

Asnomia. Complete absence of the sense of smell.

Ataraxics. The so-called tranquillizing drugs. From a Greek word meaning calmness.

Attitudes. Certain regularities in the way an individual feels, thinks and is predisposed to act towards some aspect of his environment.

Autonomic nerves. A division of the nervous system that serves the endocrine glands and the involuntary muscles of the internal organs.

Behaviour therapy. A method of treatment based on the principles of learning theory.

Behaviourists. A school of psychologists who ignored both conscious and unconscious experience, as being too subjective for scientific study, and concentrated on such patterns of behaviour as conditioned responses. Led by John B.

Watson. An influential present-day behaviourist is B. F. Skinner.

Blind Spot. The point at which the optic nerve joins the retina. Since neither rods nor cones are present, this spot is blind to any light.

British Ability Scales. A comparatively recent measure of intelligence which can be used with children up to the age of seventeen years.

Castration Complex. Supposed fear on the part of boys that they will be (and on the part of girls that they already have been) deprived of their external male genitals, as a punishment for incestuous desires.

Catatonia. Hostile form of schizophrenia, characterized either by inhibition of response, or by extreme violence.

Childhood. (1) Legally, any person who has not yet reached his eighteenth birthday anniversary. (2) Commonly, any person whose adolescence has not yet begun. (3) In psychology, the period of life between infancy and adolescence.

Choleric. Irritable. One of Galen's 'four temperaments'.

Chromosome. A microscopic, coloured body in the nucleus of a cell. Contains genes.

Climacteric. The so-called change of life. Called 'menopause' in the female.

Closure. An organizing tendency to perceive an incomplete pattern as a complete pattern.

Colour blindness. The inability to distinguish certain colours. Total colour blindness is rare, but two-colour vision occurs in one out of every fifteen men.

Compensation. The adjustment mechanism by which a person obscures the fact of some personal deficiency by concentrating on some other possession.

Compensatory movements. The smooth motion of the eye as the head is turned from side to side to view an object from various angles.

Complex. In Freudian terminology, a system of emotionally charged ideas, existing in the unconscious, which influence thought, perception, and behaviour.

Compulsion. An irrational, useless act that constantly intrudes into a person's behaviour, usually as a defence against an obsession.

Concept. An idea formed by dissociating a quality from the various other qualities with which it is associated in objects of the environment.

Conditioned response. An act of behaviour aroused by stimuli that were originally ineffective.

Conditioning. Teaching a subject to associate a response already known with a new stimulus.

Conduction deafness. Hearing loss due to a reduction in the flexibility of the joints between the three little bones in the middle ear.

Cone. A cell in the central area of the retina, shaped like a small cone, and sensitive to colours.

Conscience. The body of ideals by which a person guides or judges his actions.

Consciousness. Awareness. The totality of experience and mental processes of a person at a given moment.

Convergence. The motion of the eyes as they adjust to an object moving towards them.

Correlation. The degree of relationship between two sets of measurements arranged in pairs, expressed by a number called the 'coefficient' of correlation. If this number, symbolized by the letter 'r', is 0, there is no correlation; if 1, there is perfect correlation; if between 0 and 1, there is partial correlation.

Covert responses. Responses that are not readily observable, like silent speech.

Cue. A stimulus that symbolizes a more complex stimulus.

Defence reaction. A response pattern, or adjustive mechanism, that tends unconsciously to shield a person from some imperfection in his personality or from some threat from reality.

Delusions. Beliefs or convictions that are firmly held despite objective evidence to the contrary.

Dementia. Mental deterioration, particularly of intellect and memory.

Diffusion. An emotional state in which the aroused person makes many useless and exaggerated responses, and performs normal acts with excessive violence.

Dipsomania. Compulsive desire for alcoholic beverages.

Disorientation. A state of mental confusion, in which a person is unsure of his location or identity.

Dissociate. To separate one image, idea, or function of the personality, from another.

Dissociation. A mechanism by which a group of mental processes separates from normal consciousness and functions by itself.

Divergence. The outward motion of the eyes as they adjust to an object that is moving away from them.

Dominant trait. A trait that will be expressed in any individual who has its gene.

Double personality. The alternate identity which is suddenly assumed by some victims of amnesia.

Drive. A persistent stimulus, usually of physiological origin, that demands an adjustive response.

Dysfunction. Imperfect working of a bodily organ.

Educationally subnormal. A child whose I.Q. falls within the range of approximately 45–80.

Ego. The experiencing subject, or self. In psychoanalysis, the part of the personality that deals with reality.

Egocentrism. A mechanism by which a person gets attention and obscures inferiority through boastfulness and similar behaviour.

Eidetic image. A vivid, detailed visual image.

Emotion. An affective response, characterized by changes in feeling, behaviour, and internal excitement.

Endocrine glands. Internal organs that secrete chemical substances called hormones into the blood. Sometimes referred to as 'ductless' glands, because they do not have any tubes or ducts leading into specific parts of the body, as do such glands as the salivary and tear glands.

Endocrinology. The scientific study of the hormones secreted by our glands.

Enuresis. Involuntary bed-wetting, usually during sleep.

Environment. Every influence met by an individual after the hereditary pattern has been received through the germ plasm.

Epilepsy. A chronic disease, with many forms, whose symptoms include convulsions and periods of unconsciousness.

Ethnology. The science of the races of mankind, especially their origin, distribution, and physical differences.

Etiology. The study of the causes and conditions of a disease or abnormality.

Eugenics. Mating controlled by the laws of heredity in order to breed superior individuals.

Extinction. Weakening a conditioned

response by presenting the conditioned stimulus without reinforcement.

Extrasensory perception. Term for supposed ability to perceive objects or to receive communications without the use of the sense organs. Abbreviated E.S.P.

Extravert. As defined by Jung, a person most interested in the external world of objects and people. Contrasted to 'introvert'.

Facial vision. The ability, most highly developed in blind people, to detect the position of objects by the sense of hearing.

Factor analysis. The methods by which statisticians discover basic traits, the primary dimensions of personality, and group factors of intelligence.

Fallacy. A mistake in reasoning.

Fantasy. The satisfaction of motives in the imagination.

Fixation. A pause made by the eyes during the reading of a line of type. Also, the arrestment of emotional and other developments at an immature level.

Four humours. Four body fluids distinguished and emphasized by the ancient Greek physician Hippocrates. These were: chole, or yellow bile; melanchole, or black bile; blood; and phlegm.

Four temperaments. Four types into which Galen classified all personalities over 1,800 years ago. These were: choleric, melancholy, sanguine, and phlegmatic. Galen associated these types with Hippocrates's four 'humours'.

Fovea. The point of greatest concentration of the cone cells in the retina, and thus the point of sharpest daytime vision.

Fraternal twins. Twins developed from two ova, fertilized by two sperms. May be of same or of opposite sex.

Fugue. A flight to avoid trouble, the memory of which is later repressed.

Functional autonomy. The motive force of habits originally adopted to satisfy other motives.

Functional psychosis. A psychosis, such as schizophrenia or paranoia, which cannot be accounted for by any detectable deterioration in the victim's nervous system.

Functionalists. A school of psychologists who emphasized the way that people use mental experiences in their adjustments to the environment. Led by William James.

Gang. The private, fiercely loyal group of playmates to which the pre-adolescent child belongs.

Gene. Invisible transmitter of individual hereditary traits. Contained in a chromosome.

Generosity error. The error of rating acquaintances more favourably than strangers.

Genetics. The study of the laws of heredity.

Germ plasm. The chromosomes of sex cells (egg and sperm).

Gestalt. A German word meaning 'pattern' or 'form'. Applied to the school of psychology which emphasizes the importance of insight in learning, and the tendency to perceive wholes.

Goitre. An enlarged thyroid gland.

Gonads. The sex glands: in males, the testes; in females, the ovaries.

Group factors. Aptitudes for certain habitual ways of reasoning, or thinking symbolically.

Habit. A form of memory in which remembering is shown by the automatic performance of a learned response.

Haemophilia. An inherited condition, sex-linked to maleness, in which the blood does not clot normally.

Hallucinations. Sensory experiences for which no adequate sensory stimulus can be discovered.

Halo effect. The error of rating a person near the top or bottom in every trait if you have been favourably or poorly impressed by his excellence or deficiency in one trait.

Hebephrenia. Extremely retrogressive form of schizophrenia, characterized by silliness and childishness.

Heredity. The transmission of traits from one generation to the next through the process of sexual reproduction.

Homosexual. A person whose sexual activity involves members of the same sex.

Hormones. Chemical substances, secreted internally by the endocrine glands, that affect the workings of the nervous system, and often duplicate the effects of the nervous system.

Hypnosis. A temporary condition resembling deep sleep, in which a person exercises conscious control of his behaviour and feelings according to the suggestions of one who has hypnotized him.

Hypochondria. Also called hypochondriasis. A morbid concern with one's own health.

Hypothesis. A likely explanation assumed to be true until proven wrong.

Hysteria. The condition of a person who unconsciously converts anxiety into physical symptoms that then become more-or-less independent of the hysteric's control.

Illusion. An appearance that is not real.

Image. A subjective experience, resembling perception, in the absence of the original stimulus.

Infancy. The first three years of life.

Inferiority complex. An attitude, often unconscious, caused by strong feelings of unworthiness or lack of competence.

Insight. A sudden understanding of the relationships involved in the solving of a problem.

Insomnia. Inability to sleep under normal conditions.

Instinct. Innate, unlearned, unchangeable behaviour in response to the stimuli of a normal environment, such responses being universal to a species.

Intelligence. An aptitude for original thinking. An ability to solve new problems with facility and ingenuity. A capacity to learn and grasp new concepts and new approaches.

Intelligence quotient. A number that measures the relative rank of a person's general intelligence. Obtained by dividing mental age by chronological age, and then multiplying by 100 to remove the decimal point. Best thought of as a percentage, 100 being average.

Introspection. Self-examination of one's feelings, thoughts, and visions.

Introvert. As defined by Jung, a person most interested in his own thoughts and feelings. Contrasted to 'extravert'.

Intuition. Immediate knowledge without preliminary reasoning or examination.

Involutional melancholia. A functional psychosis of the climacteric period, characterized by extreme depression.

Kinaesthetic sense. The awareness of body movements, by which one controls co-ordination.

Korsakoff's syndrome. An organic psychosis caused by alcoholism and vitamin deficiencies, which is marked by the forgetting of recent events.

Laws of learning. Statements of influences that have been found to help or hinder learning.

Learning. A more-or-less permanent change in behaviour, caused by past experience. Can consist of one or more of three steps: (1) inventing an original solution to a problem, or thinking; (2) committing a solution to memory, or memorizing; (3) becoming efficient at applying the solution to a problem, or forming a habit.

Learning curve. A graph drawn to show the time taken by a subject to solve a given problem at successive trials.

Libido. A psychoanalytic term, meaning the total of a person's available energy. Specifically, the term is usually applied to sexual energy.

Lloyd Morgan's Canon. The warning by a nineteenth-century English biologist, not to read human qualities into animal subjects.

Lobotomy. An operation in which the connexions between the pre-frontal lobes and the more primitive parts of the brain are surgically severed, to diminish violent excitement brought on by feelings of great guilt and hate.

Mania. Psychotic excitement.

Manic-depressive psychosis. A psychotic disorder characterized by periods, usually alternating, of depression and elation.

Masochism. The inability to obtain sexual pleasure without suffering pain.

Maturation. The complete development of aptitudes.

Maze. A network of paths through which it is difficult to find the way to a goal.

Mean. Statistical term for the arithmetical average of the items in a list.

Mechanical aptitude quotient. A number that measures the relative rank of a person's mechanical aptitude. Obtained by dividing mechanical aptitude age by chronological age, and multiplying by 100. Abbreviated to M.A.Q.

Mechanisms. The various kinds of habits that people acquire in attempts to satisfy their motives.

Median. Statistical term for the item in the exact middle of a list, when the items are listed in order of increasing magnitude.

Melancholic. Depressed. One of Galen's four temperaments.

Memory. The present knowledge of a past experience.

Menopause. The stopping of the periodic menstrual flow in women, usually between the ages of forty and fifty, sometimes attended by mild personality disturbances.

Mental age. The chronological age of the normal children whose performance on intelligence tests is equalled by the child being tested.

Mental maturity. A stage in life when a person stops showing the previously continuous improvements in his ability to answer the general questions asked on intelligence tests. Reached somewhere between the ages of fourteen and eighteen.

Metabolism. All of the chemical processes in the cells of the body, including the conversion of food to energy, the storing of energy, the using of energy, the repair of tissues, and the disposing of wastes.

Mode. Statistical term for the most

common item in a list.

Motive. A tendency to activity, started by a drive, and ended by an adjustment.

Muscular dystrophy. A crippling disease in which the kinaesthetic sense, though not the intellect, is impaired.

Myxoedema. A sluggish condition due to an insufficiency of the thyroid-gland hormone thyroxin.

Negativism. A form of behaviour in which the child resists adult authority; the so-called 'no no' stage, at its peak at the age of three.

Neurasthenia. A neurotic condition whose predominant symptom is continuous fatigue.

Neurosis. An extreme, maladjustive form of an adjustment mechanism.

Neurotic. Of a neurosis. Also, a person suffering from a neurosis.

New brain. The most complex, most recently evolved part of the human brain. Controls thinking and deliberate actions.

Night blindness. An inability to see properly at night, due to a deficiency of visual purple in red cells of the retina.

Norm. A standard, derived from measurements of actual achievements.

Normal distribution. A group of test scores distributed in such a way that most of them are somewhere in the middle of the range, with fewer and fewer scores as either extreme is approached.

Objective. Factual; independent of personal bias.

Obsession. A persistent idea or desire that is recognized as being more-or-less irrational or immoral by the person to whom it continually occurs.

Oedipus complex. Supposed desire on the part of a child to replace the parent of the same sex in the affections of the parent of the other sex. Discovered and named by Freud after the legendary Greek hero who unknowingly killed his father and married his mother.

Old brain. More primitive part of the human brain. Controls automatic actions, both inborn and acquired, and contains the site of feelings and sensations.

Olfactory. Of the sense of smell.

Operant learning. A kind of conditioning of particular interest to B. F. Skinner. It contrasts to classical conditioning in that the behaviour is emitted by the organism rather than elicited by stimuli.

Optic nerve. The pathway of light stimuli from the eye to the brain.

Organ language. Colloquial and slang phrases that express the truths of psychosomatic medicine, such as 'It gripes me,' 'It breaks my heart,' and 'I haven't the guts for it.'

Organic psychosis. A psychosis, such as senile dementia, which can be shown to follow physical changes and deteriorations.

Overt responses. Responses that are readily observable, like crying or laughing.

Panic. Temporary attack of intense fear.

Paranoia. Functional psychosis marked by extreme suspiciousness of the motives of others, and fixed delusions of grandeur or persecution.

Parasite. An animal that lives on another without making any useful and fitting return.

Parasympathetic nerves. A division of the autonomic nervous system that keeps the body in normal running order.

Paresis. An organic psychosis caused

by syphilitic damage to the brain.

Perception. The act of interpreting a stimulus registered in the brain by one or more sense mechanisms.

Persistence of vision. The time lag, of one-sixteenth of a second, between the removal of a stimulus and the fading away of its after-image.

Personality. The complicated arrangement of motives that are expressed in the traits of an individual's unique mode of adjustment to his environment.

Personification. The pretence of regarding something that is not human as a person.

Phi phenomenon. The illusion of movement, in a series of still pictures seen in rapid succession, exploited in screen pictures and television, and based on persistence of vision.

Phlegmatic. Calm. One of Galen's four temperaments.

Phobia. A repressed fear transferred to an innocent object or situation.

Physiological limit of learning. The upper limit of a person's ability to learn and remember.

Physiology. The science of the normal functions of animals or their organs.

Pituitary gland. One of the endocrines, located at the base of the brain. Its secretions influence growth, sexual development, and metabolism.

Placebo. A harmless, powerless imitation medicine—for example, a sugar pill—given to an hysteric with the suggestion that it is a potent remedy.

Plateau. A period during the learning process in which no progress seems to be made. Symbolized by a straight line segment in the graph of the learning curve.

Polygraph. A machine, often called the 'lie detector', sensitive enough to detect and draw a graph of the slight changes in blood pressure, pulse rate, breathing rate, and skin electricity that usually accompany the telling of lies.

Prejudice. An extreme and usually negative attitude which is directed towards a particular class or group of people.

Primary dimensions of personality. Dimensions of personality which statistical tests have shown to have low correlations with each other, so that each dimension is separate and distinct in meaning from the others.

Progestin. A female hormone that regulates ovulation and menstruation.

Projection. The disguising of a source of conflict by attributing one's own motives to someone else.

Projective test. A test in which a person reveals his characteristic ways of feeling and thinking in the way he goes about solving a creative task.

Psychiatry. The study and treatment of mental and emotional disorders.

Psychoanalysis. The name given by Sigmund Freud in 1896 to his evolving methods of research and therapy. A school of psychology that emphasizes the importance of unconscious mental processes in normality and abnormality.

Psychodrama. A specialized technique of psychotherapy in which patients act out, usually before an audience of other patients, the roles, situations, and fantasies relevant to their personal problems.

Psychogenic. Pertaining to causes or conditions that are psychological in origin.

Psychograph. A diagram, prepared from rating scales, that shows how a person rates in each of several traits. Also known as a 'personality profile'.

Psychology. The science of individual behaviour and experience.

Psychopathic personality. A person with an imperfect or non-existent understanding of morality, and consequent antisocial or immoral conduct.

Psychosis. A mental or personality disorder, more severe than a neurosis, characterized by unrealistic behaviour that is often so dangerous or incompetent that the individual must be given custodial care.

Psychosomatic medicine. The branch of medical science and applied psychology that attempts to detect and cure those ailments whose physical symptoms express emotional stresses.

Psychosurgery. Brain surgery performed in the treatment of certain mental disorders.

Psychotherapy. The treatment of mental and emotional disorders, and mild adjustment problems, with psychological techniques.

P.T.C. Phenyl thiocarbamide, a chemical substance that some people cannot taste but which tastes bitter to the rest of the population.

Puberty. The period of attaining sexual maturity, usually beginning in girls between the ages of nine and eighteen, in boys between the ages of eleven and eighteen.

Pupillary reflex. Involuntary contraction of the pupil of the eye, caused by a sudden increase in the amount of light entering the eye.

Purkinje phenomenon. The change in a person's ability to distinguish colours as the day fades into night. Warm colours darken, while cool colours lighten.

Quickening. The first movement of the foetus in the womb.

Rating scale. A line drawn to represent a dimension of personality, on which is marked a person's position between the two opposite traits of personality at the poles of the dimension.

Rationalize. To give socially acceptable reasons for some act whose true motive is embarrassing.

Reaction formation. The disguising of a motive so completely that it is expressed in a form directly opposite to its original intention.

Reasoning. The form of thinking in which possible solutions to problems are tried out symbolically.

Recall. The form of memory in which a previous experience is remembered.

Receptor. See 'sense organ'.

Recessive trait. A trait that will not be expressed in any individual in whom its gene is paired with a corresponding dominant gene.

Recognition. The form of memory in which something is remembered when it is presented to the senses.

Reconditioning. Teaching a subject to make a response directly opposite to an undesirable conditioned response.

Reflex act. An unlearned automatic, muscular response to a stimulus.

Regression. See 'Retrogression'.

Regressive movements. Returns by the eyes to words already read.

Reinforcement. The rewarding effect of successful learning.

Reliability. Agreement between two measurements of the same thing.

Repression. An adjustment mechanism in which certain memories and motives are not allowed to enter consciousness but must operate only at unconscious levels of the personality.

Reproduction. The form of memory in which accurate copies or quotations can be made.

Response. The behaviour reaction brought about by a stimulus.

Retina. The light-sensitive, back layer

of the eye, on which images of objects are projected. It contains two kinds of receiving cells, rods and cones.

Retroactive inhibition. The interference by later learning in earlier learning.

Retrogression. A retreat by a person of a certain age level to an adjustive mechanism more appropriate to a lower age level. Called 'regression' by psychoanalysts.

Rod. A cell on the margin of the retina, shaped like a little cylinder, and sensitive only to light of low intensity.

Rorschach test. A projective test of personality in which the subject is asked to tell what he 'sees' in each one of ten ink-blots.

Saccadic movements. The jerky motions of the eye in reading.

Sadism. The inability to obtain sexual pleasure without inflicting pain.

Sanguine. Cheerful. One of Galen's four temperaments.

Schizophrenia. A functional psychosis, characterized by retrogression, fantasy, hallucinations, delusions, and general withdrawal from the environment.

Secondary reinforcer. A reinforcer which has derived its reinforcing properties from being associated with one or more primary reinforcers—e.g. in experiments monkeys have learned to work for poker chips which could later be exchanged for food. The poker chips were the secondary reinforcers which could be exchanged for the primary reinforcer of food.

Senile dementia. An organic psychosis caused by the degeneration and disappearance of nerve cells in the brains of old people.

Sensation. The act of receiving a stimulus by a sense organ.

Sense organ. A specialized part of the body, selectively sensitive to some types of change in its environment but not to others. For example, the eye.

Sex-linkage. The association of certain physical traits with the male or female sex of a person. For instance, colour blindness and baldness are linked to maleness.

Shock. An extreme degree of emotion in which the agitated person is incoherent and behaves either deliriously or stuporously.

Sibling. One of one's brothers or sisters.

Silent speech. The inaudible movements of the larynx during silent reading.

Social facilitation. The enhancement of performance in the presence of companions.

Socialization. Learning to behave in a way approved by one's family and society.

Sociology. The science of the nature, origin, and development of human social groups and community life.

Somnambulism. A dissociation in which the individual tries to carry out in his sleep acts which he unconsciously desires. Also called 'sleep-walking'.

Stereotyping. The action of assigning particular attributes to a person purely on the basis of the class or group to which he belongs.

Stimulus. Any kind of mechanical, physical, or chemical change that acts upon a sense organ.

Structuralists. A school of psychologists who claimed that complex mental experiences were really 'structures' built up from simple mental states, much as chemical compounds are built up from chemical elements. Led by Wilhelm Wundt.

Stupor. The condition of extreme depression, in which a patient says and does nothing.

Stuttering. The involuntary repetition of a sound, syllable, or word.

Subjective. About the feelings, thoughts, and visions of an individual.

Sublimation. The redirection of the energy of a motive into other channels of action.

Symbol. A stimulus that represents another stimulus.

Sympathetic nerves. A division of the autonomic nervous system that runs the body on an emergency basis when triggered by extreme cold, pain, violence, or emotion.

Syringomyelia. A rare disease in which sensitivity to heat and cold is lost, but the sense of touch is kept.

Temperament. The emotional traits of personality displayed by an individual.

Testosterone. A male sex hormone, a deficiency of which prevents the development of normal masculine traits.

Theelin. A female sex hormone, secreted through life until the menopause, that stimulates the reproductive organs and the breasts, determining the secondary sexual traits.

Thematic Apperception test. A projective test of personality in which the subject is presented with a series of illustrations and asked to write a story based on each picture.

Thinking. Discovering or inventing an original solution to a problem.

Trait. A physical or psychological quality or characteristic.

Tranquillizing drug. Any of a group of ataraxic drugs, which relax patients, giving them a feeling of peace and contentment, and freeing them from anxiety, or at least from its physical effects.

Transfer. The application of material or methods appropriate to one situation to another situation.

Trauma. A severe, sudden shock that has permanent effects upon the personality.

Traumatic neurosis. The drastic disruption of personality caused by any sudden, severe shock that is interpreted as a real threat to continued existence. If caused by military experiences, is sometimes known as 'shell shock', 'battle fatigue', and 'war neurosis'.

Trial-and-error thinking. The learning process in which a subject solves a problem only after making many random responses.

Type. A class of individuals alleged to have a particular trait. According to psychologists, an invalid concept, because individuals cannot be grouped into a few distinct classes.

Unconscious. Not consciously known or intended, but nevertheless influential in determining behaviour.

Validity. The degree to which a test measures what it is supposed to measure.

Verbal tests. Intelligence tests in which a great deal of the performance tested is in the form of words.

Vertigo. A feeling of dizziness.

Viscera. The soft inside parts of the body.

Visual purple. A chemical compound, normally found in a layer of the retina, which decomposes in the presence of light and recombines in darkness, and so is necessary for proper night vision. It depends upon vitamin A for nutrition.

Index

Related titles in the Made Simple Series

PSYCHIATRY

Made Simple

by M. T. Haslam, MA, MD, FRCP, FRC Psych

Psychiatry Made Simple provides a detailed account of the illnesses which can affect the mechanisms of brain function, their causation and symptoms, and current concepts of treatment. The author's straightforward approach aims to dispel the mystery that surrounds the subject and the book will therefore be of value to all students in the nursing, medical and social welfare professions as well as the general reader interested in a greater understanding of the mind.

368 pages   ISBN 0 434 98566 X

PHILOSOPHY

Made Simple

by Richard H. Popkin, PhD
Avrum Stroll, PhD
Advisory editor A. V. Kelly, MA (Oxon)

Philosophy Made Simple will be of particular interest to students beginning degree courses in philosophy and to those who are studying it as an ancillary subject within courses such as sociology, education, social sciences and theology. It will, in addition, be useful for a variety of liberal arts courses at adult education and other institutions. The book also provides a valuable basis for an introductory self-study course.

320 pages   ISBN 0 434 98452 3

SOCIOLOGY

Made Simple

by Jane L. Thompson, BA

Sociology Made Simple provides a stimulating and accessible introduction to some of the main concerns of contemporary sociology. The book is intended for A level GCE and first-year college students as well as undergraduates but will be of interest to the general reader who is looking for a greater understanding of society and how it works. Sections are included on social class, the family, education, youth culture, the mass media, work, industry and industrial change, poverty and welfare, politics and power, together with an outline of different sociological approaches and methods of research.

304 pages   ISBN 0 434 98508 2

CHILD DEVELOPMENT

Made Simple

by Richard Lansdown, MA, Dip Psych, PhD

Child Development Made Simple offers a basic but comprehensive introduction to the scientific study of child development, from the prenatal stage to adolescence. In addition, the text provides a full description of all the major theories of child development. All aspects of physical, mental, social and moral development are dealt with in a way that will appeal to all student teachers, nurses, health care and social workers who deal with children. Parents and parents-to-be will also find the book an invaluable guide to explain and clarify their children's development and behaviour.

272 pages   ISBN 0 434 98599 6